Maturin Murray Ballou

Due South or Cuba Past and Present

Maturin Murray Ballou

Due South or Cuba Past and Present

ISBN/EAN: 9783337002862

Printed in Europe, USA, Canada, Australia, Japan

Cover: Foto ©ninafisch / pixelio.de

More available books at **www.hansebooks.com**

DUE SOUTH

OR

CUBA PAST AND PRESENT

BY

MATURIN M. BALLOU

AUTHOR OF "DUE WEST; OR ROUND THE WORLD IN TEN MONTHS"

BOSTON AND NEW YORK
HOUGHTON, MIFFLIN AND COMPANY
The Riverside Press, Cambridge

PREFACE.

THE public favor accorded to a late volume by the author of these pages, entitled "Due West; or Round the World in Ten Months," has suggested both the publication and the title of the volume in hand, which consists of notes of a voyage to the tropics, and a sojourn in Cuba during the last winter. The endeavor has been to present a comprehensive view of the island, past and present, and to depict the political and moral darkness which have so long enshrouded it. A view of its interesting inhabitants, with a glance at its beautiful flora and vegetation generally, has been a source of such hearty enjoyment to the author that he desires to share the pleasure with the appreciative reader. The great importance of the geographical position of the island, its present critical condition, and the proposed treaty of commerce with this country, together render it at present of unusual interest in the eyes of the world. If possible, Cuba is more Castilian than peninsular Spain, and both are so Moorish as to present a fascinating study of national characteristics.

M. M. B.

CONTENTS.

CHAPTER I.
PAGE

Departure. — On Board Ship. — Arrival at Nassau. — Capital of the Bahamas. — Climate. — Soil. — Fruits and Flowers. — Magic Fertility. — Colored Population. — The Blockade Runners. — Population. — Products. — A Picturesque Local Scene. — Superstition. — Fish Story. — The Silk-Cotton Tree. — Remarkable Vegetation. — The Sea Gardens. — Marine Animal Life. — The Bahama Banks. — Burial at Sea. — Venal Officials. — Historical Characters. — The Early Buccaneers. — Diving for Drinking-Water 1

CHAPTER II.

Among the Islands. — San Salvador. — A Glimpse at the Stars. — Hayti. — The Gulf Stream. — The Caribbean Sea. — Latitude and Longitude. — The Southern Coast of Cuba. — A Famous Old Fortress. — Fate of Political Prisoners. — The Oldest City in Cuba. — The Aborigines. — Cuban Cathedrals. — Drinking Saloons. — Dogs, Horses, and Coolies. — Scenes in Santiago de Cuba. — Devoured by Sharks. — Lying at Anchor. — Wreck of a Historic Ship. — Cuban Circulating Medium. — Tropical Temperature 24

CHAPTER III.

Doubling Cape Cruz. — Trinidad. — Cienfuegos. — The Plaza. — Beggars. — Visit to a Sugar Plantation. — Something about Sugar. — An Original Character. — A Tropical Fruit Garden. — Cuban Hospitality. — The Banana. — Lottery Tickets. — Chinese Coolies. — Blindness in Cuba. — Birds and Poultry. — The Cock-Pit. — Negro Slavery, To-Day. — Spanish Slaveholders. — A Slave Mutiny. — A Pleasant Journey across the Island. — Pictures of the Interior. — Scenery about Matanzas. — The Tropics and the North contrasted 46

CHAPTER IV.

The Great Genoese Pilot. — Discovery of Cuba. — Its Various Names. — Treatment of the Natives. — Tobacco! — Flora of the Island. — Strange Idols. — Antiquity. — Habits of the Aborigines. — Remarkable Speech of an Indian King. — A Native Entertainment. — Paying Tribute. — Ancient Remains. — Wrong Impression of Columbus. — First Attempt at Colonization. — Battle with the Indians. — First Governor of Cuba. — Founding Cities. — Emigration from Spain. — Conquest of Mexico 70

CHAPTER V.

Baracoa, the First Capital. — West Indian Buccaneers. — Military Despotism. — A Perpetual State of Siege. — A Patriotic Son of Cuba. — Political Condition of the Island. — Education of Cuban Youths. — Attempts at Revolution. — Fate of General Narciso Lopez. — The Late Civil War and its Leader. — Terrible Slaughter of Spanish Troops. — Stronghold of the Insurgents. — Guerrillas. — Want of Self-Reliance. — Spanish Art, Literature, and Conquest. — What Spain was. — What Spain is. — Rise and Fall of an Empire 88

CHAPTER VI.

Geographical. — A Remarkable Weed. — Turtle-Hunting. — Turtle-Steaks in Olden Times. — The Gulf Stream. — Deep-Sea Soundings. — Mountain Range of Cuba. — Curious Geological Facts. — Subterranean Caverns. — Wild Animals. — The Rivers of the Island. — Fine Harbors. — Historic Memories of the Caribbean Sea. — Sentinel of the Gulf. — Importance of the Position. — Climate. — Hints for Invalids. — Matanzas. — Execution of a Patriot. — Valley of Yumuri; Caves of Bellamar; Puerto Principe; Cardenas 102

CHAPTER VII.

City of Havana. — First Impressions. — The Harbor. — Institutions. — Lack of Educational Facilities. — Cuban Women. — Street Etiquette. — Architecture. — Domestic Arrangements. — Barred Windows and Bullet-Proof Doors. — Public Vehicles. — Uncleanliness of the Streets. — Spanish or African! — The Church Bells. — Home-Keeping Habits of Ladies. —

Their Patriotism. — Personal Characteristics. — Low Ebb of
Social Life. — Priestcraft. — Female Virtue. — Domestic Ties.
— A Festive Population. — Cosmetics. — Sea-Bathing . . . 125

CHAPTER VIII.

Sabbath Scenes in Havana. — Thimble-Riggers and Mountebanks. — City Squares and their Ornamentation. — The Cathedral. — Tomb of Columbus. — Plaza de Armas. — Out-Door Concerts. — Habitués of Paseo de Isabella. — Superbly Appointed Cafés. — Gambling. — Lottery Tickets. — Fast Life. — Masquerade Balls. — Carnival Days. — The Famous Tacon Theatre. — The Havana Casino. — Public Statues. — Beauties of the Governor's Garden. — The Alameda. — The Old Bell-Ringer. — Military Mass 144

CHAPTER IX.

Political Inquisition. — Fashionable Streets of the City. — Tradesmen's Signs. — Bankrupt Condition of Traders. — The Spanish Army. — Exiled Patriots. — Arrival of Recruits. — The Garrote. — A Military Execution. — Cuban Milk Dealers. — Exposure of Domestic Life. — Living in the Open Air. — The Campo Santo of Havana. — A Funeral Cortége. — Punishing Slaves. — Campo de Marte. — Hotel Telegrafo. — Environs of the City. — Bishop's Garden. — Consul-General Williams. — Mineral Springs 166

CHAPTER X.

The Fish-Market of Havana. — The Dying Dolphin. — Tax upon the Trade. — Extraordinary Monopoly. — Harbor Boats. — A Story about Marti, the Ex-Smuggler. — King of the Isle of Pines. — The Offered Reward. — Sentinels in the Plaza de Armas. — The Governor-General and the Intruder. — "I am Captain Marti!" — The Betrayal. — The Ex-Smuggler as Pilot. — The Pardon and the Reward. — Tacon's Stewardship and Official Career. — Monopoly of Theatricals. — A Negro Festival 184

CHAPTER XI.

The Havana Lottery. — Its Influence. — Hospitality of the Cubans. — About Bonnets. — The Creole Lady's Face. — Love of

viii   CONTENTS.

PAGE

Flowers. — An Atmospheric Narcotic. — The Treacherous Indian Fig. — How the Cocoanut is propagated. — Cost of Living in Cuba. — Spurious Liquors. — A Pleasant Health Resort. — The Cock-Pit. — Game-Birds. — Their Management. — A Cuban Cock-Fight. — Garden of the World. — About Birds. — Stewed Owl! — Slaughter of the Innocents. — The Various Fruits 200

CHAPTER XII.

Traveling by Volante. — Want of Inland Communication. — Americans Profitable Customers. — The Cruel National Game. — The Plaza de Toros. — Description of a Bull-Fight. — The Infection of Cruelty. — The Romans and Spaniards compared. — Cry of the Spanish Mob: "Bread and Bulls!" — Women at the Fight. — The Nobility of the Island. — The Monteros. — Ignorance of the Common People. — Scenes in the Central Market, Havana. — Odd Ideas of Cuban Beggars. — An Original Style of Dude. — A Mendicant Prince . . . 219

CHAPTER XIII.

Introduction of Sugar-Cane. — Sugar Plantations. — Mode of Manufacture. — Slaves on the Plantations. — African Amusements. — The Grinding Season. — The Coffee Plantations. — A Floral Paradise. — Refugees from San Domingo. — Interesting Experiments with a Mimosa. — Three Staple Productions of Cuba. — Raising Coffee and Tobacco. — Best Soils for the Tobacco. — Agricultural Possibilities. — The Cuban Fire-Fly. — A Much-Dreaded Insect. — The Ceiba Tree. — About Horses and Oxen 236

CHAPTER XIV.

Consumption of Tobacco. — The Delicious Fruits of the Tropics. — Individual Characteristics of Cuban Fruits. — The Royal Palm. — The Mulberry Tree. — Silk Culture. — The Island once covered by Forests. — No Poisonous Reptiles. — The Cuban Bloodhound. — Hotbed of African Slavery. — Spain's Disregard of Solemn Treaties. — The Coolie System of Slavery. — Ah-Lee draws a Prize. — Native African Races. — Negroes buying their Freedom. — Laws favoring the Slaves. — Example of San Domingo. — General Emancipation 260

CHAPTER XV.

Slave Trade with Africa. — Where the Slavers made their Landing. — An Early Morning Ride. — Slaves marching to Daily Labor. — Fragrance of the Early Day. — Mist upon the Waters. — A Slave Ship. — A Beautiful but Guilty Brigantine. — A French Cruiser. — Cunning Seamanship. — A Wild Goose Chase. — A Cuban Posada. — Visit to a Coffee Estate. — Landing a Slave Cargo. — A Sight to challenge Sympathy and Indignation. — Half-Starved Victims. — Destruction of the Slave Ship 282

CHAPTER XVI.

Antique Appearance of Everything. — The Yeomen of Cuba. — A Montero's Home. — Personal Experience. — The Soil of the Island. — Oppression by the Government. — Spanish Justice in Havana. — Tax upon the Necessities of Life. — The Proposed Treaty with Spain. — A One-Sided Proposition. — A Much Taxed People. — Some of the Items of Taxation. — Fraud and Bankruptcy. — The Boasted Strength of Moro Castle. — Destiny of Cuba. — A Heavy Annual Cost to Spain. — Political Condition. — Pictures of Memory 300

DUE SOUTH.

CHAPTER I.

Departure. — On Board Ship. — Arrival at Nassau. — Capital of the Bahamas. — Climate. — Soil. — Fruits and Flowers. — Magic Fertility. — Colored Population. — The Blockade Runners. — Population. — Products. — A Picturesque Local Scene. — Superstition. — Fish Story. — The Silk-Cotton Tree. — Remarkable Vegetation. — The Sea Gardens. — Marine Animal Life. — The Bahama Banks. — Burial at Sea. — Venal Officials. — Historical Characters. — The Early Buccaneers. — Diving for Drinking-Water.

WE left Boston in a blustering snow-storm on the morning of February 25th, and reached New York city to find it also clothed in a wintry garb, Broadway being lined on either side of its entire length with tall piles of snow, like haycocks, prepared for carting away during the coming night. Next morning, when we drove to the dock to take passage on board the steamship Cienfuegos, the snow-mounds had all been removed. The mail steamer sailed promptly at the hour assigned, hauled out into the stream by a couple of noisy little tugs, with two-inch hawsers made fast to stem and stern. Before sunset the pilot left the ship, which was then headed due south for Nassau, N. P., escorted by large fields of floating ice, here and there decked with lazy snow-white sea-gulls. The sharp northwest wind, though blustering and aggressive, was in our favor, and the ship spread all her artificial wings as auxiliary to her natural motor. We doubled Cape Hatteras and Cape Lookout well in towards the shore, sighting on the afternoon of the fourth day the Island of Abaco, largest of the Bahama Isles, with its famous " Hole in the Wall " and sponge-lined shore. The woolen clothing worn when we came on board ship had already become oppressive, the cabin thermometer indicating 72° Fahrenheit. With nothing to engage the eye save the blue sky and the bluer water, the most is made of every circumstance at sea, and even trivial occurrences become notable. The playful dolphins went through their aquatic pantomime for our amusement. Half a dozen of them started off just ahead of the cutwater, and raced the ship for two hours, keeping exactly the same relative distance ahead without any apparent effort. Scores of others leaped out of the water and plunged in again in graceful curves, as though they enjoyed the sport. A tiny land bird flew on board, and was chased all over the ship by one or two juveniles until caught, panting and trembling with the unwonted exertion. Presently it was given its liberty, partook freely of bread crumbs and drank of fresh water, then assumed a perch aloft, where it carefully dressed its feathers, and after thanking its entertainers with a few cheerful notes it extended its wings and launched out into space, no land being in sight. The broken mainmast of a ship, floating, with considerable top hamper attached, was passed within a cable's length, suggestive of a recent wreck, and inducing a thousand dreary surmises. At first it was announced as the sea serpent, but its true nature was soon obvious. At midnight, March 1st, Nassau light hove in sight, dimmed by a thin, soft haze, which hung over the water, and through which the light, by some law of refraction, seemed to be coming out to meet the ship. Overhead all was bright, — almost dazzling with unnumbered stars and familiar constellations, like silver spangles on a background of blue velvet. We anchored off the island an hour before daylight, the harbor being too shallow to admit the ship. A forbidding sand bar blocks the entrance, inside of which the water is but fifteen feet deep. Indeed, Nassau would have no harbor at all were it not that nature has kindly placed Hog Island in the form of a breakwater, just off the town. The vibrating hull of the Cienfuegos was once more at rest; the stout heart-throbs, the panting and trembling, of the great engine had ceased; the wheelhouse and decks were deserted, and one was fain to turn in below for a brief nap before landing on this the most populous of the Bahamas.

The island, which was settled by Europeans as early as 1629, embraces nearly a hundred square miles, forming an oasis in the desert of waters. It is sixteen miles long and about one half as wide, containing fourteen thousand inhabitants, more or less, who can hardly be designated as an enterprising community. On first landing, everything strikes the visitor as being peculiarly foreign, — almost unique. The town is situated on the northerly front of the island, extending along the shore for a couple of miles, and back to a crest of land which rises to nearly the height of a hundred feet. This elevation is crowned by the residence of the English Governor-General, in front of which may be seen a colossal but not admirable statue of Columbus. The town boasts a small public library, a museum, theatre, several small churches, a prison, a hospital, and a bank. The government maintains one company of infantry, composed of black men, officered by whites. It must be admitted that they present a fine military appearance when on parade. Nassau has long been a popular resort for invalids who seek a soft, equable climate, and as it lies between the warm South Atlantic and the Gulf Stream it is characterized by the usual temperature of the tropics. There seemed to be a certain enervating influence in the atmosphere, under the effects of which the habitués of the place were plainly struck with a spirit of indolence. The difference between those just arrived and the regular guests of the Victoria Hotel, in this respect, could not fail to be observed. The languidly oppressive warmth imparts a certain softness to manners, a voluptuous love of idleness, and a glow to the affections which are experienced with less force at the North. Neither snow nor frost is ever encountered here, and yet it is as near to Boston or New York as is the city of Chicago. The temperature, we are told, never falls below 64° Fahrenheit, nor rises above 82°, the variations rarely exceeding five degrees in twenty-four hours. In Florida a change of twenty degrees is not unusual within the period of a single day. The thermometer stood at 73° on the first day of March, and everything was bathed in soft sunlight.

It is somewhat singular that an island like New Providence, which is practically without soil, should be so remarkably productive in its vegetation. It is surrounded by low-lying coral reefs, and is itself composed of coral and limestone. These, pulverized, actually form the earth out of which spring noble palm, banana, ceiba, orange, lemon, tamarind, almond, mahogany, and cocoanut trees, with a hundred and one other varieties of fruits, flowers, and woods, including the bread-fruit tree, that natural food for indolent natives of equatorial regions. Of course in such a soil the plough is unknown, its substitutes being the pickaxe and crowbar. However, science teaches us that all soils are but broken and decomposed rock, pulverized by various agencies acting through long periods of time. So the molten lava which once poured from the fiery mouth of Vesuvius has become the soil of thriving vineyards, which produce the priceless Lachryma Christi wine. This transformation is not accomplished in a lifetime, but is the result of ages of slow disintegration.

Among other flowering trees, some strikingly beautiful specimens of the alligator-pear in full bloom were observed, the blossom suggesting the passion-flower. While our favorite garden plants at the North are satisfied to bloom upon lowly bushes, at the South they are far more ambitious, and develop into tall trees, though sometimes at the partial expense of their fragrance. The air was full of sweet perfume from the white blossoms of the shaddock, contrasting with the deep glossy green of its thick-set leaves, the spicy pimento and cinnamon trees being also noticeable. With all this charming floral effect the bird melody which greets the ear in Florida was wanting, though it would seem to be so natural an adjunct to the surroundings. Nature's never-failing rule of compensation is manifested here: all the attractions are not bestowed upon any one class; brilliancy of feathers and sweetness of song do not go together.

The torrid zone endows the native birds with brilliant plumage, while the colder North gives its feathered tribes the winning charm of melody.

The soil of these Bahama Islands, composed of such unpromising ingredients, shows in its prolific yield how much vegetation depends for its sustenance upon atmospheric air, especially in tropical climes. The landlord of the Victoria Hotel told us, as an evidence of the fertility of the soil, that radish seeds which were planted on the first day of the month would sufficiently mature and ripen by the twenty-first — that is in three weeks — for use upon the table; and also that potatoes, tomatoes, cucumbers, and melons were relatively expeditious in ripening here after planting. Our mind reverted to the jugglers of Madras and Bombay, who made an orange-tree grow from the seed, and bear fruit before our very eyes, at a single sitting.

The luscious pineapple, zapota, mango, pomegranate, guava, star-apple, citron, custard-apple, mammee, and other fruits abound. The profuseness and variety of beautiful ferns and orchidaceous plants will also be sure to attract the attention of the Northern visitor. The rocky formation of the soil produces good natural roads, so that a long drive in the environs of Nassau is like a pleasure excursion over a well-macadamized thoroughfare. We were told of a delightful drive of fifteen miles in length which follows the sea beach the whole distance, but did not find time to test its attractions, though strongly tempted by the excellence of the roads. Here, as in other tropical regions, each month has its special floral display, although there are many, and indeed a majority, of the plants which continue to flower all the year round. We observed that the stone walls and hedges were now and again covered for short spaces with the coral-vine, whose red blossoms, so pleasing to the eye, emit no odor. The yellow jasmine was dazzlingly conspicuous everywhere, and very fragrant. Red and white roses, various species of cacti, and tube-roses bloomed before the rude thatched cabins of the negroes in the environs, as well as in the tiny front gardens of the whites in the streets of the town; while red, white, and pink oleanders grew as tall as trees, and flower here every month in the year. The night-blooming cereus abounds, opening just at sunset, and closing again at break of day. The outside leaves of this poetical flower are of a pale green, the inner ones of a pure wax-like white, and the petals light yellow. Complete, it is about eight inches long, and from twelve to fifteen in circumference.

While we drove through the suburbs, slatternly, half-clothed family groups of negroes watched us with curious eyes, and on the road aged colored men and women were occasionally met, who saluted us with grave dignity. No one seemed to be at work; sunshine was the only perceptible thing going on, ripening the fruits and vegetables by its genial rays, while the negroes waited for the harvest. Like the birds, they had no occasion to sow, but only to pluck and to eat. There was, both in and out of the town, a tumble-down, mouldy aspect to the dwellings, which seemed to be singularly neglected and permitted to lapse into decay. With the exception of the town of Nassau, and its immediate environs, New Providence is nearly all water and wilderness; it has some circumscribed lakes, but no mountains, rivers, or rivulets. The island is justly famous for the beauty and variety of its lovely flowers. It is true that the rose is not quite equal in color, development, and fragrance to ours of the North; Nature has so many indigenous flowers on which to expend her liberality that she bestows less attention upon this, the loveliest of them all. The Cherokee rose, single-leafed, now so rare with us, seems here to have found a congenial foreign home. In the suburbs of Nassau are many attractive flowers, fostered only by the hand of Nature. Among them was the triangular cactus, with its beautiful yellow blossom, like a small sunflower, supported by a deep green triangular stem.

The pendulous cactus was also hanging here and there on walls and tree trunks, in queer little jointed, pipe-stem branches. The royal palm, that king of tropical vegetation, is not very abundant here, but yet sufficiently so to characterize the place. Its roots resemble those of asparagus, and are innumerable. Another peculiarity of the palm is that it starts a full-sized trunk; therefore, not the diameter, but the height, determines its age, which is recorded by annual concentric rings clearly defined upon its tall, straight stem.

During the late civil war in the United States, when blockade runners made this place a port of call and a harbor for refitting, it was by English connivance practically a Confederate port. The officers and sailors expended their ill-gotten wealth with the usual lavishness of the irresponsible, the people of Nassau reaping thereby a fabulous harvest in cash. This was quite demoralizing to honest industry, and, as might be expected. a serious reaction has followed. Legitimate trade and industry will require years before they can reassert themselves. Sudden and seeming prosperity is almost sure to be equally transitory. We were told that, during the entire period in which the Confederates resorted here under the open encouragement and protection of England, the town was the scene of the most shameful drunken orgies from morning until night. Lewdness and crime were rampant. Officers played pitch-penny on the veranda of the Victoria Hotel with gold eagles, and affiliated openly with negresses. The evil influence upon all concerned was inevitable, and its poisonous effect is not yet obliterated.

Three quarters of the present population are negroes, but of course all trace of the aborigines has disappeared. It is curious and interesting to know what Columbus thought of them. He wrote to his royal mistress, after having explored these Bahamas, as follows: "This country excels all others as far as the day surpasses the night in splendor; the natives love their neighbors as themselves; their conversation is the sweetest imaginable, and their faces are always smiling. So gentle and so affectionate are they that I swear to your highness there is no better people in the world."

The negroes are mostly engaged in cultivating patches of pineapples, and yams, sweet potatoes, and other vegetables; a large number of the males employ themselves also in fishing and gathering sponges. It will be remembered that from this locality comes the principal supply of coarse sponge for Europe and America. There is also a considerable trade, carried on in a small way, in fine turtle-shell, which is polished in an exquisite manner, and manufactured by the natives into ornaments. Though the Bahama sponges are not equal to those obtained in the Mediterranean, still they are marketable, and Nassau exports half a million dollars' worth annually. It is a curious fact that sponges can be propagated by cuttings taken from living specimens, which, when attached to a piece of board and sunk in the sea, will increase and multiply. Thus the finest Mediterranean specimens may be successfully transplanted to the coral reefs of these islands, the only requisite to their sustenance seeming to be a coralline shore and limestone surroundings. Another important industry which gives employment to a considerable number of the inhabitants is the canning of pineapples, a process which is equivalent to preserving them for any length of time. One firm on Bay Street, as we were informed, canned and exported nearly a million of pines in one season, lately; and another, engaged in the fresh-fruit trade, shipped to the States fifteen cargoes of pines in one year, besides many thousands of cocoanuts. These are not all raised in Nassau, but this port is made the headquarters for collecting and disposing of the fruit grown upon what are termed the out-islands, as well as marketing the large product of its own soil. It is but a short drive inland to the extensive pineapple fields, where the handsome fruit may be seen in the several stages of growth, varying according to the season of the year. If intended for exportation, the fruit is gathered green; if for canning purposes, the riper it is the better. The visitor will also be impressed by the beauty and grace of the cocoanut trees, their pinnate leaves often a hundred feet from the ground, notwithstanding the bare cylindrical stem attains a thickness of only two feet.

The Royal Victoria Hotel, though bearing a loyal name, is kept by an American, and is a very substantial, capacious building, composed of native limestone, four stories high, three of which are surrounded by wide piazzas, which afford the shade so necessary in a land of perpetual summer. The native stone of which the island is composed is so soft when first quarried that it can easily be cut or sawed into any shape desired, but it hardens very rapidly after exposure to the atmosphere. The hotel will accommodate three hundred guests, and is a positive necessity for the comfort and prosperity of the place. It was built and is owned by the British government, who erected it some twenty-five years since. At the time of our arrival there was gathered under the lofty Moorish portico of the hotel a most picturesque group of negroes, of both sexes and of all ages, their ebony faces forming a strong contrast to the background of well-whitewashed walls. Some of the women were dressed in neat calico gowns, and wore broad-brimmed straw hats; some were in rags, hatless, shoeless, and barelegged; some had high-colored kerchiefs wound turban-like about their woolly heads; and some wore scarlet shawls, the sight of which would have driven a Spanish bull raving mad. There were coquettish mulatto girls with bouquets for sale, and fancy flowers wrought of shells; these last of most exquisite workmanship. Specimens of this native shell-work were sent to the Vienna Exposition, where they received honorable mention, and were afterwards purchased and presented to the Prince of Wales. Old gray-haired negroes, with snow-white beards on a black ground, offered fruits in great variety, — zapotas, mangoes, pineapples, and grape-fruit.

Others had long strings of sponges for sale, wound round their shoulders like huge snakes; some of these were good, but many were utterly useless. No one knows this better than the cunning negroes themselves, but strangers, only touching at Nassau, they do not expect to see again, and there is proverbially cheating in all trades but ours. A bright, thrifty-looking colored woman had spread out her striped shawl upon the ground, and on this arrayed a really fine collection of conch-shells for sale, delicately polished, and of choice shapes. When first brought to the surface by the divers they are not infrequently found to contain pearls imbedded in the palatable and nutritious meat. These pearls are generally of a pinkish hue, and greatly prized by the jewelers. Now and then a diver will realize a hundred dollars for one of them. From the conch-shell also come the best shell cameos. A smart half-breed offered canes of ebony, lignum vitæ, lance, and orange wood, all of native growth. He was dressed in a white linen jacket, pantaloons to match, with a semi-military cap, cocked on one side of his head, — quite a colored dude. The women who sell native-made baskets are most persistent, but if you purchase of them make your own change, for they are apt to take money away for this purpose and to forget to return. Negro nature is frail, characterized at Nassau by theft and licentiousness, but great crimes are rare. If you have occasion to hire a boat for a sail in the harbor, be sure to find and employ "Bushy," a tall, intelligent darkey, the best boatman and stroke-oar in Nassau.

Bushy showed us what he called a fish-whip, made from the whipray, a fish quite new to us, but indigenous to these waters. With a body shaped like a flounder, it has a tail often ten feet long, tapering from about one inch in thickness at the butt to an eighth of an inch at the small end. When dried this resembles whalebone, and makes a good coach-whip. There is a great variety of fish in and about the Bahamas. We saw, just landed at Nassau, a jew-fish, which takes the same place here that the halibut fills at the North, being cut into steaks and fried in a similar manner. They are among the largest of edible fish, and this specimen weighed about four hundred pounds. According to Bushy, at certain seasons of the year the jew-fish lies dormant upon the sandy bottom, and refuses to take the bait. In these transparent waters he is easily seen when in this condition, and the native fishermen then dive down and place a stout hook in his mouth! Though this may sound like a "fish story," we were assured by others of its truth. Bushy undertook to give us the names of the various fishes which abound here, but the long list of them and his peculiar pronunciation drove us nearly wild. Still a few are remembered; such as the yellow-tailed snapper, striped snapper, pork-fish, angel-fish, cat-fish, hound-fish, the grouper, sucking-fish, and so on. Both harbor and deep sea fishing afford the visitor to Nassau excellent amusement, and many sportsmen go thither annually from New York solely for its enjoyment.

The colored people of Nassau, as we were assured by one competent to speak upon the subject, form a religious community, according to the ordinary acceptation of the term. They are very fond of church-going, and of singing and shouting on all religious occasions. Nervously emotional, they work themselves up to a hysterical condition so furious as to threaten their sanity, but having naturally so little of that qualification, they are pretty safe. No people could possibly be more superstitious. They shut up and double lock the doors and windows of their cabins at night to keep out evil spirits. There are regular professional man-witches among them, persons a little shrewder and more cunning than their fellows. The very ignorant believe in a sort of fetichism, so that when a boat starts on a sponge-fishing trip, the obeah man is called upon for some coöperation and mysticism, to insure a successful return of the crew. The sponge fishermen have several hundred boats regularly licensed, and measuring on an average twenty tons each. On favorable occasions these men lay aside their legitimate calling, and become for the time being wreckers, an occupation which verges only too closely upon piracy. The intricate navigation of these waters, dotted by hundreds of small reefs and islands, and which can be traversed by only three safe channels, has furnished in former years a large amount of shipwrecked merchandise to Nassau. The wrecking business at best is extremely demoralizing, unfitting any community of men for legitimate industry, as we know very well by the experience gained on our own Florida shore. Men who have cruised fruitlessly for months in search of a profitable wreck will sometimes be tempted to decoy a ship from her proper course, and lead her upon the rocks, by a display of false lights.

In front of the Victoria Hotel are some noble specimens of the ceiba, or silk-cotton tree, as it is called here, the finest and loftiest we have seen in any country. These trees, naturally slow growers, must be over a century in age, and afford, by their widespread branches, a shade equally graceful and grateful. Like the india-rubber trees of Asia, these ceibas have at least one half of their anaconda-like roots exposed upon the surface of the ground, dividing the lower portion of the stem into supporting buttresses, a curious piece of finesse on the part of nature to overcome the disadvantage of insufficient soil. The tree bears annually a large seed-pod, packed with cotton of a soft, silky texture, and hence its name. It is, however, suitable neither for timber nor fuel, and the small product of cotton is seldom if ever gathered. The islanders are proud of a single specimen of the banyan tree of considerable size, which they show to all visitors; but it cannot be indigenous — it must have been brought in its youth from Asia. There is, however, in these West Indian isles, the black mangrove, with very similar habit to the banyan. The limbs spread to such an extent from the trunk as to require support to prevent them from breaking off or bending to the ground by their own weight; but to obviate this, nature has endowed the tree with a peculiar growth. When the branches have become so heavy as to be no longer able to support themselves, they send forth from the under side sprigs which, rapidly descending to the ground, take root like the banyan, and become supporting columns to the heavy branches above. So the writer has seen in Hindostan a vine which grew, almost leafless, closely entwined around the trees to the very top, whence it descended, took fresh root, and ascended the nearest adjoining tree, until it had gone on binding an entire grove in a ligneous rope. Long tendrils of the love-vine, that curious aerial creeper, which feeds on air alone, were seen hanging across some of the low branches of the Nassau trees, and we were told that the plant will grow equally well if hung upon a nail indoors. Emblematic of true affection, it clings, like Japanese ivy, tenaciously to the object it fixes upon. One specimen was shown to us which had developed to the size of the human hand from a single leaf carelessly pinned by a guest to one of the chamber walls of the hotel.

There are said to be six hundred of the Bahama islands, large and small, of which Nassau is the capital, and there, as already intimated, the English Governor-General resides. This numerical calculation is undoubtedly correct; many are mere rocky islets, and not more than twenty have fixed inhabitants. Is there anything more wonderful in nature than that these hundreds of isles should have been built up from the bottom of the sea by insects so small as to be microscopic? All lie north of Cuba and St. Domingo, just opposite the Gulf of Mexico, easily accessible from our own shores by a short and pleasant sea-voyage of three or four days. They are especially inviting to those persons who have occasion to avoid the rigor of Northern winters. People threatened with consumption seek Nassau on sanitary principles, and yet it was found upon inquiry that many natives die of that insidious disease, which rapidly runs its career when it is first developed in a tropical climate. To the author it would seem that consumptives might find resorts better adapted to the recovery of their health. Intermittent fever, also, is not unknown at Nassau.

The sea gardens, as they are called, situated just

off the shores of the island, are well worth a visit; where, by means of a simple instrument of wood and glass, one is enabled to look many fathoms below the surface of the water, which is here so remarkable for its transparency. These water glasses are all of home manufacture, easily improvised, being formed of a small wooden box three or four inches square, open at the top, and having a water-tight glass bottom. With the glass portion slightly submerged, one is enabled to see distinctly the beautiful coral reefs, with their marvelous surroundings. There are displayed tiny caves and grottoes of white coral of great delicacy and variety, star-fishes, sea-urchins, growing sponges, sea-fans, and gaudy-colored tropical fishes, including the humming-bird-fish, and others like butterflies with mottled fins and scales, and that little oddity the rainbow-fish. The prevailing color of this attractive creature is dark green, but the tinted margins of its scales so reflect the light as to show all the colors of the rainbow, and hence its name. When bottled in alcohol, these fairy-like denizens of the deep lose their brilliancy, which they exhibit only in their native element. This unique display is greatly enhanced in beauty by the clearness of the Bahama waters, and the reflected light from the snow-white sandy bottom, dotted here and there by curious and delicate shells of opalescent lustre. One longs to descend among these coral bowers, — these mermaid-gardens, — and pluck of the submarine flora in its purple, yellow, and scarlet freshness.

It will be remembered that Columbus wrote home to his royal patrons that the fish which abounded in the seas partook of the same novelty which characterized everything else in the New World. This was about four hundred years ago, before the great Genoese had discovered Cuba. "The fish," as he wrote, "rivaled the birds in tropical brilliancy of color, the scales of some of them glancing back the rays of light like precious stones, as they sported about the ships and flashed gleams of gold and silver through the clear water."

The surface life of these translucent waters is also extremely interesting. Here the floating jelly-fish, called, from its phosphorescence, the glow-worm of the sea, is observed in great variety, sheltering little colonies of young fishes within its tentacles, which rush forth for a moment to capture some passing mite, and as quickly return again to their shelter. One takes up a handful of the floating gulf-weed and finds, within the pale yellow leaves and berries, tiny pipe-fish, sea-horses, and the little nest-building antennarius, thus forming a buoyant home for parasites, crabs, and mollusks, itself a sort of mistletoe of the ocean. The young of the mackerel and the herring glance all about just beneath the surface near the shore, like myriad pieces of silver. Now and again that particolored formation of marine life, the Portuguese man-of-war, is observed, its long ventral fins spread out like human fingers to steady it upon the surface of the water. Verily, the German scientist who says there is more of animal life beneath the surface of the sea than above it cannot be far amiss. This seems to be the more reasonable when we consider the relative proportions of land and water. The whole surface of the globe is supposed to have an area of about two hundred million square miles. Of these only about fifty millions are dry land. Within the harbor of Nassau the divisions of shoal

and deep water presented most singular and clearly
defined lines of color, azure, purple, and orange-leaf
green, — so marked as to be visible half a mile away.
All was beneath a sky so deeply and serenely blue
as constantly to recall the arching heavens of middle
India.

The Bahama Banks is a familiar expression to
most of us, but perhaps few clearly understand the
significance of the term, which is applied to a remarkable plateau at the western extremity of the archipelago, occupying a space between two and three
hundred miles long, and about one third as wide.
These banks, as they are called, rise almost perpendicularly from an unfathomable depth of water, and
are of coral formation. In sailing over them the
bottom is distinctly seen from the ship's deck, the
depth of water being almost uniformly forty to fifty
feet. Some years since, when the author was crossing
these banks in a sailing ship, a death occurred among
the foremast hands, and the usual sea burial followed.
The corpse was sewn up in a hammock, with iron
weights at the feet, the more readily to sink it.
After reading the burial service the body was
launched into the sea from a grating rigged out of a
gangway amidship. The waters were perfectly calm,
and the barque had but little headway. Indeed, we
lay almost as still as though anchored, so that the
body was seen to descend slowly alongside until it
reached the calcareous, sandy bottom, where it assumed an upright and strangely lifelike position, as
though standing upon its feet. An ominous silence
reigned among the watching crew, and it was a
decided relief to all hands when a northerly wind
sprang up, filling the canvas and giving the vessel
steerage way.

So many years have passed since the occurrence of the scene just related that we may give its sequel without impropriety, though, at the same time, we expose the venal character of Spanish officials. The man we buried on the Bahama Banks had died of small-pox, though no other person on board showed any symptoms of the disease. On entering the harbor of Havana, three days later, we had been hailed from Moro Castle and had returned the usual answer. A couple of doubloons in gold made the boarding officer conveniently blind, and a similar fee thrust quietly into the doctor's hand insured a "clean bill of health," under which we were permitted to land! The alternative was twenty-one days' quarantine.

Fort Montague, mounting four rusty guns, "with ne'er a touch-hole to any on 'em," as Bushy informed us, stands upon a projecting point about a mile from the town of Nassau, the road thither forming a delightful evening promenade, or drive. The fort is old, crumbling, and time-worn, but was once occupied by the buccaneers as a most important stronghold commanding the narrow channel. These sea-robbers imposed a heavy tax upon all shipping passing this way, and for many years realized a large income from this source. It was only piracy in another form. Most vessels found it cheaper to pay than to fight. When the notorious Black Beard had his headquarters at Nassau, he sought no such pretext, but preyed upon all commerce alike, provided the vessels were not too well armed to be captured. This notorious pirate had an innate love for cruelty, and often tortured his captives without any apparent purpose, after the fashion of our Western Indians. When the English lashed the mutineers of Delhi and

Cawnpore to the muzzles of their cannon and blew them to pieces, they were enacting no new tragedy; legend and history tell us that Black Beard, the pirate of the Windward Passage, set them that example many years before. His rule was to murder all prisoners who would not join his ship, and those whom he took fighting, that is, with arms in their hands, were subjected to torture, one form of which was that of lashing captives to the cannon's mouth and applying the match. Fort Montague is not occupied by even a corporal's guard to-day, and is of no efficiency whatever against modern gunnery. The reader will thus observe that the principal business which has engaged Nassau heretofore has been wrecking, buccaneering, privateering, and blockade running.

Some noted characters have found an asylum here, first and last. After Lord Dunmore left Virginia he sought official position and made a home on the island. He was appointed governor, and some of the buildings erected by him are still pointed out to the visitor, especially that known as the Old Fort, just back of the Victoria Hotel, crowning the height. His summer seat, known as the Hermitage, is a quaint old place, still in fair condition, and surrounded by oaks and cocoanut trees, near the sea. Such matters do not often get into history, but legend tells us that some strange orgies took place at the Hermitage, where the play was for heavy stakes, and the drinking was of a similar excessive character.

Another well-known individual who sought to make a home here, and also to escape from all former associations, was the notorious Blennerhasset, a name familiar in connection with Aaron Burr. After his trial, it will be remembered that he suddenly disappeared, and was heard of no more. He left his country for his country's good, changing his name to that of Carr. His objective point was Nassau; there his undoubted talent and legal ability were duly recognized and he was appointed government attorney, officiating in that capacity for a number of years. Having deserted his first wife, he found another to console him upon the island. At last wife number one appeared upon the island. She had discovered his hiding-place, and a domestic war ensued. Wife number two carried the day and the rightful spouse was sent away and paid an annuity to keep away. The pretended Mr. Carr is said to have finally lapsed into habits of excessive intemperance, and to have found a stranger's grave on the island.

Much of the drinking water, and certainly the best in use at Nassau, as well as on some of the neighboring islands, is procured in a remarkable, though very simple manner, from the sea. Not far from shore, on the coral reefs, there are never-failing fresh water springs, bubbling up from the bottom through the salt water with such force as clearly to indicate their locality. Over these ocean springs the people place sunken barrels filled with sand, one above another, the bottoms and tops being displaced. The fresh water is thus conducted to the surface through the column of sand, which forms a perfect filterer. Such a crude arrangement is only temporary, liable to be displaced by any severe storm which should agitate the surrounding waters. If destroyed in the hurricane season, these structures are not renewed until settled weather. In so small and low lying an island as that of Nassau, it is very plain that this crystal liquid, pure and tasteless, cannot come from any rainfall upon the soil, and its existence, therefore, suggests a problem, the solving of which we submit to the scientists.

On the arid shores of the Persian Gulf, where rain so seldom falls, and where there are no rills to refresh the parched soil, fresh water is also obtained from submerged springs beneath the salt water. Here it is brought to the surface by divers, who descend with a leather bag, the mouth of which being opened over the bubbling spring is quickly filled and closed again, being drawn to the surface by those who are left there to assist the diver, who hastens upward for air. In descending his feet are weighted with stones, which being cast off at the proper moment, he naturally rises at once to the surface. This operation is repeated until a sufficient quantity of fresh water is procured. There is no mystery, however, as to the source of these springs. The rain first falls on the distant mountains, and finding its way downward through the fissures of rocky ledges, pursues its course until it gushes forth in the bed of the gulf.

CHAPTER II.

Among the Islands. — San Salvador.— A Glimpse at the Stars. — Hayti. — The Gulf Stream. — The Caribbean Sea. — Latitude and Longitude. — The Southern Coast of Cuba. — A Famous Old Fortress. — Fate of Political Prisoners. — The Oldest City in Cuba. — The Aborigines. — Cuban Cathedrals. — Drinking Saloons. — Dogs, Horses, and Coolies. — Scenes in Santiago de Cuba. —Devoured by Sharks. — Lying at Anchor. — Wreck of a Historic Ship. — Cuban Circulating Medium. — Tropical Temperature.

AFTER leaving Nassau we stood northward for half a day in order to get a safe and proper channel out of the crooked Bahamas, where there is more of shoal than of navigable waters, leaving a score of small islands behind us inhabited only by turtles, flamingoes, and sea birds. But we were soon steaming due south again towards our objective point, the island of Cuba, five hundred miles away. San Salvador was sighted on our starboard bow, the spot where Columbus first landed in the New World, though even this fact has not escaped the specious arguments of the iconoclasts. Nevertheless, we gazed upon it with reverent credulity. It will be found laid down on most English maps as Cat Island, and is now the home of two or three thousand colored people. San Salvador is nearly as large as New Providence, and is said to claim some special advantages over that island in the quality of its fruits. It is claimed that the oranges grown here are the sweetest and best in the world, the same excellence being attributed to its abundant yield of pineapples and other tropical fruits.

There are so many of these small islands in the Bahama group that the geographers may be excused for the heterogeneous manner in which they have placed them on the common maps. To find their true and relative position one must consult the sailing-charts, where absolute correctness is supposed to be found, a prime necessity in such intricate navigation. The total population of the Bahamas has been ascertained, by census, to be a fraction less than forty thousand.

The voyager in these latitudes is constantly saluted by gentle breezes impregnated with tropical fragrance, intensified in effect by the distant view of cocoanut, palmetto, and banana trees, clothing the islands and growing down to the water's very edge. As we glide along, gazing shoreward, now and again little groups of swallows seem to be flitting only a few feet above the water for a considerable distance, and then suddenly disappearing beneath the waves. These are flying-fish enjoying an air bath, either in frolic or in fear; pursued, may be, by some aqueous enemy, to escape from whom they essay these aerial flights. The numerous islands, very many of which are uninhabited, have yet their recorded names, more or less characteristic, such as Rum Key, Turk's Island, — famous for the export of salt, — Bird Rock, Fortune Island, Great and Little Inagua, Crooked Island, and so on, all more or less noted for the disastrous wrecks which have occurred on their low coralline shores. Our Northern cities are largely dependent upon the Bahamas for their early annual supplies of pineapples, cocoanuts, oranges, bananas, and some vegetables, in which they are all more or less prolific. Here also is the harvest field of the conchologist, the beaches and coral reefs affording an abundant supply of exquisitely colored shells, of all imaginable shapes, including the large and valuable conch-shell, of which many thousand dollars' worth are annually exported, the contents first serving the divers for food.

It was interesting to remain on deck at night and watch the heavens, as we glided silently through the phosphorescent sea. Was it possible the grand luminary, which rendered objects so plain that one could almost read fine print with no other help, shone solely by borrowed light? We all know it to be so, and also that Venus, Mars, Jupiter, and Saturn shine in a similar manner with light reflected from the sun. It was curious to adjust the telescope and bring the starry system nearer to the vision. If we direct our gaze upon a planet we find its disk sharply defined; change the direction and let it rest upon a star, and we have only a point of light, more or less brilliant. The glass reveals to us the fact that the star-dust which we call the Milky Way is an aggregation of innumerable single suns. Sweeping the arching blue with the telescope, we find some stars are golden, some green, others purple, many silvery-white, and some are twins. Probably there is no such thing as stars of the first and second magnitude, as the common expression names them. It is most likely only a question of distance which regulates the brightness to our vision. Science reduces the distances of heavenly bodies from our earth to figures, but they are so immense as to be simply bewildering. At the North the moon is silvery, but in tropical skies at night it becomes golden, glowing, and luxurious in its splendor, never pale and wan as it seems with us.

When the lonely lighthouse which marks Cape

Maysi, at the easterly point of Cuba, hove in sight on the starboard bow, the dim form of the mountains of Hayti was also visible on the opposite horizon. A subterranean connection is believed to exist between the mountain ranges of the two islands.

When the outline of the Haytian mountains was in view, it was very natural to express a wish to visit the island at some convenient time. This led to some intelligent and interesting remarks from a compagnon de voyage, who had resided for two years at Port-au-Prince, the capital. "Unless you are compelled to land there," said he, "I advise you to avoid Hayti." He fully confirmed the reports of its barbarous condition, and declared it to be in a rapid decadence, as regarded every desirable element of civilization. In the country, a short distance from either Gonaives, Jacmel, or Port-au-Prince, where the mass of the negro population live, Voudou worship and cannibalism are quite common at the present time. The influence of the Voudou priests is so much feared by the government that the horrible practice is little interfered with. When the officials are forced to take cognizance of the crime, the lightest possible punishment is imposed upon the convicted parties. The island of San Domingo is about half the size of Cuba, Hayti occupying one third of the western portion, the rest of the territory belonging to the republic of San Domingo. "As to Port-au-Prince," said our informant, "it is the dirtiest place I have ever seen in any part of the world." Nevertheless, the historic interest clustering about the island is very great. It was the seat of the first Spanish colony founded in the New World. Its soil has been bathed in the blood of Europeans as well as of its aboriginal inhabitants. For three hundred years it was the arena of fierce struggles between the French, Spaniards, and English, passing alternately under the dominion of each of these powers, until finally, torn by insurrection and civil war, in 1804 it achieved its independence. The city of San Domingo, capital of the republic, is the oldest existing settlement by white men in the New World, having been founded in 1494 by Bartholomew Columbus. It contains to-day a little less than seven thousand inhabitants.

We gave Cape Maysi a wide berth, as a dangerous reef makes out from the land, eastward, for a mile or more. The fixed light at this point is a hundred and thirty feet above sea level, and is visible nearly twenty miles off shore.

We were running through the Windward Passage, as it was called by the early navigators, and whence one branch of the Gulf Stream finds its way northward. The Gulf Stream! Who can explain the mystery of its motive power; what keeps its tepid waters in a course of thousands of miles from mingling with the rest of the sea; whence does it come? The accepted theories are familiar enough, but we do not believe them. Maury says the Gulf of Mexico is its fountain, and its mouth is the Arctic Sea. The maps make the eastern shore of Cuba terminate as sharply as a needle's point, but it proved to be very blunt in reality, as it forms the gateway to the Caribbean Sea, where the irregular coast line runs due north and south for the distance of many leagues. It is a low, rocky shore for the most part, but rises gradually as it recedes inland, until it assumes the form of hills so lofty as to merit the designation of mountains.

There was on board of our ship an intelligent resident of Santiago, who was enthusiastic in his description of the plains and valleys lying beyond the hills which stood so prominently on the coast, — hills probably older than any tongue in which we could describe them. The Scriptural Garden of Eden has absolutely been placed here by supposition on the part of traveled people. The temperature is simply perfect, if we are to believe our informant; the vegetation is of a primitive delicacy and beauty unequaled elsewhere; the fruits are fabulously abundant and of the most perfect flavor; the water bubbles forth from springs of crystal purity, and the flora is so lovely as to inspire the most indifferent beholder with delight. "It is called the Garden of Cuba," said the American Consul of Cienfuegos, "but many go further, and declare it to be the location of the original Paradise." Certain it is that the few Americans who have sought this so highly praised region, though compelled to deny themselves the ordinary comforts to be found in more accessible resorts, have admitted with emphasis that nature, pure and undefiled, was here to be enjoyed in unstinted measure.

The hills bordering the shore and extending some distance inland contain much undeveloped mineral wealth, such as iron, silver, and gold. A mine of the former product is now being profitably worked by an American company, and the ore regularly shipped to Pennsylvania for smelting. This ore has special properties which render it more than usually valuable, and it is even claimed to be the best iron mine in the world. There is a strangely solitary and inhospitable appearance about this portion of the island, devoid as it is of all human habitations, and fringed either with long reaches of lonely snow-white beach or rugged brown rocks. The volcanic appearance of the land is significant of former upheavals, and this immediate region is still occasionally troubled with geological chills and fever.

The nights of early March in this latitude were exceedingly beautiful, and solemnly impressive was the liberal splendor of the sky. The full moon looked down upon and was reflected by waters of perfect smoothness. River navigation could not have been more quiet than were these nights on the blue Caribbean Sea. The air was as mild as June in New England, while at night the Southern Cross and the North Star blazed in the horizon at the same time. As we steered westward after doubling the cape, both of these heavenly sentinels were seen abeam, the constellation on our port side, and the North Star on the starboard. Each day, at the noon hour, the passengers were interested in watching the officers of the ship while they were "taking the sun," to determine the latitude and longitude. Shall we put the process into simple form for the information of the uninitiated? When the sun reaches the meridian, or culminating point of ascension, the exact moment is indicated by the instrument known as a quadrant, adjusted to the eye of the observer. The figures marked on the quadrant give the latitude of the ship at the moment of meridian. The ship's time is then made to correspond, that is to say, it must indicate 12 o'clock, M., after which it is compared with the chronometer's Greenwich time, and the difference enables the observer to determine the longitude. As fifteen miles are allowed to the minute, there will be nine hundred miles to the hour. The importance of absolute correctness in the chronometer will at once be realized, since, were it only three minutes out of the way, it would render the calculation as to longitude wrong by nearly fifty miles, which might be, and doubtless often has been, the cause of wrecking a ship upon rocks laid down upon the charts, but supposed to be far away. With the chronometer and the quadrant observation correctly ascertained, the sailing-master can prick off his exact situation on the chart. So long as the weather will permit a clear view of the sun at noon, the ship's precise location on the wide waste of waters can be known; but when continuous cloudy weather prevails, the ship's course is calculated by what is called dead reckoning, depending upon the speed and distance run as indicated by the log, which is cast hourly under such circumstances, and becomes the main factor in calculating the position of the ship. Of course the result cannot be very accurate, but is a dernier ressort. When land is in sight no observation is necessary, as the bearing of the ship is then unmistakably defined.

The sea was like molten sapphire as we glided swiftly along the southern coast of Cuba, watching the gracefully undulating shore. The mountains rose higher and higher, until they culminated in the lofty peak of Pico Turquino (blue mountain), over ten thousand feet high, as lately ascertained by actual measurement. There are coves and bays along this coast where oysters *do* grow upon trees, ridiculous as the assertion first strikes the ear. The mangrove-trees extend their roots from the shore into the sea, to which the oysters affix themselves, growing and thriving until plucked by the fishermen. They are small and of an inferior species compared with those of our own coast, but are freely eaten in the island. Near the shore hereabouts are many islets containing from three to five square miles, some of which are quite barren, while others are delicious gardens, full of tropical fruit trees, flowers, and odoriferous plants, where Paul and Virginia might have felt quite at home, wandering hand in hand.

Soon after passing the remarkably sheltered port of Guantanamo, which was for nearly a century the most notorious piratical rendezvous in the West Indies, the famous castle of Santiago is seen. It is known as Moro Castle, but it antedates the more familiar Moro of Havana by a full century. This antique, yellow, Moorish-looking stronghold — which modern gunnery would destroy in about eight minutes — is picturesque to the last degree, with its crumbling, honeycombed battlements, and queer little flanking turrets, grated windows, and shadowy towers. It is built upon the face of a lofty dun-colored rock, upon whose precipitous side the fortification is terraced. It stands just at the entrance of the narrow channel leading to the city, so that in passing in one can easily exchange oral greetings with the sentry on the outer battlement. What strikingly artistic pictures the light and shade together formed with those time-stained walls, as we steamed slowly by them! On the ocean side, directly under the castle, the sea has worn a gaping cave, so deep that it has not been explored within the memory of the people living in the neighborhood. The broad and lofty entrance is in form as perfect an arch as could be drawn by the pencil of a skillful architect. As is usual with such formations all over the world, there is a romantic legend concerning the cave related as connected with the olden time, and there is also a prevailing superstition that no one attempting to explore it will live to return.

In passing up the channel two or three little forts of queer construction are seen, supplementing the larger one, placed upon jutting headlands. The Moro of Santiago is now used as a prison for political offenders; its days of defensive importance ended with the period of the buccaneers, against whose crude means of warfare it was an ample protection. As we steamed past it that sunny afternoon, stimulated by the novelty of everything about us, a crowd of pallid, sorrowful faces appeared at the grated windows, watching us listlessly. Two days later five of them, who were condemned patriots, were led out upon those ramparts and shot, their bodies falling into the sea, and eight were sent to the penal settlement of Ceuta. Spain extends no mercy to those who dare to raise their hands or voices in favor of freedom; her political existence is sustained only in an atmosphere of oppression and cruelty. Every page of her history is a tableau of bloodshed and torture. The narrow winding channel which leads from the open sea to the harbor passes through low hills and broad meadows covered with rank verdure, cocoanut groves, and little fishing hamlets. Thrifty laurels, palms with their graceful plumes of foliage, and intensely green bananas line the way, with here and there upon the banks a pleasant country house in the midst of a pretty garden of flowering shrubs. So close is the shore all the while that one seems to be navigating upon the land, gliding among trees and over greensward rather than on blue water. Presently we pass a sharp angle of the hills into a broad, sheltered bay, and before us lies the quaint, rambling old city of Santiago de Cuba, built upon a hillside, like Tangier in Africa, and nearly as Oriental as that capital of Morocco. The first most conspicuous objects to meet the eye are the twin towers of the ancient cathedral which have withstood so many earthquakes. The weather-beaten old quartermaster on our forecastle applies the match to his brass twelve-pounder, awaking a whole broadside of echoes among the mountains, the big chain rushes swiftly through the hawse-hole, and the ship swings at her anchor in the middle of the picturesque bay.

A boat was promptly secured with which to land at this ancient city, founded by Velasquez. From the moment one touches the shore a sense of being in a foreign land forces itself upon the new-comer. The half-unintelligible language, the people, the architecture, the manners, the vegetation, even the very atmosphere and the intensity of the sunshine, are novel and attractive. It is easy to convey our partial impressions of a new place, however unique it may be, but not our inward sensations. The former are tangible, as it were, and may be depicted; the latter are like atmospheric air, which cannot be seen, but is felt. The many-colored, one-story houses of Santiago are Moorish in architecture, ranged in narrow streets, which cross each other at right angles with considerable regularity, but with roadways in an almost impassable condition, lined with sidewalks of ten or fifteen inches in width. These thoroughfares were once paved with cobblestones, but are now characterized by dirt and neglect, a stream of offensive water constantly percolating through them, in which little naked children are at play. No wonder that the city is annually decimated by yellow fever; the surprise is that it does not prevail there every month in the year. The boys and girls of the lower classes, white and black, are not thought to require clothing until they are about nine years of age. A few negresses were observed sitting on the ground, at the corners of the streets, beside their baskets containing sweet cakes, mouldy biscuits, bananas, and grape-fruit, the uninviting appearance of which seemed to indicate that they were in the last stage of collapse. Was it possible any one could eat such stuff? As we passed and repassed these patient waiters, certainly no purchasers appeared. How the forty-five thousand inhabitants manage to achieve a living it would be difficult to imagine, for the town seemed to be as dead and void of all activity as Cordova, in far-off Spain, the sleepiest city in all Europe. Santiago has not a single bookstore within its limits. No other place in Christendom, with so numerous a population, could exist, outside of Spain, without some literary resort. There are here three or four spacious two-story club-houses, with some pretension to neatness and social accommodations; but then no Cuban town of any size would be complete without these anti-domestic institutions, where the male population may congregate for evening entertainment. The interior arrangements of these club-houses were entirely exposed to view, as we passed by the iron-grated windows, devoid of curtains, blinds, or screens of any sort, and extending from ceiling to floor.

Santiago dates back to the year of our Lord 1514, making it the oldest city in the New World, next to San Domingo, and it will be remembered as the place whence Cortez sailed, in 1519, to invade Mexico.

Here also has been the seat of modern rebellion against the arbitrary and bitterly oppressive rule of the home government. The city is situated six hundred miles southeast of Havana, and, after Matanzas, comes next to it in commercial importance, its exports reaching the handsome annual aggregate of eight millions of dollars. It is the terminus of two lines of railways, which pass through the sugar districts, and afford transportation for this great staple. Three leagues inland, among the mountains, are situated the famous Cobre copper mines, said to be of superior richness, and whence, in the days of their active working, four million dollars' worth of the ore has been exported in one year. This was the amount shipped in 1841, and so late as 1867 six thousand tons were exported in ten months. Not content with realizing a very large income from the mines by way of taxes upon the product, the Spanish government increased these excise charges to such an extent as to absorb the entire profits of the works and kill the enterprise, so that the rich ores of Cobre now rest undisturbed in the earth. It seems there is an Indian village near the copper mines, whose people are represented to be the only living descendants of the aborigines, — the Caribs whom Columbus found here on first landing. Careful inquiry, however, led us seriously to doubt the authenticity of the story. Probably this people are peculiar in their language, and isolation may have caused them to differ in some respects from the inhabitants of the valley and plains, but four centuries must have destroyed every trace of the early inhabitants of Cuba. Having been from the very outset enslaved and brutally treated by the Spaniards, it is believed that as early as the year of our Lord 1700 they had utterly disappeared, and some historians say no trace even was to be found of the native race one century after the settlement of the island by Europeans.

The head of the Church of Rome in Cuba is located here, it being an archbishop's see; and the elaborate ceremonials which occasionally take place attract people from the most distant cities of the island. We chanced to be present when the bishop was passing into the cathedral, clothed in full canonicals and accompanied by church dignitaries bearing a canopy above his head. Observing our little party as strangers, though in the midst of a stately ceremony, the bishop graciously made us a sign of recognition. The cathedral of Santiago is the largest in Cuba, but extremely simple in its interior arrangements; and so, indeed, are all the churches on the island. As to the exterior, the façade resembles the cathedral of Havana, being of the same porous stone, which always presents a crumbled and mottled surface. The inside decorations are childish and fanciful, consisting mostly of artificial flowers of colored paper, crudely formed by inexperienced hands into stars, wreaths, and crosses. One innovation was noticed in this church: a saint on the right of the altar was mounted upon a wooden horse, with spear in rest à la militaire, forming a most incongruous figure. In the church of Matanzas, visited a week or two later, the effigy of our Saviour was observed to be half dressed in female attire, a glaring absurdity which the author has once before seen in the Spanish convent-church of Burgos. In the Matanzas church alluded to, boys and girls of nine and ten years were seen at the confessional. Could absurdity be carried to a greater height? These with negro women form nearly all the audiences to be met with in the Cuban churches, unless upon festal occasions. The men manifest their indifference by their absence, and white women are scarcely represented. Besides the cathedral, Santiago has three or four other old churches, small and dilapidated, within whose sombre walls one seems to have stepped back into the fifteenth century. Upon strolling accidentally into one of these we felt a chill suffuse the whole system, like that realized on descending into a dark, undrained cellar.

The multiplicity and gaudiness of the drinking-saloons and bar-rooms were particularly noticeable in passing along the principal streets, and all were doing a thriving business, judging from appearances. The Cubans drink lightly, but they drink often, and are especially addicted to gin, which is dealt out to them at an extraordinarily low price. It appears that people can consume a much larger quantity of spirituous liquors here without becoming intoxicated than they can do at the North. It is very rare to see a person overcome by this indulgence in Cuba, and yet, as was afterwards observed in Cienfuegos, Matanzas, and Havana, the common people begin the day with a very liberal dram, and follow it up with frequent libations until bed-time, — tippling at every convenient opportunity. A few of the better class of private houses were constructed with courts in the centre, where flowers and tropical fruits were growing luxuriantly. These dwellings were confined to no special quarter of the town, but were as often found next to a commercial warehouse or a negro shanty as elsewhere. The dogs, horses, and Chinese coolies were all in wretched condition. One might count the ribs of the first two a long way off, while the latter were ragged, lame, half-starved, and many of them blind. Animals are the recipients of the severest sort of usage both in Cuba and Spain. Few vehicles were to be seen, as merchandise is mostly transported on the backs of mules and ponies, and these animals are seldom shod.

The town is lighted with gas, or rather it was so illuminated a few weeks since; but it was quietly whispered about that the corporation had failed to pay for this service last year, and that the monopoly itself was on the verge of bankruptcy, like nearly everything else of a business character in Cuba. The gaslights certainly appeared pale and sickly enough, as though only half confirmed in the purpose of giving any light at all, and were prematurely extinguished in many of the streets. In the shops, whose fronts were all open, like those of Canton and Yokohama, the clerks were to be seen in their shirt sleeves, guiltless of vests or collars, coquetting over calicoes and gaudy-colored merinos with mulatto girls decked in cheap jewelry, and with negresses wearing enormous hoop-earrings. At the approach of evening the bar-rooms and saloons, with a liberal display of looking-glasses, bottles of colored liquors, gin, and glitter, were dazzling to behold. The marble tables were crowded with domino and card players, each sipping at intervals his favorite tipple. The sidewalks are so narrow that the pedestrian naturally seeks the middle of the street as a pathway, and the half a dozen victorias and four volantes which form the means of transportation in Santiago, and which are constantly wandering about in search of a job, manage to meet or to overtake one perpetually; causing first a right oblique, then a left oblique, movement, with such regularity as to amount to an endless zigzag. We did not exactly appreciate the humor of this annoyance, but perhaps the drivers did. After climbing and descending these narrow, dirty streets by daylight and by gaslight, and watching the local characteristics for a few hours, one is only too happy to take a boat back to the ship, and leave all behind.

A desire for a cold bath and a good swim is natural in this climate after sunset, but beware of indulging this inclination in the waters of Santiago. Under that smooth, inviting surface, glistening beneath the rays of a full moon, lurk myriads of sharks. They are large, hungry, man-eating creatures, the tigers of the ocean, and the dread of all local boatmen here. To fall overboard in these waters, however good a swimmer one may be, is simply to be devoured. At Singapore, Sumatra, or Batavia, a Malay will for a consideration dive into the waters of the Malacca Straits, armed with a long, sharp knife, boldly attack a shark, and rip open his bowels at the moment when he turns on his side to give the deadly bite. But on that coast this dreaded fish appears singly; it is rare to see two of them together; while Santiago harbor seems to swarm with them, the dark dorsal fin of the threatening creatures just parting the surface of the sea, and betraying their presence. Lying at anchor between our ship and the shore was a trig Spanish corvette, — an American-built vessel, by the way, though belonging to the navy of Spain. It was curious at times to watch her crew being drilled in various martial manœuvres. While an officer was exercising the men at furling topsails, a few days before our arrival, a foretopman fell from aloft into the sea. Under ordinary circumstances and in most waters, the man could easily have been saved, but not so in this instance. He did not even rise to the surface. A struggle for portions of his body between half a dozen ravenous sharks was observed alongside the corvette, and all was quickly over. The fore-topman had been torn limb from limb and instantly devoured.

The over-stimulated brain felt no inclination for sleep on this first night in the harbor, the situation was so novel, and the night itself one to suggest poetic thoughts. The moon was creeping slowly across the blue vault, like a great phantom mingling with the lambent purity of the stars. We sat silently watching the heavens, the water, and the shore ; saw the lights go out one after another among the clustering dwellings, and the street gas-burners shut off here and there, until by and by the drowsy town was wrapped in almost perfect darkness. Only the ripple of the sea alongside the ship broke the silence, or the sudden splash of some large fish, leaping out of and falling back into the water. It seemed as though no sky was ever before of such marvelous blue depth, no water so full of mystery, no shore so clad in magic verdure, and no night ever of such resplendent clearness. The landing-steps and grating had been rigged out from a broad porthole on the spar deck, where a quartermaster was awaiting the return of the purser and a party of gentlemen who were making late, or rather early, hours on shore ; for it was nearly two o'clock in the morning, and the weary seaman, who had sat down at his post on the grating, was snoring like a wheezy trombone. The measured tread fore and aft of the second officer, who kept the anchor watch, was the only evidence of wakefulness that disturbed our lonely mood. A similar night scene was vividly called to mind as experienced in Typhoon Bay, below Hong Kong, a few years since.

In the harbor, next morning, a sunken wreck was pointed out to us, which was partially visible at low tide, not far from the shore. Only the ribs and stanchions are still held together by the stout keel timbers and lower sheathing. This wreck has lain there unheeded for years, yet what a story these old timbers might tell, had they only a tongue with which to give voice to their experience! — literally the experience of ages. We refer to the remains of the old St. Paul, one of the ships of the great Spanish Armada that Philip II. sent to England in 1588, being one of the very few of that famous flotilla that escaped destruction at the time. What a historical memento is the old wreck! After a checkered career, in which this ancient craft had breasted the waves of innumerable seas and withstood the storms of nearly three centuries, she was burned to the water's edge here in the harbor of Santiago a few years since, and sunk, where her remains now lie, covered with slime and barnacles, — a striking emblem of the nation whose flag she once proudly bore. During the last years of her career afloat she was used for transporting troops from Europe, and as a Spanish guard-ship in these seas by the local government. It is doubtful if it is generally known that this relic of the Spanish Armada is in existence. Curio-hunters, once put upon the scent, will probably soon reduce these ancient timbers to chips, and a crop of canes and snuff-boxes, more or less hideous and more or less counterfeit, will ensue.

MONEY IN CUBA.

Here we got our first experience of the present currency, — the valueless circulating medium of Cuba. When one has occasion to visit the island it is best to take American funds, either in bank-bills or gold, sufficient to meet all ordinary expenses. Our bank-bills and our gold are both at a premium. This will also save all necessity for drawing on home through any local bankers, who have a way of charging for the accommodation quite after the style of everything Spanish. The hotel-keepers will require their pay on the basis of Spanish gold, but will cheerfully allow a premium of six per cent. on American gold or American bank-bills. As to the banks in Cuba, all are shaky, so to speak; several have lately failed, and the others might as well do so. It is not long since the president of the Havana Savings Bank placed a pistol at his temple and blew his brains out. Mercantile credit may be said to be dead, and business nearly at a standstill. Commercial honesty is hardly to be expected from a bankrupt community, where the people seem only to be engaged in the sale and purchase of lottery tickets, a habit participated in by all classes.

What little gold and silver coin there is found in circulation is mutilated; every piece of money, large and small, has been subjected to the ingenious punch, and thus has lost a portion of its intrinsic value. American gold and silver, not having been thus clipped, justly commands a six per cent. premium.

The circulating medium upon the island is paper scrip, precisely similar to that used in this country before the resumption of specie payment. This scrip is dirty beyond endurance, and one absolutely hesitates to take it in making change.

When our currency became soiled and torn we could exchange it for new, but there is no such facility in Cuba. One dollar of our money will purchase $2.45 of this scrip. It passes current, and really seems to answer the necessities of trade, but even the Cubans are not deceived by it. They know that it is really worthless, being based upon nothing, and issued indiscriminately by a bankrupt government. The paper-mill grinds it out in five, ten, twenty, and fifty cent pieces as fast as it can be put into circulation, while no one knows how much has been issued. But one thing is known; namely, that every authorized issue of a given sum has been enormously exceeded in amount.

Within about five years, or less, an issue of bank-bills and of this small currency was entrusted to an establishment in the United States, when fourteen millions of dollars were printed in *addition* to the amount authorized! All were duly receipted for and signed by corrupt Spanish officials, who coolly divided these millions among themselves! The Captain-General of Cuba during whose administration this financial stroke was accomplished came to the island a poor man, and returned to Spain in two years possessed of three million dollars!

There is no more beautiful or safe harbor in the world than that of Santiago de Cuba, commercially speaking, as it is completely land-locked and protected on all sides from storms; but for the same reason it is as close and hot an anchorage as can be found in the tropics. An intelligent resident gave us 80° Fahrenheit as the average temperature of the year, though the thermometer showed a more ambitious figure during our brief stay. There are but two seasons, the wet and the dry, the latter extending from September to May. The city might have an excellent water supply if there were sufficient enterprise among the citizens to cause it to be conducted by pipes from the springs in the neighboring hills. It is now wretchedly deficient in this respect, causing both suffering and ill health in a climate especially demanding this prime necessity of life.

CHAPTER III.

Doubling Cape Cruz. — Trinidad. — Cienfuegos. — The Plaza. — Beggars. — Visit to a Sugar Plantation. — Something about Sugar. — An Original Character. — A Tropical Fruit Garden. — Cuban Hospitality. — The Banana. — Lottery Tickets. — Chinese Coolies. — Blindness in Cuba. — Birds and Poultry. — The Cock-Pit. — Negro Slavery, To-Day. — Spanish Slaveholders. — A Slave Mutiny. — A Pleasant Journey across the Island. — Pictures of the Interior. — Scenery about Matanzas. — The Tropics and the North contrasted.

To reach Cienfuegos, our next objective point, one takes water conveyance, the common roads in this district being, if possible, a degree worse than elsewhere. It is therefore necessary to double Cape Cruz, and perform a coasting voyage along the southern shore of the island of about four hundred miles. This is really delightful sailing in any but the hurricane months; that is, between the middle of August and the middle of October. It would seem that this should be quite a commercial thoroughfare, but it is surprising how seldom a sailing-vessel is seen on the voyage, and it is still more rare to meet a steamship. Our passage along the coast was delightful: the undulating hills, vales, and plains seemed to be quietly gliding past us of their own volition; the tremor of the ship did not suggest motion of the hull, but a sense of delight at the moving panorama so clearly depicted. No extensive range of waters in either hemisphere is so proverbially smooth as the Caribbean Sea, during eight months of the year, but a stout hull and good seamanship are demanded during the remaining four, especially if coming from the northward over the Bahama Banks and through the Windward Passage, as described in these chapters.

The city of Trinidad, perched upon a hillside, is passed at the distance of a few miles, being pleasantly situated more than a league from the coast. The town of Casilda is its commercial port. This arrangement was adopted in the early days as a partial protection against the frequent inroads of the buccaneers, who ceased to be formidable when separated from their ships. Trinidad was once the centre of the prosperous coffee trade of Cuba, but is now, and has been for many years, commercially wrecked. It is very beautifully located, with Mount Vijia for its background, in what is declared to be the healthiest district upon the island. But it is an ancient city, comparatively deserted, its date being nearly contemporary with that of Santiago. Cienfuegos, its successful business rival, is on the contrary quite modern, exhibiting many features of thrift and activity, and is counted the third commercial city of Cuba. Like Cardenas, it is called an American capital. It has some twenty-five thousand inhabitants, a large proportion of whom speak English, nine tenths of its commerce being with the United States. In this immediate neighborhood Columbus, on his second voyage, saw with astonishment the mysterious king who spoke to his subjects only by signs, and that group of men who wore long white tunics like the monks of mercy, while the rest of the people were entirely naked. The town is low and level, occupying a broad plane. The streets are of fair width, crossing each other at right angles, and are kept neat and clean. The harbor is an excellent and spacious one, admitting of vessels being moored at the wharves, a commercial convenience unknown at Santiago, Matanzas, or Havana. The navies of all the world might rendezvous here and not crowd each other. Three rivers, the Canudo, Saludo, and Danuyi, empty into the bay, and each is navigable for a considerable distance inland, a matter of great importance in a country so devoid of good roads. The parti-colored houses are of the usual Cuban type, mostly of one story, built with a patio or open courtyard in the centre, well filled with flowering plants, among which were observed the attractive coral-tree, which resembles a baby palm, and the universal banana.

The Plaza of Cienfuegos forms a large, well-arranged square, where an out-door military concert is given twice a week, a universal practice in all Cuban cities. It is laid out with excellent taste, its broad paths nicely paved, and the whole lighted at night with numerous ornamental gas-lamps. The vegetation is both attractive and characteristic, consisting of palms, laurels, and flowering shrubs, mingled with which are some exotics from the North, which droop with a homesick aspect. Plants, like human beings, will pine for their native atmosphere. If it be more rigorous and less genial at the North, still there is a bracing, tonic effect, imparting life and strength, which is wanting in the low latitudes. On one side of this fine square is the government house and barracks, opposite to which is an open-air theatre, and in front is the cathedral with any number of discordant bells. The little English sparrow seems to be ubiquitous, and as pugnacious here as on Boston Common, or the Central Park of New York. Boyish games are very similar the world over: young Cuba was playing marbles after the orthodox fashion, knuckle-down. It was very pitiful to behold the army of beggars in so small a city, but begging is synonymous with the Spanish name, both in her European and colonial possessions. Here the maimed, halt, and blind meet one at every turn. Saturday is the harvest day for beggars in the Cuban cities, on which occasion they go about by scores from door to door, carrying a large canvas bag. Each family and shop is supplied with a quantity of small rolls of bread, specially baked for the purpose, and one of which is nearly always given to the applicant on that day, so the mendicant's bag becomes full of rolls. These, mixed with vegetables, bits of fish, and sometimes meat and bones when they can be procured, are boiled into a soup, thus keeping soul and body together in the poor creatures during the week.

Cienfuegos is situated in the midst of a sugar-producing district, where soil and climate are both favorable, and over twenty large plantations are to be seen within a radius of two or three leagues. The export from them, as we were informed by the courteous editor of "La Opinion," a local paper, aggregates thirty thousand hogsheads annually. The visitor should not fail to make an excursion to some representative plantation, where it is impossible not to be much interested and practically informed. One of these sugar estates, situated less than two leagues from the town, was found to be furnished with a complete outfit of the most modern machinery, which had cost the proprietor a quarter of a million dollars. It was working with the usual favorable results, though at the present price of sugar no profit can accrue to the planter. The plantation presented a busy scene. During the grinding season the machinery is run night and day, but is obliged to lie idle for eight months out of the year.

In the uncultivated fields through which we passed when driving out to the sugar estate, the prickly pear grew close to the ground in great luxuriance, as it is seen on our Western prairies. Its thick leaves, so green as to be dense with color, impart the effect of greensward at a short distance. On close inspection it was seen to be the star cactus, which like the Northern thistle kills all other vegetation within its reach. Here and there the wild ipecacuanha with its bright red blossom was observed, but the fields, except those devoted to the cane, were very barren near Cienfuegos.

Sugar-cane is cultivated like Indian corn, which it also resembles in appearance. It is first planted in rows, not in hills, and must be hoed and weeded until it gets high enough to shade its roots. Then it may be left to itself until it reaches maturity. This refers to the first laying out of a plantation, which will afterwards continue fruitful for years by very simple processes of renewal. When thoroughly ripe the cane is of a light golden yellow, streaked here and there with red. The top is dark green, with long narrow leaves depending, — very much like those of the corn stalk, — from the centre of which shoots upwards a silvery stem a couple of feet in height, and from its tip grows a white fringed plume, of a delicate lilac hue. The effect of a large field at its maturity, lying under a torrid sun and gently yielding to the breeze, is very fine, a picture to live in the memory ever after. In the competition between the products of beet-root sugar and that from sugar-cane, the former controls the market, because it can be produced at a cheaper rate, besides which its production is stimulated by nearly all of the European states through the means of liberal subsidies both to the farmer and to the manufacturer. Beet sugar, however, does not possess so high a percentage of true saccharine matter as does the product of the cane, the latter seeming to be nature's most direct mode of supplying us with the article. The Cuban planters have one advantage over all other sugarcane producing countries, in the great and inexhaustible fertility of the soil of the island. For instance: one to two hogsheads of sugar to the acre is considered a good yield in Jamaica, but in Cuba three hogsheads is the average. Fertilizing of any sort is rarely employed in the cane-fields, while in beet farming it is the principal agent of success.

Though the modern machinery, as lately adopted on the plantations, is very expensive, still the result achieved by it is so much superior to that of the old methods of manufacture that the small planters are being driven from the market. Slave labor cannot compete with machinery. The low price of sugar renders economy imperative in all branches of the business, in order to leave a margin for profit. A planter informed the author that he should spread all of his molasses upon the cane-fields this year as a fertilizer, rather than send it to a distant market and receive only what it cost. He further said that thousands of acres of sugar-cane would be allowed to rot in the fields this season, as it would cost more to cut, grind, pack, and send it to market than could be realized for the manufactured article. Had the price of sugar remained this year at a figure which would afford the planters a fair profit, it might have been the means of tiding over the chasm of bankruptcy which has long stared them in the face, and upon the brink of which they now stand. But with a more than average crop, both as to quantity and quality, whether to gather it or not is a problem. Under these circumstances it is difficult to say what is to become, financially, of the people of Cuba. Sugar is their great staple, but all business has been equally depressed upon the island, under the bane of civil wars, extortionate taxation, and oppressive rule.

If you visit Cienfuegos you will take rooms at the Hotel Union, as being the least objectionable of the two public houses which the city contains, and there you will make the acquaintance of Jane, who is an institution in herself. Indeed, she will doubtless board your ship when it first arrives, so as to enlighten you concerning the excellences of the Union over its rival establishment, which will also be sure to be represented. Jane is interpreter and general factotum of that delectable posada, the Union, and being the only one in the house who speaks either French or English, she becomes an important factor in your calculations. Jane's nationality is a pleasing mystery, but she may be classed as a Portuguese quadroon. Venus did not preside at her birth, but, by means of the puff-ball and egg-shell powder, she strives to harmonize her mottled features. Being interpreter, waitress, hotel-runner, and chambermaid, she is no idler, and fully earns the quarter eagle you naturally hand her at leave-taking. In visiting the neighboring sugar plantation Jane acts as your guide, on which occasion her independence will be sure to challenge admiration. She salutes slave or master with equal familiarity, conducts you through each process of the elaborate works, from the engine to the crushing mill, and so on, until you reach the centrifugal machine, where the glistening crystals of pure sugar fall into an open receptacle ready for packing and shipment. She takes you into the slave-quarters among the pickaninnies, hens, pigs, and pigeons, looking on blandly and chewing huge pieces of cane while you distribute the bright ten cent pieces with which you filled your pocket at starting. If Jane slyly pinches a papoose and causes it to yell, it is only for fun; she means no harm, though the dusky mite gets smartly slapped by its mother for misbehaving. The cabin floor of bare earth is sure to be covered with these little naked, sprawling objects, like ants. On the way back to town Jane orders the postilion to drive into the private grounds of a palatial Cuban residence, where she boldly announces herself and party to the proprietor in good rolling Spanish. It is the home of Señor N——, a wealthy merchant of the city. We are received as though we belonged to the royal family. The hospitable owner speaks English fluently, and answers our thousand and one questions with tireless courtesy, takes us into his superb fruit garden (of which more anon), then introduces us to his domestic quarters, where everything appears refined, faultlessly neat, and tasteful. If you go to the railroad station, as usual the evening before departure, in order to secure tickets and get your baggage labeled, — for the cars start in the morning before daylight, — Jane will accompany you, riding by your side in the victoria. Excuse her if she orders the calash thrown back, as she appears bonnetless in a loud, theatrical costume, trimmed with red and yellow, and carrying a bouquet in her freckled hands. It is her opportunity, and she looks triumphantly at the street loungers in passing. If you are charged on your bill a Delmonico price for a mythical lunch to be taken with you on the journey to Matanzas, and which Jane has forgotten to put up, pay without wrangling; it saves time and temper.

The tropical garden which we visited just outside of Cienfuegos embraced a remarkable variety of trees, including some thrifty exotics. Here the mango, with its peach-like foliage, was bending to the ground with the weight of its ripening fruit; the alligator pear was marvelously beautiful in its full blossom, suggesting, in form and color, the passion-flower; the soft delicate foliage of the tamarind was like our sensitive plant; the banana trees were in full bearing, the deep green fruit (it is ripened and turns yellow off the tree) being in clusters of a hundred, more or less, tipped at the same time by a single, pendent, glutinous bud nearly as large as a pineapple. The date-palm, so suggestive of the far East, and the only one we had seen in Cuba, was represented by a choice specimen, imported in its youth. There was also the star-apple tree, remarkable for its uniform and graceful shape, full of the green fruit, with here and there a ripening specimen; so, also, was the favorite zapota, its rusty-coated fruit hanging in tempting abundance. From low, broad-spreading trees depended the grape-fruit, as large as an infant's head and yellow as gold, while the orange, lime, and lemon trees, bearing blossoms, green and ripe fruit all together, met the eye at every turn, and filled the garden with fragrance. The cocoanut palm, with

THE BANANA. 55

its tall, straight stem and clustering fruit, dominated all the rest. Guava, fig, custard-apple, and breadfruit trees, all were in bearing. Our hospitable host plucked freely of the choicest for the benefit of his chance visitors. Was there ever such a fruit garden before, or elsewhere? It told of fertility of soil and deliciousness of climate, of care, judgment, and liberal expenditure, all of which combined had turned these half a dozen acres of land into a Gan Eden. Through this orchard of Hesperides we were accompanied also by the proprietor's two lovely children, under nine years of age, with such wealth of promise in their large black eyes and sweet faces as to fix them on our memory with photographic fidelity.

Before leaving the garden we returned with our intelligent host once more to examine his beautiful specimens of the banana, which, with its sister fruit the plantain, forms so important a staple of food in Cuba and throughout all tropical regions. It seems that the female banana tree bears more fruit than the male, but not so large. The average clusters of the former comprise here about one hundred, but the latter rarely bears over sixty or seventy distinct specimens of the cucumber-shaped product. From the centre of its large broad leaves, which gather at the top, when it has reached the height of twelve or fifteen feet there springs forth a large purple bud ten inches long, shaped like a huge acorn, though more pointed. This cone hangs suspended from a strong stem, upon which a leaf unfolds, displaying a cluster of young fruit. As soon as these are large enough to support the heat of the sun and the chill of the rain, this sheltering leaf drops off, and another unfolds, exposing its little brood of fruit; and so the process goes on until six or eight rings of young bananas are started, forming, as we have said, bunches numbering from seventy to a hundred. The banana is a herbaceous plant, and after fruiting its top dies; but it annually sprouts up again fresh from the roots. From the unripe fruit, dried in the sun, a palatable and nutritious flour is made.

No matter where one may be, in town or country, in the east or west end of the island, Santiago or Havana, the lottery-ticket vender is there. Men, women, and children are employed to peddle the tickets, cripples especially being pressed into the service in the hope of exciting the sympathies of strangers and thus creating purchasers. It may be said to be about the only prosperous business at present going on in this thoroughly demoralized island. Half the people seem to think of nothing else, and talk of dreaming that such and such combinations of numbers will bring good luck. Some will buy only even numbers, others believe that the odd ones stand the best chance of winning; in short, all the gambling fancies are brought to bear upon these lotteries. Enough small prizes are doled out to the purchasers of tickets, by the cunning management, to keep hope and expectation ever alive in their hearts, and to coax out of them their last dollar in further investments. "If," said a native resident of Matanzas to us, "these lotteries, all of which are presided over by the officials, are honestly conducted, they are the one honest thing in which this government is concerned. Venal in everything else, why should they be conscientious in this gambling game?" No one believes in the integrity of the government, but, strange to say, the masses have implicit faith in the lotteries.

At one corner of our hotel in Cienfuegos, there sat upon the sidewalk of the street a blind beggar, a Chinese coolie, whose miserable, poverty-stricken appearance elicited a daily trifle from the habitués of the house. Early one morning we discovered this representative of want and misery purchasing a lottery ticket. They are so divided and subdivided, it appears, as to come even within the means of the street beggars! Speaking of blindness, the multiplicity of people thus afflicted, especially among negroes and coolies, led to the enumeration of those met with in a single day; the result was seventeen. On inquiry it was found that inflammation of the eyes is as common here as in Egypt, and that it runs a rapid and fatal course, — fatal to the sight after having once attacked a victim, unless it receives prompt, judicious, and scientific treatment.

The Chinese coolies, who are encountered in all parts of the island, but more especially in the cities, are almost invariably decrepit, poverty-stricken mendicants, and very frequently blind. They are such as have been through their eight years' contract, and have been brought to their present condition by ill-treatment, insufficient food, and the troubles incident to the climate. In the majority of cases these coolies have been cheated out of the trifling amount of wages promised to them, for there is no law in Cuba to which they can appeal. There are laws which will afford the negro justice if resorted to under certain circumstances, but none for the coolies. There are some few Chinamen who have survived every exigency, and are now engaged in keeping small stores or fruit stands, cigar making, and other light employments, their only hope being to gain money enough to carry them back to their native land, and to have a few dollars left to support them after getting there. There are no Chinese laundries in Cuba; John cannot compete with the black women in this occupation, for they are natural washers and ironers. John is only a skillful imitator. He proves most successful in the cigarette and cigar factories, where his deft fingers can turn out a more uniform and handsome article than the Cubans themselves. Machinery is fast doing away with hand-made cigarettes. At the famous establishment of La Honradez, in Havana, which we visited some weeks later, one machine was seen in operation which produced ten thousand complete cigarettes each hour, or a million per day! Still this same establishment employed some fifty Chinese in order to supply its trade with the hand-made article, for home consumption. The Cubans prefer to unroll and readjust a cigarette before lighting it. This cannot be done with the machine-made article, which completes its product by a pasting process. The three machines (an American patent) at the Honradez factory turn out three millions of cigarettes per day, and this is in addition to those which are hand-made by the Chinese.

The landlord of the Hotel Union, at Cienfuegos, will give you plenty of fruit and cheap Cataline wine, but the meat which is served is poor and consists mostly of birds. Any other which may be set before you will hardly be found to be a success, but then one does not crave much substantial food in this climate. There is a small wild pigeon which forms a considerable source of food in Cuba, and which breeds several times in a year. They are snared and shot in large numbers for the table, but do not show any signs of being exterminated. Ducks and water-fowl generally abound, and are depended upon to eke out the short supply of what we term butcher's meat. Three quarters of the people never partake of other meat than pigeons, poultry, and wild ducks. Eggs are little used as food, being reserved for hatching purposes. All families in the country and many in the cities make a business of raising poultry, but the product is a bird of small dimensions, not half the size of our common domestic fowls. They are very cheap, but they are also very poor. The practice is to keep them alive until they are required for the table, so that they are killed, picked, and eaten, all in the same hour, and are in consequence very tough. As the climate permits of hens hatching every month in the year, the young are constantly coming forward, and one mother annually produces several broods; chickens, like tropical fruits, are perennial.

Sunday is no more a day of rest in Cienfuegos than it is in other Roman Catholic countries; indeed, it seemed to be distinguished only by an increase of revelry, the activity of the billiard saloons, the noisy persistency of the lottery-ticket venders, the boisterousness of masquerade processions, and a general public rollicking. The city is not large enough to support a bull-ring, but cock-pits are to be found all over the island, and the Sabbath is the chosen day for their exhibitions. It must be a very small and very poor country town in Cuba which has not its cock-pit. The inveterate gambling propensities of the people find vent also at dominoes, cards, checkers, and chess in the bar-rooms, every marble table being in requisition for the purpose of the games on Sundays. Having noticed the sparse attendance at the cathedral, we remarked to Jane that the church was quite empty, whereupon she replied with a significant leer, "True, Señor, but the jail is full." More than once an underlying vein of sarcasm was observed in the very pertinent remarks of which Jane was so happily delivered.

There are comparatively few slaves to be found on the plantations or elsewhere in the vicinity of Cienfuegos: in fact, slavery is rapidly disappearing from the island. "Slave labor is more costly than any other, all things considered," said a sugar planter to us. "I do not own one to-day, but I have owned and worked six hundred at a time," he added. "We pay no tax on the laborers we hire, but on slaves we pay a heavy head-tax annually." An edict has been promulgated by the home government, which went into force last year, and which frees one slave in every four annually, so that on January 1, 1888, all will have become free. In the mean time the commercial value of slaves has so decreased in view of their near emancipation that they are not appraised on an average at over fifty or sixty dollars each. The law has for a period of many years provided that any slave who pays to his master his appraised value shall at once receive his free papers. Many purchase their liberty under this law, and then hire themselves to the same master or to some other, as they may choose, — at low wages, to be sure, but including food and shelter. Slaves have always been entitled by law in Cuba to hold individual property independent of their masters, and there are few smart ones who have not accumulated more or less pecuniary means during their servitude. They have had no expenses to meet in the way of supporting themselves. That has devolved upon their owners, so that whatever money they have realized by the several ways open to them has been clear profit. Many slaves have anticipated the period of their legal release from servitude, and more will do so during the present year. We also heard of planters who, realizing the inevitable, have manumitted the few slaves whom they still held in bondage, and hiring them at merely nominal wages, believed they saved money by the operation.

It will be seen, therefore, that slavery as an institution here is virtually at an end. Low wages will prevail, and this is necessary to enable the planters to compete with the beet sugar producers of Europe. In truth, it is a question how long they will be able to do so at any rate of wages. The modern machinery being so generally adopted by the sugar-cane planters, while remarkably successful, both as to the quality and the quantity of the juice it expresses from the cane, not only is expensive in first cost, but it requires more intelligent laborers than were found serviceable with the old process. To supply the places of the constantly diminishing slaves, emigrants, as they were called, have heretofore been introduced from the Canary Islands; men willing to contract for a brief period of years, say eight or ten, as laborers, and at moderate wages. These people have proved to be good plantation hands, though not so well able to bear the great heat of the sun as were the negroes; otherwise they were superior to them, and better in all respects than the Chinese coolies, who as workers on the plantations have proved to be utter failures. The mortality among these Mongolians, as we learned from good authority, had reached as high as sixty-seven per cent. within eight years of their date of landing in Cuba, that being also the period of their term of contract. None have been introduced into the island for several years. This coolie importation, like the slave-trade with Africa, was a fraud and an outrage upon humanity, and never paid any one, even in a mercenary point of view, except the shipowners who brought the deceived natives from the coast of China. Slavery in Cuba and slavery in our country were always quite a different thing, and strange to say the laws of the Spanish government were far more favorable and humane towards the victims of enforced labor than were those established in our Southern States. When the American negro ceased to be a slave, he ceased to cultivate the soil for his master only to cultivate it for himself. Not so in the tropics. The Cuban negro, in the first place, is of a far less intelligent type than the colored people in the States; secondly, the abundance of natural food productions in the low latitudes, such as fruit, fish, and vegetables, requires of the negro only to pluck and to eat; clothing and shelter are scarcely needed, and virtually cost nothing where one may sleep in the open air without danger every night in the year; and finally, the negro of the tropics will not work unless he is compelled to.

There is a certain class of the Spanish slaveholders who have always fought against negro emancipation in any form, — fought against manifest destiny as well as against sound principles, fought indeed against their own clear interest, so wedded were they to the vile institution of slavery. Yet to every thinking man on the island, it is clearly apparent that human slavery in Cuba, as everywhere else, has proved to be a disturber of the public peace, and has retarded more than anything else the material and moral progress of the entire people. It is but a short time since that the editor of a Havana newspaper, the "Revista Economica," was imprisoned in Moro Castle, and without even the pretense of a trial afterwards banished from the island, because he dared to point out the fact in print that the freeing of the slaves would prove a mutual benefit to man and master, besides being a grand act of humanity. Two years since the slaves on a large plantation near Guines refused to work on a holiday which had always heretofore been granted to them; whereupon the soldiery were called in to suppress what was called a mutiny of the blacks, resulting in nine negroes being shot dead, and many others put in chains to be scourged at leisure. Doomed as we have shown slavery to be, still it dies hard in Cuba.

In the vicinity of Cienfuegos, Santiago, and Trinidad, in the mountain regions of the eastern district, there are many lawless people, — banditti, in fact, who make war for plunder both upon native and foreign travelers, even resorting in some cases to holding prisoners for ransoms. Several aggravating instances of the latter character came to our knowledge while we were on the spot. Since these notes were commenced five of these robbers have been captured, including the leader of the band to which they belonged, a notorious outlaw named Clemente Martinez. They were taken by means of a stratagem, whereby they were decoyed into an ambush, surrounded, and captured red-handed, as they fought furiously, knowing that they had no mercy to expect at the hands of the soldiers. It was the civil guard at Rancho Veloz who made this successful raid into the hills, and every one of the prisoners was summarily shot. Such off-hand punishment is dangerous, but in this instance it was no more prompt than just. It is necessary, therefore, to carry arms for self-defense upon the roads in some parts of the island, and even the countrymen wear swords when bringing produce to market. Residents having occasion to go any distance inland take a well-armed guard with them, to prevent being molested by the desperate refugees who lurk in the hill country. Undoubtedly many of these lawless bands are composed of former revolutionists, who are driven to extremes by want of food and the necessities of life.

Our journey was continued from Cienfuegos to Havana, by way of Matanzas, crossing the island nearly at right angles. The traveler plunges at once by this route into the midst of luxuriant tropical nature, where the vegetation is seen to special advantage, characterized by a great variety of cacti and parasitic growth, flowering trees and ever graceful palms, besides occasional ceibas of immense size. Though the landscape, somehow, was sad and melancholy, it gave rise to bright and interesting thoughts in the observer: doubtless the landscape, like humanity, has its moods. Vegetation, unlike mankind, seems here never to grow old, never to falter; crop succeeds crop, harvest follows harvest; nature is inexhaustible, — it is an endless cycle of abundance. Miles upon miles of the bright, golden-green sugar-cane lie in all directions, among which, here and there, is seen the little cluster of low buildings constituting the negroes' quarters attached to each plantation, and near by is the tall white chimney of the sugar-mill, emitting its thick volume of wreathing smoke, like the funnel of a steamboat. A little on one side stands the planter's house, low and white, surrounded by beautiful shade trees and clustering groups of flowers. Scores of dusky Africans give life to the scene, and the sturdy overseer, mounted on his little Cuban pony, dashes back and forth to keep all hands advantageously at work. One large gang is busy cutting the tall cane with sharp, sword-like knives; some are loading the stalks upon ox-carts; some are driving loads to the mill; some feeding the cane between the great steel crushers, beneath which pours forth a ceaseless jelly-like stream, to be conducted by iron pipes to the boilers; men, women, and children are spreading the crushed refuse to dry in the sun, after which it will be used for fuel. Coopers are heading up hogsheads full of the manufactured article, and others are rolling up empty ones to be filled.

Some years ago, when the author first visited Cuba, the overseer was never seen without his long, cutting whip, as well as his sword and pistols. The latter he wears to-day, but the whip is unseen. The fact is, the labor on the plantations is now so nearly free labor that there is little if any downright cruelty exercised as of yore. Or, rather, we will qualify the remark by saying that there has been a vast improvement in this respect on the side of humanity. The shadow of the picture lies in the past. One could not but recall in imagination the horrors which so long characterized these plantations. The bloodthirsty spirit of the Spanish slaveholders had free scope here for centuries, during which time the invaders sacrificed the entire aboriginal race; and since then millions of Africans have been slowly murdered by overwork, insufficient food, and the lash, simply to fill the pockets of their rapacious masters with gold. Few native Cubans are sugar-planters. These estates are almost universally owned and carried on by Spaniards from the European peninsula, or other foreigners, including Englishmen and Americans.

Occasionally, in the trip across the island, we passed through a crude but picturesque little hamlet having the unmistakable stamp of antiquity, with low straggling houses built of rude frames, covered at side and roof with palm bark and leaves; chimneys there were none, — none even in the cities, — charcoal only being used for cooking purposes, and which is performed in the open air. About the door of the long, rambling posada, a dozen or more horses were seen tied to a long bar, erected for the purpose, but no wheeled vehicles were there. The roads are only fit for equestrians, and hardly passable even for them. At rare intervals one gets a glimpse of the volante, now so generally discarded in the cities, and which suggested Dr. Holmes's old chaise, prepared to tumble to pieces in all parts at the same time. The people, the cabins, and the horses, are all stained with the red dust of the soil, recalling the Western Indians in their war paint. This pigment, or colored dirt, penetrates and adheres to everything, filling the cars and decorating the passengers with a dingy brick color. It was difficult to realize that these comparatively indifferent places through which we glided so swiftly were of importance and the permanent abode of any one. When the cars stop at the small way-stations, they are instantly invaded by lottery-ticket sellers, boys with tempting fruit, green cocoanuts, ripe oranges, and bananas, — all cheap for cash. And here too is the guava seller, with neatly sealed cans of the favorite preserve. Indeed, it seems to rain guava jelly in Cuba. Others offer country cheese, soft and white, with rolls, while in a shanty beside the road hot coffee and "blue ruin" are dealt out to thirsty souls by a ponderous mulatto woman. There are always a plenty of the denizens of the place, in slovenly dresses and slouched hats, hands in pockets, and puffing cigarettes, who do the heavy standing-round business. Stray dogs hang about the car-wheels and track to pick up the crumbs which passengers throw away from their lunch-baskets. Just over the wild-pineapple hedge close at hand, half a score of naked negro children hover round the door of a low cabin; the mother, fat and shining in her one garment, gazes with arms akimbo at the scene of which she forms a typical part. The engineer imbibes a penny drink of thin Cataline wine and hastens back to his machine, which has been taking water from an elevated cistern beside the track, the bell rings, the whistle sounds, and we are off to repeat the process and the picture, six or eight leagues further on. Take our advice and don't attempt to make a meal at one of these stations. The viands are wretchedly poor, and the price charged is a swindle.

As we approach Matanzas the scene undergoes a radical change. Comfortable habitations are multiplied, passable roads appear winding gracefully about the country, groves and gardens spring into view, with small and thrifty farms. Superb specimens of the royal palm begin to appear in abundance, always suggestive of the Corinthian column. Scattered over the hills and valleys a few fine cattle are seen cropping the rank verdure. There is no greensward in the tropics, and hay is never made. The scenery reminds one of Syria and the Nile.

One sees some vegetable and fruit farms, but sugar raising absorbs nearly every other interest, the tobacco leaf coming next, now that coffee is so neglected. The farmer ploughs with the crooked branch of a tree, having one handle with which to guide the crude machine, — just such an instrument as is used for the purpose in Egypt to-day, and has been used there for thousands of years. The cattle are mostly poor, half-starved creatures, — starved amid a vegetation only too rank and luxuriant. The dairy receives no attention in Cuba. Butter is seldom made; the canned article from this country, thin and offensive, is made to answer the purpose. The climate is too hot to keep butter or cream without ice, and that is expensive. Human beings, men, women, and children, look stunted and thin, possessing, however, wonderfully fine eyes, large, lustrous, and ebony in hue; eyes that alone make beauty; but the physiognomists have long since learned that eyes of themselves are no indication of character or moral force.

The thermometer had stood since early morning at 83°, during the long ride from Cienfuegos. It was hot and dusty. Notwithstanding the ceaseless novelty of the scene, one became a little fatigued, a little weary; but as we approached Matanzas, the refreshing air from off the Gulf of Mexico suddenly came to our relief, full of a bracing tonic, and rendering all things tolerable. The sight of the broad harbor, lying with its flickering surface under the afternoon sun, was beautiful to behold.

After all, these tropical regions lack the delicious

freshness of the greensward, of new foliage, and the fine fragrance of the rural North; they need the invigorating sleep of the seasons from which to awake refreshed and blooming. Where vegetation is growing and decaying at the same time, there can never be general freshness and greenness; eternal summer lacks interest; we crave the frost as well as the sunshine. Compensation follows fast upon the heels of even a Northern winter. The tropical loveliness of the vegetation in this attractive land indicates what Cuba should be, but is not.

Having accompanied the reader across many degrees of latitude, effecting a landing and reaching the interior of Cuba, let us now pass to other considerations of this interesting and important island.

CHAPTER IV.

The Great Genoese Pilot. — Discovery of Cuba. — Its Various Names. — Treatment of the Natives. — Tobacco! — Flora of the Island. — Strange Idols. — Antiquity. — Habits of the Aborigines. — Remarkable Speech of an Indian King. — A Native Entertainment. — Paying Tribute. — Ancient Remains. — Wrong Impression of Columbus. — First Attempt at Colonization. — Battle with the Indians. — First Governor of Cuba. — Founding Cities. — Emigration from Spain. — Conquest of Mexico.

THE island of Cuba was discovered by the great Genoese pilot, on the 28th day of October, 1492. The continent of America was not discovered until six years later, — in 1498. The name of Columbus flashes a bright ray over the mental darkness of the period in which he lived, for the world was then but just awakening from the dull sleep of the Middle Ages. The discovery of printing heralded the new birth of the republic of letters, and maritime enterprise received a vigorous impulse. The shores of the Mediterranean, thoroughly explored and developed, had endowed the Italian States with extraordinary wealth, and built up a very respectable mercantile marine. The Portuguese mariners were venturing farther and farther from the peninsula, and traded with many distant ports on the extended coast of Africa.

To the west lay what men supposed to be an illimitable ocean, full of mystery, peril, and death. A vague conception that islands hitherto unknown might be met afar off on that strange wilderness of waters was entertained by some minds, but no one thought of venturing in search of them. Columbus alone, regarded merely as a brave and intelligent seaman and pilot, conceived the idea that the earth was spherical, and that the East Indies, the great El Dorado of the century, might be reached by circumnavigating the globe. If we picture to ourselves the mental condition of the age and the state of science, we shall find no difficulty in conceiving the scorn and incredulity with which the theory of Columbus was received. We shall not wonder that he was regarded as a madman or as a fool; we are not surprised to remember that he encountered repulse upon repulse as he journeyed wearily from court to court, and pleaded in vain to the sovereigns of Europe for aid to prosecute his great design. The marvel is that when door after door was closed against him, when all ears were deaf to his earnest importunities, when day by day the opposition to his views increased, when, weary and footsore, he was forced to beg a bit of bread and a cup of water for his fainting and famishing boy at the door of a Spanish convent, his reason did not give way, and his great heart did not break with disappointment.

But he felt himself to be the instrument of a higher power, and his soul was then as firm and steadfast as when, launched in his frail caravél upon the ocean, he pursued day after day and night after night, amidst a murmuring, discontented, and even mutinous crew, his westward path across the trackless waters. No doubt he believed himself to be inspired, or at least specially prompted from above. This was shown by his tenacious observance of all ceremonies of the Church, in his unaffected piety, and in that lofty and solemn enthusiasm which was a characteristic of his whole life. This must have been the secret in no small degree of the power he exerted so successfully over his semi-barbarous followers, who were more affected by awe than by fear. It was the devout and lofty aspect of their commander which controlled his sailors under circumstances so trying. We can conceive of his previous sorrows, but what imagination can form an adequate conception of his hopefulness and gratitude when the tokens of the neighborhood of land first greeted his senses? What rapture must have been his when the keel of his barque first grounded on the shore of San Salvador, and he planted the royal standard in the soil, as the Viceroy and High-Admiral of Spain in the New World! No matter what chanced thereafter, a king's favor or a king's displeasure, royal largesses or royal chains, that moment of noble exultation was worth a lifetime of trials.

Columbus first named Cuba "Juana," in honor of Prince John, son of Ferdinand and Isabella. Subsequently the king named it Fernandina. This was changed to Santiago, and finally to Ave Maria; but the aboriginal designation has never been lost, Cuba being its Indian and only recognized name. The newcomers found the land inhabited by a most peculiar race, hospitable, inoffensive, timid, fond of the dance and the rude music of their own people, yet naturally indolent, from the character of the climate they inhabited. They had some definite idea of God and heaven, and were governed by patriarchs or kings, whose word was their only law, and whose age gave them undisputed precedence. They spoke the dialect of the Lucayos, or Bahamas, from which islands it is presumed by historians they originated; but it would seem more reasonable to suppose that both the people of the Bahamas and of the West India isles came originally from the mainland; that is, either north or south of the Isthmus of Panama. In numbers they were vaguely estimated at a million, a calculation the correctness of which we cannot but doubt. Reliable local authority, Cubans who have made a study of the early history of the island, assured the author that the aborigines at the time of Velasquez's first settlement, say in 1512, could not have exceeded four hundred thousand. They had but few weapons of offense or defense, and knew not the use of the bow and arrow. Being a peaceful race and having no wild animals to contend with, their ingenuity had never been taxed to invent weapons of warfare against man or beast. The natives were at once subjected by the new-comers, who reduced them gradually to an actual state of slavery, and proving hard task-masters, the poor overworked creatures died by hundreds, until they had nearly disappeared. The home government then granted permission to import negroes from the coast of Africa to labor upon the soil and to seek for gold, which was known to exist in the river courses. Thus commenced the foreign slave-trade of the West Indies, King Ferdinand himself sending fifty slaves from Seville to labor in the mines, and from that time this plague spot upon humanity has festered on the island. It should be remembered in this connection that previous to the discoveries of Columbus, negro slavery had been reduced to a system by the Moors, and thus existed in Spain before the days of the great Genoese.

The Spaniards were not content with putting the aborigines to labor far beyond their power of endurance on the soil where they were born, but shipped them by hundreds to Spain to be sold in the slave-market of Seville, the proceeds being turned into the royal treasury. Columbus himself was the promoter of this outrageous return for the hospitality he had received at the hands of the natives. Irving apologetically says he was induced to this course in order to indemnify the sovereigns of Castile and Leon for the large expense his expedition had been to them. The fact that the great navigator originated the slave-trade in the New World cannot be ignored, though it detracts in no small degree from the glory of his career.

Although the conquerors have left us but few details respecting these aborigines, still we know with certainty from the narrative of Columbus, and those of some of his most intelligent followers, that they were docile, artless, generous, but inclined to ease; that they were well-formed, grave, and far from possessing the vivacity of the natives of the south of Europe. They expressed themselves with a certain modesty and respect, and were hospitable to the last degree. Reading between the lines of the records of history, it is manifest that after their own rules and estimates, their lives were chaste and proper, though it was admissible for kings to have several wives. Moreover, though living in a state of nudity, they religiously observed the decencies of life, and were more outraged by Spanish lasciviousness than can be clearly expressed. This debasing trait, together with the greed for gold exhibited by the new-comers, disabused the minds of the natives as to the celestial origin of their visitors, a belief which they at first entertained, and which the Spaniards for mercenary purposes strove to impress upon them. The labor of this people was limited to the light work necessary to provide for the prime wants of life, beyond which they knew nothing, while the bounteous climate of the tropics spared the necessity of clothing. They preferred hunting and fishing to agriculture; beans and maize, with the fruits that nature gave them in abundance, rendered their diet at once simple, nutritious, and entirely adequate to all their wants. They possessed no quadrupeds of any description, except a race of voiceless dogs, as they were designated by the early writers, — why we know not, since they bear no resemblance to the canine species, but are not very unlike a large rat. This animal is trapped and eaten by the people on the island to this day, having much of the flavor and nature of the rabbit.

The native Cubans were of tawny complexion and beardless, resembling in many respects the aborigines of North America, and as Columbus described them in his first communication to his royal patrons, were "loving, tractable, and peaceable; though entirely naked, their manners were decorous and praiseworthy." The wonderful fecundity of the soil, its range of noble mountains, its widespread and well-watered plains, with its extended coast line and excellent harbors, all challenged the admiration of the discoverers, so that Columbus recorded in his journal these words: "It is the most beautiful island that eyes ever beheld, — full of excellent ports and profound rivers." And again he says; "It excels all other countries, as far as the day surpasses the night in brightness and splendor." The spot where the Spaniards first landed is supposed to be on the east coast, just west of Nuevitas. "As he approached the island," says Irving, "he was struck with its magnitude and the grandeur of its features: its airy mountains, which reminded him of Sicily; its fertile valleys and long sweeping plains, watered by noble rivers; its stately forests; its bold promontories and stretching headlands, which melted away into remotest distance."

Excursions inland corroborated the favorable impression made by the country bordering upon the coast. The abundance of yams, Indian corn, and various fruits, together with the plentifulness of wild cotton, impressed the explorers most favorably. Their avarice and greed were also stimulated by the belief that gold was to be found in large quantities, having received enough to convince them of its actual presence in the soil, but in the supposition that the precious metal was to be found in what is termed paying quantities they were mistaken.

The Spaniards were not a little surprised to see the natives using rude pipes, in which they smoked a certain dried leaf with apparent gratification. Tobacco was indigenous, and in the use of this now universal narcotic, these simple savages indulged in at least one luxury. The flora was strongly individualized. The frangipanni, tall and almost leafless, with thick fleshy shoots, decked with a small white blossom, was very fragrant and abundant; here also was the wild passion-flower, in which the Spaniards thought they beheld the emblems of our Saviour's passion. The golden-hued peta was found beside the myriad-flowering oleander, while the undergrowth was braided with cacti and aloes. The poisonous manchineel was observed, a drop of whose milky juice will burn the flesh like vitriol. Here the invaders also observed and noted the night-blooming cereus. They were delighted by fruits of which they knew not the names, such as the custard-apple, mango, zapota, banana, and others, growing in such rank luxuriance as to seem miraculous. We can well conceive of the pleasure and surprise of these adventurous strangers, when first partaking of these new and delicate products. This was four hundred years ago, and to-day the same flora and the same luscious food grow there in similar abundance. Nature in this land of ceaseless summer puts forth strange eagerness, ever running to fruits, flowers, and fragrance, as if they were outlets for her exuberant fecundity.

The inoffensive, unsuspicious natives shared freely everything they possessed with the invaders. Hospitality was with them an instinct, fostered by nature all about them; besides which it was a considerable time before they ceased to believe their guests superior beings descended from the clouds in their winged vessels. The Indians lived in villages of two or three hundred houses, built of wood and palm-leaf, each dwelling containing several families, the whole of one lineage, and all were governed by caciques or kings, the spirit of the government being patriarchal.

We are told by Las Casas, who accompanied Velasquez in all his expeditions, that "their dances were graceful and their singing melodious, while with primeval innocence they thought no harm of being clad only with nature's covering." The description of the gorgeous hospitality extended to these treacherous invaders is absolutely touching in the light of our subsequent knowledge. They reared no sacred temples, nor did they seem to worship idols, and yet some few antiquities have been preserved which would seem to indicate that the natives possessed grotesque images, half human and half animal, like Chinese gods in effect. These were wrought so rudely out of stone as hardly to convey any fixed idea; vague and imperfect, it is not safe to define them as idolatrous images. They might have been left here by a previous race, for, as we are all aware, respectable authorities hold that this part of the world was originally peopled by Carthaginians, Israelites, Egyptians, Hindoos, and Africans. Columbus, in his second voyage to the West Indies, found the stern-post of a vessel lying on the shore of one of the Leeward isles, which was strongly presumptive evidence that a European ship had been in these waters before him. The fact that at this writing, as already described, there lies in the harbor of Santiago the wreck of the old St. Paul, which must be over three centuries old, shows how long a piece of marine architecture may last, submerged in salt water.

An idol similar to those referred to was dug up in Hayti, and is now believed to be in the British Museum, drawings of which the author has seen, and which resemble original religious emblems examined by him in the caves of Elephanta, at Bombay. This emblem, carved by a people unacquainted with the use of edge tools, is believed by antiquarians to afford a degree of light as to the history of worship of the ancient inhabitants of Hispaniola, and also to form a collateral support of the conjecture that they sprang from the parent stock of Asia. According to Las Casas, the native Cubans had a vague tradition of the formation of the earth, and of all created things; of the deluge, of the ark, the raven, and the dove. They knew the tradition of Noah also, according to the same high authority, but for our own part we do not believe that the aborigines had any knowledge of this Biblical story. Their priests were fanatics and kept the people in fear by gross and extravagant means; but as to any formulated system of religious worship, it may be doubted if the aborigines of Cuba recognized any at the time of its discovery by Columbus. Unbroken peace reigned among them, and they turned their hands against no other people.

These aborigines exhibited many of the traits universally evinced by savage races, such as painting their bodies with red earth and adorning their heads with the feathers of brilliant birds. Much of the soil is red, almost equal to a pigment, for which purpose it was employed by the natives. They lived mostly in the open air, weaving themselves hammocks in which they slept, suspended among the trees. The cotton which they spun grew wild, but tobacco they planted and cultivated after a rude fashion. The iguana and the voiceless dog, already spoken of, were hunted and eaten, the former of the lizard family, the latter scarcely more than fifteen inches long. They had domestic birds which they fattened and ate. Their only arms were lances tipped with sea-shells, and a sort of wooden sword, both of which were more for display than for use. Fish they caught in nets and also with hooks made of bones. Their boats, or canoes, were formed of the dug-out trunks of trees, and some of these canoes, as Columbus tells us, were sufficiently large to accommodate fifty men. An ancient writer upon this subject says the oars were well formed and properly fitted, but were used only with the power of the arms, that is as paddles, no rowlocks being cut in the boat. The speed attained by them was remarkable, reaching four leagues an hour when an effort to that end was made by the occupants. A large canoe, made from the straight trunk of a mahogany tree, is described as having been five feet in width and seventy-five feet long. This craft was propelled by twenty-five oarsmen on each side, a steersman in the stern, and a lookout at the prow. This was a cacique's barge, in which he made visits of state along shore and up the rivers.

History has preserved a remarkable and characteristic speech made by a venerable cacique, who approached Columbus with great reverence on the occasion of his second visit to Cuba, and who, after presenting him with a basket of ripe fruit, said: " Whether you are divinities or mortal men, we know not. You have come into these countries with a force, against which, were we inclined to resist, it would be folly. We are all therefore at your mercy ; but if you are men, subject to mortality like ourselves, you cannot be unapprised that after this life there is another, wherein a very different portion is allotted to good and bad men. If therefore you expect to die, and believe, with us, that every one is to be rewarded in a future state according to his conduct in the present, you will do no hurt to those who do none to you." This was duly interpreted to Columbus by a native whom he had taken to Spain, and who had there acquired the Spanish language. His name was Didacus, and the date of the speech was July 7, 1492. The truth of this version is attested by Herrera and others.

The reception which Bartholomew Columbus, who was appointed Deputy Governor in the absence of the Admiral, afterwards met with in his progress through the island to collect tribute from the several caciques manifested not only kindness and submission, but also munificence. Having heard of the eagerness of the strangers for gold, such of them as possessed any brought it forth and freely bestowed it upon the Spaniards. Those who had not gold brought abundance of cotton. One cacique in the interior, named Behechio, invited the Deputy Governor to a state entertainment, on which occasion he was received with great ceremony. As he approached the king's dwelling, the royal wives, thirty in number, carrying branches of palm in their hands, came forth to greet the guest with song and dance. These matrons were succeeded by a train of virgins. The first wore aprons of cotton, the last were arrayed only in the innocence of nature, their hair flowing long and freely about their shoulders and necks. Their limbs were finely proportioned, and their complexions, though brown, were smooth, shining, and lovely. The Spaniards were struck with admiration, believing that they beheld the dryads of the woods and the nymphs of the ancient fables. The branches which they bore were delivered to the strangers with low obeisance, indicating entire submission. When the Spaniards entered the rural palace, amid songs and the rude music of the people, they found there a plentiful and, according to the Indian mode of living, a sumptuous banquet prepared for them.

After the repast the guests were each conducted to separate lodgings, and each provided with a cotton hammock. On the next day feasting and games were resumed; dancing and singing closed each evening for four consecutive days, and when the Deputy Governor and his people departed, they were laden with gifts by their generous entertainers, who also accompanied them far on their way. This episode will perhaps serve better to give us a just insight into the condition and character of the aborigines of Cuba at that early period than any amount of detailed description possibly could.

These aborigines, according to Las Casas, had no tradition even, touching their own origin, and when asked about it only shook their heads and pointed to the sky. Antiquarians have endeavored to draw some reliable or at least reasonable deductions from the collection of bones and skeletons found in the mountain caves of the island, but no conclusion worthy of record has ever been arrived at. Still, upon these evidences some scientists pin their faith that Cuba was a portion of the primitive world. Speaking of these caves, there are many subterranean openings on the island, down which rivers of considerable size abruptly disappear, not again to be met with, though it is reasonably presumed that they find their way through the rocks and soil to the sea-coast.

During the ten years subsequent to its discovery, Columbus visited and partially explored the island at four different times, the last being in 1502, four years previous to his death, which took place at Valladolid in 1506. It seems singular to us that his investigations left him still ignorant of the fact that Cuba was an island, and not a part of a new continent. This conviction remained with him during his lifetime. It was not until 1511 that the Spaniards commenced to colonize the island, when Diego Columbus, then Governor of San Domingo, sent an expedition of three hundred men for the purpose, under the command of Diego Velasquez, whose landing was disputed by the natives. A period of ten years had served to open their eyes to Spanish lust and love of gold, and from having at first regarded them as superior beings, entitled to their obedience, they were finally thus driven to fight them in self-defense. But what could naked savages, armed only with clubs and spears, accomplish against Europeans, trained soldiers, furnished with firearms, protected by plate armor, and accompanied by bloodhounds, — men who had learned the art of war by fighting successfully with the valiant Moors? The natives were at once overpowered and hundreds were slaughtered. From that time forth they became the slaves of their conquerors; a fact which reconciles us in some degree in the light of poetical justice to the fact that Amerigo Vespucci, who followed in the footsteps of others, yet took the honors of discovery so far as to give his name to the largest quarter of the globe.

Diego Velasquez, the earliest Governor of the island, appears to have been an energetic and efficient magistrate, and to have administered affairs with vigor and intelligence. He did not live, however, in a period when justice ever erred on the side of mercy, and his harsh and cruel treatment of the aborigines will always remain a stain upon his memory. The native population soon dwindled away under the sway of the Spaniards, who imposed tasks upon them far beyond their physical powers of endurance. The victims of this hardship had no one to befriend them at that time, and no one has done them justice in history. The few glimpses of their character which have come down to us are of a nature greatly to interest us in this now extinct race. Their one fault was in trusting the invaders at all. At the outset they could have swept them from the face of the earth, but, once permitted to establish themselves, they soon became too powerful to be driven out of the land. A native chief, whose only crime was that of taking up arms in defense of the integrity of his little territory, fell into the hands of Velasquez, and was cruelly burned at the stake, near what is now the town of Yara, as a punishment for his patriotism. The words of this unfortunate but brave chief (Hatuey), extorted by the torments which he suffered, were: "I prefer hell to heaven, if there are Spaniards in heaven!"

In point of energetic action and material progress, Velasquez reminds us of a later Governor-General, the famous Tacon. In a single decade, Velasquez founded the seven cities of Baracoa, Santiago de Cuba, Trinidad, Bayamo, Puerto del Principe, St. Spiritus, and, on the south coast near Batabano, Havana, since removed to its present site. He caused the mines to be opened and rendered them profitable, introduced valuable breeds of cattle, instituted agricultural enterprise, and opened a large trade with San Domingo, Jamaica, and the Spanish peninsula. Population increased rapidly, thousands of persons emigrating annually from Europe, tempted by the inviting stories of the returned explorers. Emigration schemes were approved and fostered by the home government, and thus a large community was rapidly divided among the several cities upon the island. Still this new province was considered mainly in the light of a military depot by the Spanish throne, in its famous operations at that period in Mexico. The fact that it was destined to prove the richest jewel in the Castilian crown, and a mine of wealth to the Spanish treasury, was not dreamed of at that date in its history. Even the enthusiastic followers of Cortez, who sought that fabulous El Dorado in the New World, had no promise for this gem of the Caribbean Sea; but, in spite of every side issue and all contending interests, the island continued to grow in numbers and importance, while its native resources were far beyond the appreciation of the home government.

Thus Cuba became the headquarters of the Spanish power in the West, forming the point of departure for those military expeditions which, though circumscribed in numbers, were yet so formidable in the energy of the leaders, and in the arms, discipline, courage, fanaticism, and avarice of their followers, that they were amply adequate to carry out the vast scheme of conquest for which they were designed. It was hence that Cortez embarked for the conquest of Mexico; a gigantic undertaking, a slight glance at which will recall to the mind of the reader the period of history to which we would direct his attention.

Landing upon the continent (1518) with a little band scarcely more than half the complement of a modern regiment, Cortez prepared to traverse an unknown country, thronged by savage tribes with whose character, habits, and means of defense he was wholly unacquainted. This romantic adventure, worthy of the palmiest days of chivalry, was finally crowned with success, though checkered with various fortunes, and stained with bloody episodes that prove how the threads of courage and ferocity are inseparably blended in the woof and warp of Spanish character. It must be remembered, however, that the spirit of the age was harsh, relentless, and intolerant, and that if the Aztecs, idolaters and sacrificers of human victims, found no mercy at the hands of the fierce Catholics whom Cortez commanded, neither did the Indians of our own section of the continent fare much better at the hands of men professing to be disciples of a purer faith, and coming to these shores, not as warriors, but themselves persecuted fugitives.

The Spanish generals who invaded Mexico encountered a people who had attained a far higher point of civilization than their red brethren of the outlying Caribbean Islands, or those of the northeastern portion of the continent. Vast pyramids, imposing sculptures, curious arms, fanciful garments, various kinds of manufactures, the relics of which strongly interest the student of the past, filled the invaders with surprise. There was much that was curious and startling in their mythology, and the capital of the Mexican empire presented a strange and fascinating spectacle to the eyes of Cortez. The rocky amphitheatre in the midst of which it was built still remains unchanged, but the great lake which surrounded it, traversed by causeways and covered with floating gardens laden with flowers, is gone.

The star of the Aztec dynasty set in blood. In vain did the inhabitants of the conquered city, roused to madness by the cruelty and extortion of the victors, expel them from their midst. Cortez refused to flee farther than the shore; the light of his burning galleys rekindled the desperate valor of his followers, and Mexico fell, as a few years after did Peru under the perfidy and sword of Pizarro, thus completing the scheme of conquest, and giving Spain a colonial empire far more splendid than that of any other power in Christendom.

Of the agents in this vast scheme of territorial aggrandizement, we see Cortez dying in obscurity and Pizarro assassinated in his palace, while retributive justice has overtaken the monarchy at whose behest the richest portions of the Western Continent were violently wrested from their native possessors.

CHAPTER V.

Baracoa, the First Capital. — West Indian Buccaneers. — Military Despotism. — A Perpetual State of Siege. — A Patriotic Son of Cuba. — Political Condition of the Island. — Education of Cuban Youths. — Attempts at Revolution. — Fate of General Narciso Lopez. — The Late Civil War and its Leader. — Terrible Slaughter of Spanish Troops. — Stronghold of the Insurgents. — Guerrillas. — Want of Self-Reliance. — Spanish Art, Literature, and Conquest. — What Spain was. — What Spain is. — Rise and Fall of an Empire.

BARACOA lies one hundred miles northeast from Santiago, and was the capital of the island as first established by Velasquez. Here Leo X. erected in 1518 the first cathedral in Cuba. The town is situated on the north coast, near the eastern extremity of the island, having a small but deep harbor, and a considerable trade in the shipping of sugar and fruits to this country. The population at present numbers about six thousand. Five years after the settlement of Baracoa, the capital was moved to Santiago de Cuba, where it remained until 1589, when Havana was formally declared to be the capital of the island, its first Captain-General being Juan de Tejada. The city was captured and partially destroyed by a French pirate in 1638, and afterwards suffered a like catastrophe at the hands of the buccaneers of combined nationality, embracing some disaffected Spaniards. So late as 1760 Havana was captured and held by the English, under the Duke of Albemarle, but was restored to Spain, after a brief occupancy, in 1763. The first grand impulse to the material prosperity of the city, anomalous though it may seem, was given through its capture by the British. It is true that the victors seized everything by force, but they also taught the listless people how to repair their losses, and how to multiply prosperity. The port of Havana, accustomed heretofore to receive the visits of half a score of European vessels annually, suddenly became the rendezvous of a thousand ships in the same period of time, much tò the surprise of the inhabitants. Bourbon in nature as the Spaniards were and still are, they could not but profit by the brilliant example of their enemies, and from that time forward the city grew rapidly in commercial importance, and has continued to do so, notwithstanding the rivalry of Matanzas, Santiago, Cienfuegos, and other ports, as well as the drawbacks of civil war and business stagnation.

These buccaneers of the West Indies, to whom we have so often alluded, were composed mostly of English, French, and Dutch adventurers, whose bitter hatred the Spaniards early incurred. They were for a long time their terror and scourge, being the real masters of the ocean in these latitudes. They feared no enemy and spared none, while by shocking acts of needless cruelty they proved themselves fiends in human shape. Among these rovers there were often found men particularly fitted for the adventurous career they had adopted, men who combined remarkable executive ability with a spirit of daring bravery and a total disregard of all laws, human and divine. By a few such leaders the bands of freebooters were held in hand, and preserved their organization for many years; obedience to the word of their chief, after he was once chosen as such, being the one inviolable law of their union. The romance of the sea owes its most startling chapters to the career of these pirates. Sometimes their principal rendezvous was at the Isle of Pines; at others further north among the Bahamas, Nassau being one of their favorite resorts.

In the mean time, under numerous and often changed Captains-General, the island of Cuba increased in population by free emigration from Spain, and by the constant importations of slaves from Africa. It may be said to have been governed by a military despotism from the very outset to the present time; and nothing short of such an arbitrary rule could maintain the connection between the island and so exacting a mother country, more than three thousand miles across the ocean. Accordingly we find the Captain-General invested with unlimited power. He is in fact a viceroy appointed by the crown of Spain, and accountable only to the reigning sovereign for his administration of the colony. His rule is absolute. He has the power of life and death in his hands. He can by his arbitrary will send into exile any person who resides in the island whom he considers inimical to the interests of the home government. Of the exercise of this power instances are constantly occurring, as in the case of the editor of the "Revista Economica," already recorded. He can at will suspend the operation of the laws and ordinances, can destroy or confiscate property, and in short, the island may be said to be in a perpetual state of siege.

Such is the infirmity of human nature that few individuals can be safely trusted with despotic power; accordingly we find no Captain-General whose administration will bear the test of rigid examination. Indeed, the venality of a majority of these officials has been so gross as to have passed into a proverb. It is not to be expected that officers from Spain should consult the true interests of the Cubans; they are not sent hither for that purpose, but merely to look after the revenue of the crown, and to swell it to the very uttermost. The office of Governor-General is of course a brilliant prize, for which there are plenty of aspirants eagerly struggling, while the means by which a candidate is most likely to succeed in obtaining the appointment presupposes a character of an inferior order. This official knows that he cannot count on a long term of office, and hence he makes no effort to study the interests or gain the good-will of the people over whom he presides. He has a twofold object only in view: namely, to keep the revenue well up to the mark, and to enrich himself as speedily as possible. The princely salary he receives — fifty thousand dollars per annum, with a palace and household attendants supplied — is but a portion of the income which, by a system of peculation, he is enabled to divert to his private coffers. As a rule, the Captain-General comes out to Cuba a poor man, and returns a rich one, however brief his term of office.

Occasionally during the lapse of years a true and patriotic man has filled this important post, when the remarkable elements of prosperity contained within the limits of this peerless land were rapidly developed and advanced. Such an one was Don Luis de las Casas, whose name is cherished by all patriotic Cubans, as also is that of Don Francisco de Arrango, an accomplished statesman and a native of Havana. He was educated in Spain, and designed to follow the law as a profession. This man, being thoroughly acquainted with the possibilities of the island and the condition and wants of his countrymen, succeeded in procuring the amelioration of some of the most flagrant abuses of the colonial system. In his argument for reform before the home government, he told them that serious dissent permeated every class of the community, and was bid in return to employ a still more stringent system of rule. To this Arrango replied that force was not remedy, and that to effectually reform the rebellious they must first reform the laws. His earnest reason carried conviction, and finally won concession. By his exertions the staple productions of the island were so much increased that the revenue, in place of falling short of the expenses of the government as his enemies had predicted, soon yielded a large surplus. He early raised his voice against the iniquitous slave trade, and suggested the introduction of white labor, though he admitted that the immediate and wholesale abolition of slavery was impracticable. This was the rock on which he split, as it regarded his influence with the Spaniards in Cuba, that is, with the planters and rich property holders. Slavery with them was a sine qua non. Many of them owned a thousand Africans each, and the institution, as an arbitrary power as well as the means of wealth, was ever dear to the Spanish heart. Former and subsequent Captains-General not only secretly encouraged the clandestine importation of slaves, after issuing an edict prohibiting it, but profited pecuniarily by the business. It was owing to his exertions that the duty on coffee, spirits, and cotton was remitted for a period of ten years, and that machinery for the sugar plantations was allowed to be imported into Cuba from the United States free of all duty.

The patriotic services of Arrango were appreciated by the court of Madrid, although he was at times the inflexible opponent of its selfish schemes. The Cross of Charles III. showed the esteem in which he was held by that monarch. With a modesty which did him honor he declined to accept a title of nobility which was afterwards tendered to him by his king. This patriotic son of Cuba was at heart a republican, and declared that the king could make noblemen, but God only could make gentlemen. In 1813, when, by the adoption of the Constitution of 1812, Cuba became entitled to representation in the general Cortes, — a privilege but briefly enjoyed, — he went to Madrid as a deputy, and there achieved the crowning glory of his useful life: namely, the opening of the ports of the island to foreign trade. In 1817 he returned to his native land with the rank of Counselor of State and Financial Intendant of Cuba, also possessing the Grand Cross of the Order of Isabella. He died in 1837, at the age of seventy-two, after a long and eminently useful life, bequeathing large sums of money for various public purposes in his native isle.

When the invasion of Spain, which took place in 1808, produced the Constitution of 1812, Cuba was considered entitled, as we have stated, to enjoy its benefits, and it was so announced by royal statute; but political revolution at home and a manifest restiveness upon the island finally led in 1836 to the revoking of this royal statute, which had never been practically operative, and the old Constitution was proclaimed.

Up to this period of time the various political events at home had disturbed but slightly the tranquillity of this rich province of Spain. The Cubans, although sensible of the progress of public intelligence and wealth under the protection of a few enlightened governors and through the influence of some distinguished and patriotic individuals, still felt that these advances were slow, partial, and limited. The most intelligent realized that there was no regular system; that the public interests were sure to suffer, confided to officials entrusted with unlimited power. They frequently saw themselves betrayed by a cupidity which impelled the authorities to enrich themselves in every possible way at the expense of general suffering. Added to these sources of discontent was the powerful influence exerted by the spectacle of the rapidly increasing greatness of the United States, where a portion of the Cuban youths were wont to receive their education. No matter in what political faith these youths had left home, they were sure to return republicans.

There also were the examples of Mexico and Spanish South America, which had recently conquered with their blood their emancipation from monarchy. Liberal ideas were naturally diffused by Cubans who had traveled either in Europe or North America, there imbibing the spirit of modern civilization. But with a fatuity and obstinacy which has always characterized her, the mother country resolved to ignore all causes of discontent, and their significant influence as manifested by the people of the island. In place of yielding to the popular current and introducing a liberal and mild system of government, she drew the reins yet tighter, curtailing many former privileges. Thus it was that blind persistence in the fatal principle of despotic domination relaxed the natural bonds uniting Cuba and the mother country, and infused gall into the hearts of the governed. Obedience still continued, but it was the dangerous obedience of terror, not the secure and instinctive spirit of loyalty.

This severity on the part of the home government has naturally given rise to several attempts to cast off the Spanish yoke. The first occurred in 1823, when Simon Bolivar offered to aid the disaffected party by throwing an invading force into the island. Another was made in 1826, and a third in 1828. In 1848 a conspiracy was formed at Cienfuegos and Trinidad to establish Cuban independence, under the leadership of General Narciso Lopez; but finding that his plans were premature, he escaped to this country, and here arranged a descent upon the island, which he led in person: this was in 1850. General Lopez, however, was not seconded by the timid natives, though they had freely pledged themselves to do so, and his expedition, after winning one decisive battle and several important skirmishes, was at last overpowered and its leader promptly executed. General Lopez was an adopted citizen of Cuba, and was married to one of her daughters. He was executed at the age of fifty-two.

The Lopez expedition would seem to have been the most serious and best organized attempt at revolution in Cuba by invasion, though there have been formidable attempts since. From 1868 to 1876 Cuba may be said to have been in a state of chronic civil war. This outbreak was led by Carlos Manuel de Cespedes, an able lawyer and wealthy planter of Bayamo, in the eastern department of the island. He raised the standard of independence on his estate, Demajagua, supported at the outset by less than fifty men. This was in October, 1868, and by the middle of November he had an organized army of twelve thousand men; poorly armed, it must be admitted, but united in purpose and of determined will. That portion of the island contiguous to Santiago, and between that city and Cienfuegos, was for a long period almost entirely in possession of the patriot forces. Here many sanguinary battles were fought with varying fortune, at terrible sacrifice of life, especially on the part of the government troops, over one hundred thousand of whom, first and last, are known to have perished in that district. Spain actually sent one hundred and forty-five thousand enlisted men to Cuba during the eight years of active warfare. Of this number those who finally returned to the European peninsula were but a few hundreds! It was publicly stated in the Cortes of Madrid that not enough of that immense force ever returned to fill a single regiment! The climate was far more fatal to these soldiers than were patriot bullets. The warfare was conducted by the native Cubans mostly on the guerrilla plan, and was ten times more destructive to the imported soldiers than to themselves. Discipline counted for little or nothing in contending with men who fought singlehanded and from ambush, decimating the ranks of an invading column, who in turn could only fire at random.

Exhaustion and promised concessions, which were, as usual with the Spanish government, never fulfilled, finally brought this struggle to an end; but it cost Spain many millions of dollars and the lives of over a hundred and fifty thousand men, saying nothing of the destruction of an enormous amount of property on the island, belonging to loyal Spaniards. Miles upon miles of thrifty plantations, with all their buildings and machinery, were laid waste, and remain so to this day.

Since 1876 there have been roving bands of insurgents in existence, causing the authorities more or less serious trouble, leading them at times to make serious attempts at their entire suppression. But the mountains and half-inaccessible forests of the eastern department still serve to secrete many armed and disaffected people, whose frequent outbreaks are made public by the slow process of oral information. The press is forbidden to publish any news of this character. Thus it will be seen that, although the spirit of liberty may slumber in the island, it is by no means dead, nor is the intense hatred which exists between the home-born Spaniard and the native Cuban growing less from year to year. Indeed, the insurrection of Trinidad and Cienfuegos (1868) still smoulders, and any extreme political exigency would be liable to cause it to blaze forth with renewed force. The region where the insurgents have always made their rendezvous, and which they have virtually held for years, is nearest to Guantanamo and Santiago. This mountainous district is the resort of all runaway slaves, escaped criminals, and those designated as insurgents. These together form at the present time a roving community of several hundred desperate men. These refugees, divided into small bands, make predatory raids upon travelers and loyal planters, as we have described, to keep themselves supplied with the necessities of life other than those afforded by the prolific hand of Nature. Occasionally they are organized by some fresh leader, some daring native, stimulated by a spirit of patriotism, and possessing some executive ability; then follows a systematic outbreak of just sufficient importance to harass the government, and to form, perhaps, an excuse for demanding a fresh regiment of victims from the European peninsula. Such a guerrilla contest engages the worst passions of the combatants, and quarter is neither asked nor given when they come face to face. The bloodthirsty acts of both sides, as related to the author during his late visit to the spot, are too horrible to record in these pages. It is not legitimate warfare, but rather wholesale murder, which characterizes these occasions, and there is no expedient of destruction not resorted to by both the refugees and the pursuing soldiers. The nature of the country favors the revolutionists, and determines their mode of conflict. Thus far, when the irregular bands have been strong enough to meet these detachments of regulars sent into their neighborhood to capture them, they have nearly always beaten them gallantly, and this has served to perpetuate their hopes, desperate as is a cause which only outlaws, escaped criminals, and slaves dare to fight for. These people appear to be well supplied with arms and ammunition, which it is said are smuggled to them from sympathizers in this country, particularly from Florida. Though their ranks are supposed to embrace but small numbers, still they form a nucleus at all times, about which discontented spirits may gather. Thus it is found necessary to quarter a foreign army of thirty thousand soldiers upon the people at the present time, while half the navy of Spain lies anchored in the ports of the island.

One great drawback and defect in the character

of the native Cubans is a want of self-reliance. The remedy for the outrageous oppression under which they have so long struggled lies within themselves; "for they can conquer who believe they can." In the consciousness of strength is strength, but the Creole republicans have never yet evinced the necessary degree of true manhood to challenge general outside sympathy, or to command the respect of other nationalities. The numerous revolutionary outbreaks upon the island — so frequent in the last half century as to be chronic — have all been of the most insignificant character, compared with the importance of the occasion and the object in view. These efforts have mostly been made from without, almost entirely unsupported from within the borders of Cuba, with the exception of that of 1868. It appears incredible that an intelligent people, within so short a distance of our Southern coast, constantly visited by the citizens of a free republic, and having the example of successful revolt set them by the men of the same race, both in the North and the South, weighed down by oppression almost without parallel, should never have aimed an effectual blow at their oppressors. It would seem that the softness of the unrivaled climate of those skies, beneath which it is luxury only to exist, has unnerved this people, and that the effeminate spirit of the original inhabitants had descended in retribution to the posterity of their conquerors.

In closing these brief chapters relating to the early history of the island of Cuba, and in bringing the record up to our own period, some natural reflections suggest themselves as to the present condition of the mother country. We follow with more than passing interest the condition of Spain, whose history is so closely interwoven with our own. From the close of the fifteenth century our paths have run on in parallel lines, but while we have gone on increasing in power and wealth, she has sunk in the scale of decadence with a rapidity no less surprising than has been the speed of our own progress. At the commencement of the sixteenth century Spain threatened to become the mistress of the world, as Rome had been before her. She may be said to have at that period dominated Europe. In art she was in the very foremost position: Murillo, Velasquez, Ribera, and other famous painters were her honored sons. In literature she was also distinguished: both Cervantes and Lope de Vega contributed to her greatness and lasting fame. While, in discoverers and conquerors, she sent forth Columbus, Cortez, and Pizarro. The banners of Castile and Aragon floated alike on the Pacific and the margin of the Indian Ocean. Her ships sailed in every sea, and brought home freights of fabulous value from all the regions of the earth. Her manufacturers produced the richest silks and velvets; her soil yielded corn and wine; her warriors were adventurous and brave; her soldiers inherited the gallantry of the followers of Charles V.; her cities were the splendid abodes of luxury, refinement, and elegance. She was the court of Europe, the acknowledged leader of chivalry and of grandeur.

This is the picture of what Spain was at no remote period of time, but in her instance we have an example showing us that states are no more exempt than individuals from the mutability of fate. So was it with Egypt, Babylon, Assyria, and Rome, though in their case we look far back into the vista of history to recall the change, whereas in the instance of

DECLINE OF THE SPANISH EMPIRE.

Spain we are contemporary witnesses. From a first-class power, how rapidly she has sunk into comparative insignificance! She has been shorn of her wealthy colonies, one after another, in the East and in the West, holding with feeble grasp a few inconsiderable islands only besides this gem of the Antilles, the choicest jewel of her crown. Extremely poor and deeply indebted, she has managed for years to extort by means of the most outrageous system of taxation a large share of her entire revenue from the island of Cuba, her home population having long since become exhausted by over-burdensome imposts. Her nobles of to-day are an effeminate, soulless, and imbecile race, while the common people, with some excellent qualities, are yet ignorant, cruel, and passionate. The whole country is divided against itself, the tottering throne being with difficulty upheld. Even the elements have of late seemed to combine against her, decimating whole cities of her southern possessions by earthquakes, and smiting her people with pestilence.

This simple statement of her present situation is patent to all who read and observe. It is not an overdrawn picture. In it the moralist beholds the retributive justice of providence. As Spain in the plenitude of her power was ambitious, cruel, and perfidious, so has the measure which she meted out to others been in return accorded to herself. As with fire and sword she swept the Aztec and the Incas from Mexico and Peru, so was she at last driven from these genial countries by their revolted inhabitants. The spoiler has been despoiled, the victor has been vanquished, and thus has Spain met the just fate clearly menaced by the Scriptures to those who smite with the sword.

CHAPTER VI.

Geographical. — A Remarkable Weed. — Turtle-Hunting. — Turtle-Steaks in Olden Times. — The Gulf Stream. — Deep-Sea Soundings. — Mountain Range of Cuba. — Curious Geological Facts. — Subterranean Caverns. — Wild Animals. — The Rivers of the Island. — Fine Harbors. — Historic Memories of the Caribbean Sea. — Sentinel of the Gulf. — Importance of the Position. — Climate. — Hints for Invalids. — Matanzas. — Execution of a Patriot. — Valley of Yumuri; Caves of Bellamar; Puerto Principe; Cardenas.

HAVING thus briefly glanced at the historical and political story of Cuba, — whose very name seems bathed in sunshine and fragrance, yet bedewed with human tears, — let us now consider its peculiarities of climate, soil, and population, together with its geographical characteristics. The form of the island is quite irregular, resembling the blade of a Turkish scimitar slightly curved back, or that of a long narrow crescent, presenting its convex side to the north. It stretches away in this shape from east to west, throwing its western end into a curve, as if to form a barrier to the outlet of the Gulf of Mexico, and as if at some ancient period it had formed a part of the American continent; severed on its north side from the Florida peninsula by the wearing of the Gulf Stream, and from Yucatan, on its southwestern point, by a current setting into the Gulf. Two broad channels are thus formed, by either of which the Mexican Gulf is entered.

These channels are nearly of the same width, somewhat exceeding a hundred miles each, the northern passage being a few miles the broader. The Bahama Banks extend along its northern coast-line about fifty or sixty miles distant, where commences the group of many small isles known as the Bahamas, and of which we have already treated. On her eastern extreme, near Cape Maysi, Cuba is within about fifty miles of the western shore of Hayti, from which it is separated by the Windward Passage. The southern shore is washed by the Caribbean Sea, which is also here and there interspersed with small islands of little importance. One hundred and fifty miles due south lies the British island of Jamaica, with a superficial area of over four thousand square miles. Still further to the eastward, on the other side of Hayti, lies Porto Rico (like Cuba a Spanish possession), and the two groups of islands known as the Leeward and Windward isles. These are of various nationalities, including English, French, and Dutch, thus completing the entire region familiarly known to us as the West Indies.

In approaching the coast from the Windward isles, the observant traveler will notice the fields of what is called gulf-weed, which floats upon the surface of the sea. It is a unique genus, found nowhere except in these tropical waters, and must not be confounded with the sea-weed encountered by Atlantic steamers off the Banks of Newfoundland, and about the edges of the Gulf Stream in that region. This singular and interesting weed propagates itself on the waves, and there sustains, as on the shore of New Providence, zoöphytes and mollusks which also abound in these latitudes. The poetical theory relating to this sargasso, and possibly to the animals that cling to it, is that it marks the site of an Atlantic continent sunk long ages since, and that, transformed from a rooting to a floating plant, it wanders round and round as if in search of the rocks upon which it once grew. The southern shore of Cuba presents much of special interest to the conchologist in the variety and beauty of the sea-shells that abound upon its beaches. The water is of an exquisite color, a brilliant green, very changeable, like liquid opal. Were an artist truthfully to depict it, he would be called color-mad. Northern skies are never reflected in waters of such fanciful hues. Some beautiful specimens of white corals are found here, but they are not a characteristic of the coast.

On that portion bordering the Old Bahama Channel, and also opposite the Isle of Pines, which Columbus named Evangelista, — on this south shore, large numbers of turtles are taken annually, which produce the best quality of tortoise-shell. It is strange that the habits of these creatures down here in the Caribbean Sea should so closely resemble those of the tiny tortoises described by Thoreau as frequenting Walden Pond. The female turtle digs the hole in which to deposit her eggs on the sandy beach, just above the margin of high tide, generally choosing a moonlight night for the purpose. The hole is often so large that the turtle will require an hour of industrious labor to dig it to her entire satisfaction. Observing the strictest silence, the turtle-hunter steals upon the animal, and with a single motion turns it upon its back, rendering it utterly helpless, after which it can be secured at will. Thousands are annually caught in this manner.

It is a curious fact worth recalling to memory that

four hundred years ago, when Columbus first landed upon the island, he found that the aborigines kept turtle corrals near the beach, amply supplied with these animals. From them they procured eggs, and also furnished themselves with the only meat which it was possible to obtain, if we except that of the little "voiceless dog" which they hunted, and such birds as they could snare. Probably as many turtles were taken by those Carib Indians in 1492 as are caught by the fishermen this year of our Lord, in the same waters, showing how inexhaustible is the supply of Neptune's kingdom. Modern epicures may not therefore claim any distinction as to the priority of discovery touching turtle soup and turtle steaks, both of which were certainly indulged in by the Caribs in Columbus' time, and probably they were in vogue many centuries previous.

One neither departs from nor approaches the Cuban shore without crossing that marvelous ocean river, the Gulf Stream, with banks and bottom of cold water, while its body and surface are warm. Its color, in the region of the gulf where it seems to have its rise, is indigo blue, so distinct that the eye can follow its line of demarkation where it joins the common waters of the sea in their prairie-green. Its surface temperature on the coast of the United States is from 75° to 80° Fahrenheit. Its current, of a uniform speed of four to five miles per hour, expends immense power in its course, and moves a body of water in the latitude of the Carolina coast fully two hundred miles wide. This aqueous body exceeds in quantity the rivers of the Mississippi and the Amazon multiplied one thousand times. Its temperature diminishes very gradually, while it moves thousands of leagues, until one branch loses itself in Arctic regions, and the other breaks on the coast of Europe. It is well known to navigators that one branch of the Gulf Stream finds its outlet northward from the Caribbean Sea through the Windward Passage, and that here the current extends to the depth of eight hundred fathoms ; the width, however, in this section is not over ten miles. It will be nothing new to tell the reader that the sea, especially in its proximity to the continents, has a similar topographical conformation beneath its surface. The bottom consists of hills, mountains, and valleys, like the surface of the earth upon which we live. A practical illustration of the fact is afforded in the soundings taken by the officers of our Coast Survey in the Caribbean Sea, where a valley was found giving a water depth of three thousand fathoms, twenty-five miles south of Cuba. The Cayman islands, in that neighborhood, are the summit of mountains bordering this deep valley at the bottom of the sea. It is known to extend over seven hundred miles, from between Cuba and Jamaica nearly to the head of the bay of Honduras, with an average breadth of eighty miles. How suggestive the subject of these submarine Alps! Thus the island of Grand Cayman, scarcely twenty feet above sea level, is the top of a mountain twenty thousand five hundred and sixty-eight feet above the bottom of the submarine valley beside which it rises. — an altitude exceeding that of any mountain on the North American continent. A little more than five miles, or say twenty-seven thousand feet, is the greatest depth yet sounded at sea.

With an extensive coast-line particularly well adapted for the purpose, smuggling is at all times successfully carried on in Cuba, stimulated by an almost prohibitory tariff. It is well understood that many of the most prosperous merchants in Havana are secretly engaged in this business. The blindness of minor officials is easily purchased. The eastern department of the island is most notorious for this class of illegal trade. It was through these agencies that the revolutionists were so well supplied with arms, ammunition, and other necessities during the eight years of civil war. While we are writing these lines, the cable brings us news of a fresh landing of "filibusters" on the shores in this immediate neighborhood.

Cuba is the most westerly of the West Indian isles, and compared with the others has nearly twice as much superficial extent of territory, being about as large as England proper, without the principality of Wales. Its greatest length from east to west is very nearly eight hundred miles; its narrowest part is over twenty miles, and its average width about forty miles. The circumference of the island is set down at two thousand miles, and it is supposed to contain thirty-five thousand square miles. The face of the interior is undulating, with an average level of three hundred feet above the surface of the sea. The narrow form of the island, and the chain of mountains which divides it throughout its whole length, leave a limited course for its rivers, and consequently most of these in the rainy season become torrents, and during the rest of the year are nearly dried up. Those streams which sustain themselves at all seasons are well stocked with fine fish, and afford to lovers of the piscatory art admirable sport. Near their mouths some of the rivers, like those of the opposite coast of Florida, are frequented by crocodiles.

The chain of mountains running through the centre of the island, more or less broken in its course, is lofty in the east, but gradually diminishes in elevation towards the west, until it becomes a series of gently undulating hills of one or two hundred feet above sea level, ceasing as a connected range in the vicinity of Matanzas. On the easterly end this range of mountains approaches the south coast between Puerto Principe and Trinidad. The country lying between Cape Cruz, Cape Maysi, and the town of Holguin has the highest elevations; the most lofty point, Turquino, lately measured, has a height of ten thousand eight hundred feet. Illustrative of the great revolutions which the globe has undergone in its several geological epochs, petrified shells and bivalves are found on the summits of these highest peaks, surrounded by coral rocks, both of which differ entirely from those at present existing on the shores of the Antilles. An immense bowlder was pointed out to us on the summit of La Gran Piedra, at an elevation of five thousand feet, of totally different composition from any other rocks on the island. The great mystery is how such a mass of solid stone could have got there. Most of these mountains are thickly wooded, some of them to their very tops, and appear to be in a perpetual state of verdure. There are mahogany trees in these hills reported to be of almost fabulous dimensions, besides other trees of great age. Some idea of the excellence of the timber grown in Cuba may be had from the fact that over one hundred Spanish ships of war — some of which were of the largest size, mounting a hundred and twenty guns — have been built from native stock at the port of Havana.

Copper ore is found in abundance, as well as silver

and iron, in the mountains. Snow is never known to fall even in these elevated districts, and of course in no other part of the island. In the interior, the extreme heat of the low-lying sea-coast and cities is not experienced, and the yellow fever is unknown. Low, level swampy land is found only on the southern coast, where there are some wild deer, wild cats and dogs, which are hunted; the former introduced into Cuba half a century since, the two latter descended from domestic animals. Large tracts of undulating country are without trees, affording good pasturage. In some of the mountains are extensive caves, not unlike the caves of Bellamar near the city of Matanzas, in which are still to be found the bones of an unknown race, while several of these elevations are so precipitous as to be nearly inaccessible.

Travelers who have visited the Bay of Biscay, on the French and Spanish shore near Biarritz, have observed how the rocks have been worn into caverns, arches, alcoves, and honeycombed formations by the action of the waters for centuries. Just so the soft limestone strata beneath the surface of Cuba, in many portions of the island, have been hollowed out, tunneled, and formed into caves, by the tremendous downpour and wash of tropical rains. So the action of the sea has created a cave under Moro Castle, at the mouth of the harbor of Havana, as well as under that other Moro which stands guard over the entrance of Santiago de Cuba. The existence of these subterranean caverns has often led to serious accidents. In some instances buildings which were by chance erected just over them have suddenly been swallowed up as though by an earthquake.

Many of the rivers are navigable for short distances.

The longest is the Cauto, in the eastern department, which, rising in the Sierra del Cobre, passes between Holguin and Jiguani, and empties on the south coast a little north of Manzanillo. It is navigable for half its length, between fifty and sixty leagues. The river Ay has falls in its course two hundred feet high, and a natural bridge spanning it, nearly as remarkable as that of Virginia. The Sagua le Grande is navigable for five leagues, and the same may be said of the river Sasa. The Agabama, emptying on the south coast near Trinidad, is also partially navigable. There are two hundred and sixty rivers in all, independent of rivulets and torrents. So abundantly is the island supplied with fresh-water springs, especially on the south side, that the pure liquid filters through the fissures of the stratified rock in such quantities as to form, by hydrostatic pressure, springs in the sea itself some distance from the shore. The sulphurous and thermal springs of San Diego are the resort of numerous invalids annually, who come hither from Europe and America.

The coast and harbors of Cuba are carefully marked for the purpose of navigation by eighteen well-placed lighthouses, visible from fifteen to twenty miles at sea, according to the importance of the surrounding points. That which stands in Moro Castle, on the south side of the harbor's entrance at Havana, is eighty feet in height and about a hundred and fifty from the level of the sea. It is visible in clear weather twenty miles from shore. In honor of a former Governor-General this lighthouse bears the inscription "O'Donnell, 1844," in mammoth letters. So plain and safe is the entrance to this harbor, which in the narrowest part is some hundred yards wide, that a pilot is hardly necessary, though foreign vessels generally take one. There is little or no tide on this part of the coast, the variations never exceeding two feet. No regular ebb and flow is therefore observable, but when the land breeze rises there is a very slight tide-way setting out of the harbor. No country in the world of the size of this island has so many large and fine harbors. They number twenty-nine on its northern side and twenty-eight on the southern. The well-defined water-line along the yellow, rusty rocks of the coast shows the mark of ages, and also that there has been no upheaval since the land took its present shape. Where there are no regular harbors the shore is indented with numerous deep channels forming inlets, safe only for native boatmen, as the winding course of the blue waters covers myriads of sunken rocks. On the southern side, opposite the Isle of Pines, there are some beautiful reaches of beach, over which the gentle surf rolls continuously with a murmur so soft as to seem like the whispered secrets of the sea. Yet what frightful historic memories brood over these deep waters of the Archipelago, where for nearly two centuries floated and fought the ships of sea-robbers of every nationality, and where the cunning but guilty slave-clippers, fresh from the coast of Africa, loaded with kidnapped men and women, made their harbor! With all their dreamy beauty, the tropics are full of sadness, both in their past and present history.

The occasional hurricanes, which prove so disastrous to the Bahamas and other isles in the immediate vicinity of Cuba, rarely extend their influence to its shores, but the bursts of fury which these usually tranquil seas sometimes indulge in are not excelled in violence in the worst typhoon regions.

The nearest port of the island to this continent is Matanzas, lying due south from Cape Sable, Florida, a distance of a hundred and thirty miles. Havana is located some sixty miles west of Matanzas, and it is here that the island divides the entrance to the Gulf of Mexico, whose coast-line, measuring six thousand miles, finds the outlet of its commerce along the shore of Cuba, almost within range of the guns in Moro Castle. Lying thus at our very door as it were, this island stands like a sentinel, guarding the approaches of the Gulf of Mexico, whose waters wash the shores of five of the United States, and by virtue of the same position barring the entrance of the great river which drains half the continent of North America. Nor does the importance of the situation end here. Cuba keeps watch and ward over our communication with California by way of the isthmus. The peculiar formation of the southeastern shore of this continent, and the prevalence of the trade-winds, with the oceanic current from east to west, make the ocean passage skirting the shore of Cuba the natural outlet for the commerce also of Venezuela, New Granada, Costa Rica, and Nicaragua. It is not surprising, therefore, when we realize the commanding position of the island, that so much of interest attaches to its ultimate destiny.

Cuba seems formed to become the very button on Fortune's cap. No wonder that the Abbé Raynal pronounced it to be the boulevard of the New World, or that the Spanish historian called it the fairest emerald in the crown of Ferdinand and Isabella. Under any other government in Christendom than that of Spain, the island would to-day have been one vast smiling garden, for its natural advantages are absolutely unequaled. To oppress and rob its inhabitants has been the unvarying policy of the home government from first to last. The undisguised system has been to extort from them every farthing possible in the way of taxes. No legitimate business could sustain itself against the enormous exactions of the Spanish rule. Coffee and cotton planting have been absolutely driven out of the island by the taxes imposed upon their production. In short, the mother country has carried her system of oppression and despotism in Cuba to the utmost stretch of human audacity.

Probably no place has a finer or more desirable climate than has the main portion of Cuba, with the clear atmosphere of the low latitudes, no mist, the sun seldom obscured, and a season of endless summer. We do not wonder that the Northern invalid turns instinctively towards so inviting a clime, where Nature in all her moods is so regal. The appearance of the sky at night is far brighter and more beautiful than at the North. The atmosphere does not seem to lose its transparency with the departure of the day. Sunset is remarkable for its soft mellow beauty, all too brief to a New England eye accustomed to the lingering brilliancy of our twilights. For more than half a century the island has been the resort of invalids from colder climes in search of health, especially those laboring under pulmonary affections. Such have rarely failed to realize more or less benefit from the mild and equable temperature. The climate so uniformly soft and soothing, the vegetation so thriving and beautiful, the fruits so delicious and abundant, give it a character akin to fairyland. Here Nature seems ever in a tender, loving mood, the very opposite of her cold temperament at the North.

The best time to visit the island, for those who do so in search of health, is from the beginning of January to the middle of May. It is imprudent to remain in the cities of Cuba later than the latter period, as the fever season then commences. The invalid will find that very many physical comforts, and some things deemed imperative at home, must be sacrificed here as quite unattainable : such, for instance, as good beds, strict cleanliness, good milk, and sweet butter. The climatic advantages must suffice for such deprivations. During the greater portion of the year it is dry and hot, the rainy season commencing in June and ending in September. The northeast trade-winds blow over the island from March to October, and though it is especially important to avoid all draughts in the tropics, still one can always find a sufficiently cool and comfortable temperature somewhere, when the trade-wind prevails. To persons in the early stages of consumption this region holds forth great promise of relief; the author can bear witness of remarkable benefit having been realized in many instances. At the period of the year when New England invalids most require to avoid the rigors of the prevailing east winds, namely, in February, March, April, and early May, the island of Cuba is in the glory of high summer, and enjoying the healthiest period of its annual returns. When consumption originates in the island, — as was also found to be the case at Nassau, — it runs its course to a fatal end with such rapidity that the natives consider it to be a contagious disease. Early in May the unacclimated would do well to leave, taking passage up the Gulf to New Orleans, or across the Gulf Stream, which here runs thirty-two miles in width, to Key West, Florida, thence by boat to Tampa Bay, and by railroad to Sanford, and by the St. John's River to St. Augustine, enjoying a brief stay at the latter places, where every requisite convenience can be enjoyed. Jacksonville should not be missed, and by coming north thus slowly and pleasantly, the change of climate is not realized, and June weather will greet the returning traveler with genial warmth.

Owing to the proximity of the northwestern part of Cuba to our own continent, the climate is somewhat variable, and at a height of five hundred feet above the level of the sea, ice is sometimes, though rarely formed; but, as has already been said in these notes, snow never falls upon the island. At long intervals Cuba has been visited by brief hailstorms, and persons who tell you this will add, "but we never have known it in our day." In the cities and near the swamps, the yellow fever, that scourge of all hot climates, prevails from the middle of June to the last of October; but in the interior of the island, where the visitor is at a wholesome distance from humidity and stagnant water, it is no more unhealthy than our own cities in summer. It is doubtful if Havana, even in the fever season, is any more unhealthy than New Orleans at the same period of the year. Fevers of different degrees of malignity prevail from May to November, and occasionally throughout the year. Among these the yellow fever is the most dangerous, and sooner or later all resident foreigners seem to suffer from it, as a sort of acclimation; once experienced, however, one is seldom attacked a second time. In the ports yellow fever is often induced by carelessness and exposure; excesses on the part of foreign sailors are frequently the cause of its fatal attack upon them. The thermometer is never known to rise so high in Havana or Santiago, the opposite extremes of the island, as it does sometimes in New York and Boston. The average temperature is recorded as being 77°, maximum 89°, minimum 50° Fahrenheit. We have been thus elaborate as regards this matter because it is of such general interest to all invalids who annually seek an equable clime.

The principal cities are Havana, with a population of nearly three hundred thousand; Matanzas, with fifty thousand; Puerto Principe, thirty thousand; Cienfuegos, twenty-five thousand.; Trinidad, fourteen thousand; San Salvador, ten thousand; Manzanillo, Cardenas, Nuevitas, Sagua la Grande, and Mariel. Among its largest and finest harbors those of Havana, Santiago de Cuba, Nipe, and Nuevitas are the best; the bay of Matanzas is also large, but shallow. This city stands next to Havana in population, but not in commercial importance. It is said to be healthier than the capital, but it lacks those attractions of life and gayety which are essential even to invalids to render them contented. The streets are wide, and many of the Moorish characteristics of Spanish cities, so common in both this island and the European peninsula, are wanting here. It was built much later and more under foreign direction than Havana. The secret of the superior health of Matanzas over that of the capital is undoubtedly because of its better drainage and general cleanliness.

Located in one of the most fertile portions of the island, the city extends up the picturesque and verdant hills by which the bay is surrounded, in the form of an amphitheatre. The fortifications are of rather a meagre character, and could not withstand a well-organized attack for half an hour. Modern improvements in the construction of heavy guns and projectiles have rendered all the forts in Cuba of no importance as a means of defense against a first-class invading fleet. The custom house is the most prominent building which strikes the eye on approaching the city by water; though built of stone, it is only one story in height, and was erected at the commencement of the present century. On the heights above the city the inhabitants have planted their country seats, from whence the view of the widespreading bay forms a delightful picture. The climate is thought to be especially adapted for the cure of throat and lung diseases, and the city is annually resorted to by those seeking relief from these troubles, as also by those afflicted with neuralgia and rheumatism. The first land made by southern-bound steamers from Boston and New York is the Monte del Pan, or Bread Mountain, forming a lofty background for the city. There are three large churches in Matanzas, a well appointed and spacious theatre, a bull-ring, and cock-pits. Statistics show that the custom-house receipts of the port reach about two million dollars annually. There are two railroads connecting the city with Havana, one of which runs also to the interior southeasterly to Cienfuegos, Sagua, and Villa Clara, intersecting a rich sugar-producing country, from whence it brings a large amount of freight to the coast for shipment. On these Cuban roads one rides in American-built cars, drawn by American engines, and often run by American engineers. Railroads were in use in Cuba before they were adopted in any other Spanish-speaking country, and there are now nearly a thousand miles in active operation on the island.

Matanzas is bounded on the north by the river Yumuri, and on the south by that of San Juan. The town is built upon the site of a former Indian village, known to the early discoverers by the name of Yucayo. It is upon the whole a well-built city, containing some small public squares and a pretty Plaza de Armas, like that of Havana, ornamented with choice trees and flowers, with a statue of Ferdinand VII. in its centre. It was in this square that Gabriel Concepcion de la Valdez, a mulatto poet and patriot of Cuba, was shot by the soldiers of the line. He was accused of complicity with the slave insurrection of 1844, when the blacks attempted to gain their freedom. At the time of his execution the first volley fired by the troops failed to touch a vital spot, and the brave victim, bleeding from many wounds, still stood erect, facing his executioners. He then pointed to his heart, and said in a calm clear voice, "Aim here!" The order was at once obeyed, and the second volley sent the heroic man to that haven where there is no distinction as to color. This martyr, of whom comparatively little is known to the public, possessed all the true elements of a poet. Many of his productions have been preserved in print, and some were translated and republished in England a few years since.

The Plaza of Matanzas is small, smaller even than that of Cienfuegos, but it presents within its circumscribed space a great variety of tropical trees and flowers, over which stand, sentinel-like, a few royal palms with their ashen-gray stems and concentric rings. The star of Bethlehem, fifteen feet high, was here seen full of lovely scarlet blossoms; the southern jasmine, yellow as gold, was in its glory; mignonette, grown to a graceful tree of twenty feet in height, was fragrant and full of blossoms, close beside the delicate vinca, decked in white and red. Some broad-leaved bananas were thriving in the Plaza, while creeping all over that tree and shrub combined, the Spanish bayonet, were pink, purple, and white morning-glories, at once so familiar and suggestive. Opposite the Plaza are several government offices, and two or three very large, fine club-houses, remarkable for the excellence of their appointments and the spaciousness of the public rooms. Club life prevails in Matanzas, as usual at the expense of domestic life, just as it does in Havana, being very much like London in this respect. It is forbidden to discuss politics in these clubs, the hours being occupied mostly over games of chance, such as cards, dominoes, chess, and checkers. Gambling is as natural and national in Cuba as in China. Many Chinese are seen about the streets and stores of Matanzas, as, indeed, all over the island — poor fellows who have survived their apprenticeship and are now free. They are peaceful, do not drink spirits, work from morning until night, never meddle with politics, and live on one half they can earn, so as to save enough to return to their beloved native land. You may persuade him to assent to any form of religion as a temporary duty, but John is a heathen at heart, and a heathen he will die.

The famous afternoon drive of Matanzas was formerly the San Carlos Paseo. It has fine possibilities, and is lined and beautifully ornamented with thrifty Indian laurels. It overlooks the spacious harbor and outer bay, but is now utterly neglected and abandoned; even the roadway is green with vegetation and gullied with deep hollows. It is the coolest place in the city at the evening hour, but the people have become so poor that there are hardly a dozen private vehicles owned in the city, and, consequently, its famous drive is deserted. Matanzas, like all the cities of Cuba, is under the shadow of depressed business, the evidences of which meet one on all hands.

The two objects of special interest to strangers who visit Matanzas are, first, the valley of the Yumuri, which may be described briefly as a narrow gorge four miles long, through which flows the river of the same name. The view of this lovely valley will recall, to any one who has visited Spain, the Vega of Granada. There are several positions from which to obtain a good view of the valley, but that enjoyed from the Chapel of Monserrate, on the hill just back of the town, is nearest, and was most satisfactory to us. The view includes a valley, peaceful, tropical, and verdant, embracing plantations, groves, and farms, in the midst of which the river glides like a silver thread through the verdure, and empties into the Bay of Matanzas. The universal belief is that this vale was once a vast, deep lake, walled across the present seaward opening of the valley, from whence a fall may have existed as a natural overflow. Some fearful convulsion of nature rent this bowl and precipitated the lake into the ocean, leaving only the river's course.

The second object of note which the visitor will not willingly miss is a sight of the famous caves of Bellamar, situated about two leagues from the city proper. It is customary to make this trip in a volante, and it is quite the thing to ride, at least once, in this unique vehicle, the only article ever invented in Cuba. The road to the caves is extremely rough, and this vehicle is best adapted to pass over the irregularities. If there are only gentlemen of the party, go on horseback. On entering the caves the visitor should throw off any extra clothing that can conveniently be left behind, as it is very warm within, and on coming out, unless one has an extra garment to put on, too great a change of temperature will be realized. These singular caves lead three hundred feet and more beneath the surface, and present beauties to the eye incident to all such subterranean formations. They were discovered accidentally, a few years since, by some stone quarriers, who, on opening into them, imagined they had broken the crust of the earth. In driving to the caves the Bay Street road, through the city, should be taken, which forms one of the finest thoroughfares of any Cuban town. The architecture of the dwellings is that of combined Italian, Grecian, and Moorish, ornamented with colonnades and verandas of stone and iron. Fine as the façades of these houses are, — none above one story in height, — they present a faded and forlorn aspect, a sort of dead-and-alive appearance, yet in accordance with life and business, not only in Matanzas, but all over the island. This one boulevard of Matanzas ends by the shore of the bay, where the fine marine view will cause you to forget all other impressions for the moment, but you will not tarry here. Turning eastward you soon strike the road to the caves, and *such* a road — it is like the bed of a dry mountain torrent.

Persons visiting Matanzas must make up their minds to be content with indifferent hotel accommodations. In fact there are no really good hotels in

Cuba; those which exist are poor and expensive. On the inland routes away from the cities there are none, and the humble hostelries, or posadas, as they are called, are so indifferent in point of comforts as not to deserve the name of inns. As a rule, invalids rarely go beyond the cities to remain over night. Brief and pleasant sojourns may be made at Havana, Cienfuegos, Matanzas, and Sagua la Grande, from whence excursions can be made by rail or otherwise and return on the same day. Let us qualify these remarks, as applied to the Hotel Louvre at Matanzas. There was a degree of picturesqueness about this establishment which was not without its attraction, and it was certainly the most cleanly public house in which we found a temporary home while on the island. Its rooms surrounded a bright clean court, or patio, planted with creeping vines, palmettos, bananas, and some fragrant flowering shrubs. The dining-room is virtually out of doors, being open on all sides, and opposite the hotel is a small plaza with tropical trees, backed by an old, musty church, whose bell had the true Spanish trick of giving tongue at most inopportune moments. The rooms of the Louvre are quite circumscribed as to space, and the partitions separating the apartments do not reach to the ceiling, so that privacy, night or day, is out of the question. The floors are all tiled in white marble, and the attendance is courteous. One does not look for a choice bill of fare in Cuba, and therefore will not be disappointed on that score. You will be charged Fifth Avenue prices, however, if you do not get Fifth Avenue accommodations. If you have learned in your travels to observe closely, to study men as well as localities, to enjoy Nature in her ever·

varying moods, and to delight in luxurious fruits, flowers, and vegetation, you will find quite enough to occupy and amuse the mind, and make you forget altogether the grosser senses of appetite.

Puerto Principe is the capital of the central department of Cuba, and is located well inland. The trade of the place, from the want of water carriage, is inconsiderable, and bears no proportion to the number of its inhabitants, which aggregates nearly thirty-one thousand. The product of the neighborhood, to find means of export, must first make its way twelve and a half leagues to Nuevitas, from whence, in return, it receives its foreign supplies. The two places are now, however, connected by a railroad. Puerto Principe is about one hundred and fifty leagues from Havana. Its original location, as founded by Velasquez in 1514, was at Nuevitas, but the inhabitants, when the place was feeble in numbers, were forced to remove from the coast to avoid the fierce incursions of the pirates, as did the people of Trinidad, who removed from the harbor of Casilda.

Cardenas is situated a hundred and twenty miles from Havana on the north coast, and is the youngest town of note in Cuba, having been founded so late as 1827. It has a population of between four and five thousand. Its prosperity is mostly owing to the great fertility of the land by which it is surrounded. It is called the American city, because of the large number of Americans doing business here, and also because the English language is so universally spoken by the people who reside in the place. The Plaza contains an excellent marble statue of Columbus, and is tastefully ornamented with tropical verdure. In the harbor of Cardenas is seen one of those curious springs of fresh water which bubble up beneath the salt sea. The city is the centre of a sugar-producing district, and a considerable portion of the sugar crop of the vicinity of Havana is also shipped from this port to America. It is connected with both the metropolis and Matanzas by rail, and is well worthy of a visit by all who can find the necessary time for doing so.

Between Havana and Nuevitas, along the northern slope of the island, are many vast tracts of unimproved land of the best quality. Much of it is overgrown with cedar, ebony, mahogany, and other valuable timber; but a large proportion is savanna or prairie, which might, with little difficulty, be reduced to cultivation. The timber alone, which is often found in large compact bodies, would pay the cost of the land and the expense of clearing it. Many branches of agriculture are neglected which might be made very remunerative, but it will never be brought about except by foreign capital and tact. The natives have not the requisite enterprise and industry. While these chapters are passing through the press, the home government is discussing in the Cortes the propriety of making a large loan to the Cubans for the purpose of bringing the lands above referred to into market, as well as rendering others accessible. But it is doubtful if anything practical is accomplished, unless foreign interest should be enlisted.

CHAPTER VII.

City of Havana. — First Impressions. — The Harbor. — Institutions. — Lack of Educational Facilities. — Cuban Women. — Street Etiquette. — Architecture. — Domestic Arrangements. — Barred Windows and Bullet-Proof Doors. — Public Vehicles. — Uncleanliness of the Streets. — Spanish or African! — The Church Bells. — Home-Keeping Habits of Ladies. — Their Patriotism. — Personal Characteristics. — Low Ebb of Social Life. — Priestcraft. — Female Virtue. — Domestic Ties. — A Festive Population. — Cosmetics. — Sea-Bathing.

HAVANA is a thoroughly representative city, — Cuban and nothing else. Its history embraces in no small degree that of all the island, being the centre of its talent, wealth, and population. It has long been reckoned the eighth commercial capital of the world. Moro Castle, with its Dahlgren guns peeping out through the yellow stones, and its tall sentinel lighthouse, stands guard over the narrow entrance of the harbor; the battery of La Punta on the opposite shore answering to the Moro. There are also the long range of cannon and barracks on the city side, and the massive fortress of the Cabanas crowning the hill behind the Moro. All these are decorated with the red and yellow flag of Spain, — the banner of blood and gold. So many and strong fortifications show how important the home government regard the place.

The harbor or bay is shaped like one's outspread hand, with the wrist for an entrance, and is populous with the ships of all nations. It presents at all times a scene of great maritime activity. Besides the national ships of other countries and those of Spain, mail steamers from Europe and America are coming and going daily, also coasting steamers from the eastern and southern shores of the island, added to regular lines for Mexico and the islands of the Caribbean Sea. The large ferry steamers plying constantly between the city and the Regla shore, the fleet of little sailing boats, foreign yachts, and rowboats, glancing in the burning sunlight, create a scene of great maritime interest.

The city presents a large extent of public buildings, cathedrals, antique and venerable churches. It has been declared in its prosperity to be the richest place for its number of square miles in the world, but this cannot be said of it at the present time. There is nothing grand in its appearance as one enters the harbor and comes to anchor, though Baron Humboldt pronounced it the gayest and most picturesque sight in America. Its multitude of churches, domes, and steeples are not architecturally remarkable, and are dominated by the colossal prison near the shore. This immense quadrangular edifice flanks the Punta, and is designed to contain five thousand prisoners at a time. The low hills which make up the distant background are not sufficiently high to add much to the general effect. The few palm trees which catch the eye here and there give an Oriental aspect to the scene, quite in harmony with the atmospheric tone of intense sunshine. Unlike Santiago or Matanzas, neither the city nor its immediate environs is elevated, so that the whole impression is that of flatness, requiring some strength of background to form a complete picture. The martial appearance of the Moro and the Cabanas, bristling with cannon, is the most vivid effect of the scene, taken as a whole. It might be a portion of continental Spain broken away from European moorings, and floated hither to find anchorage in the Caribbean Sea. One is also reminded of Malta, in the farther Mediterranean, and yet the city of Valetta, bright, sunny, and elevated, is quite unlike Havana, though Fortress St. Angelo overlooks and guards the place as the Moro does this tropical harbor, and Cuba is the Italy of America.

The waters of the harbor, admittedly one of the finest in the world, are most of the time extremely dirty. Many years ago a canal was commenced which was designed to create a flowage calculated to keep the harbor clear of the constantly accumulating filth, but it was never finished, and there remains an evidence of Spanish inefficiency, while the harbor continues to be a vast cesspool. It would be supposed that in a fever-haunted region, great attention would be bestowed upon the matter of drainage, but this is not the case in Havana, or other cities of the island. Most of the effort made in this direction is surface drainage, the liquid thus exposed quickly evaporating in the hot sunshine, or being partially absorbed by the soil over which it passes.

Havana contains numerous institutions of learning: a Royal University, founded in 1733, a medical and law school, and chairs of all the natural sciences. In spite of their liberal purposes and capabilities, however, there is a blight hanging over them. Pupils enlist cautiously and reluctantly. Among other schools there is a Royal Seminary for girls, scarcely more than a name, a free school of sculpture and painting, and a mercantile school, with a few private institutions of learning. There is a fairly good museum of natural history, and just outside the city a botanical garden. Still the means of education are very limited in Cuba, an evidence of which is the fact that so many of her youth of both sexes are sent to this country for educational purposes. An order was at one time issued by the government prohibiting this, but its arbitrary nature was so very outrageous, even for a Spanish government, that it was permitted to become a dead letter. What are called free schools, as we use the term, are not known in the island; the facilities for obtaining even the simplest education are very poor. Boys and girls, so far as any attempt is made to educate them, are taught separately, and really under the eye of the Church. Priests and nuns are the agents, the former notoriously making a cloak of their profession for vile and selfish purposes. If we speak decidedly upon this subject, yet we do so with less emphasis than do the Cubans. The girls are taught embroidery and etiquette, considered to be the chief and about the only things necessary for them to know. These young girls are women at the age of thirteen or fourteen, and frequently mothers of families before they are twenty. Of course they fade early. In domestic life the husband is literally lord and master, the wife, ostensibly at least, is all obedience. There is no woman's rights association on the island, nor even a Dorcas society. While young and unmarried, the ladies are strict adherents to all the conventionalities of Spanish etiquette, which is of the most exacting character, but after marriage the sex is perhaps as French as the Parisians, and as gay as the Viennese, under the stimulus of fast and fashionable society.

The reason of the edict issued by the government

forbidding parents to send their children to this country for educational purposes was obvious. The young Cubans during their residence here imbibed liberal ideas as to our republican form of government, which they freely promulgated and advocated on their return to their native island. Even those who had been educated in France or England, and they were numerous, readily sympathized with the pupils returned from America, and became a dangerous element. Long before the first Lopez expedition, these sons of planters and rich merchants had formed themselves into a secret society, with the avowed purpose of freeing Cuba sooner or later from the Spanish yoke.

The low-lying, many-colored city of Havana, called San Cristobel, after the great discoverer, was originally surrounded by a wall, though the population has long since extended its dwellings and business structures far into what was, half a century since, the suburbs. A portion of the old wall is still extant, crumbling and decayed, but it has mostly disappeared. The narrow streets are paved or macadamized, and cross each other at right angles, like those of Philadelphia, but in their dimensions reminding one of continental Toledo, whose Moorish architecture is also duplicated here. There are no sidewalks, unless a narrow line of flagstones can be so called, and in fact the people have less use for them where nearly every one rides in a victoria, the fare being but sixteen cents per mile. A woman of respectability is scarcely ever seen walking in the streets, unless she is a foreigner, or of the lower class, such as sellers of fruit, etc. Those living in close proximity to the churches are sometimes seen proceeding to early mass, accompanied by a negress carrying a portable seat, or a bit of carpet on which to kneel upon the marble floor of the cathedral. But even this is exceptional. Cuban etiquette says that a lady must not be seen on the streets except in a vehicle, and only Americans, English, and other foreigners disregard the rule.

The architecture of the dwelling-houses is exceedingly heavy, giving them the appearance of great age. They are built of the porous stone so abundant upon the island, which, though soft when first worked into suitable blocks, becomes as hard as granite by exposure to the atmosphere. The façades of the town houses are nearly always covered with stucco. Their combination of colors, yellow, green, and blue, harmonizes with the glowing atmosphere of the tropics. This will strike the stranger at first as being very odd; there is no system observed, the tenant of each dwelling following his individual fancy as to the hue he will adopt, a dingy yellow prevailing. Standing upon the Campo de Marte and looking in any direction, these changing colors give a picturesque effect to the range of buildings which surround the broad field. In this vicinity the structures are nearly all of two full stories, and many with rows of lofty pillars supporting broad verandas, including one or two palaces, one fine large club-house, some government offices, and the Telegrafo Hotel. These varying colors are not for fancy alone, they have a raison d'être; namely, to absorb the sharp rays of the constant sunshine. But for some toning down of the glare, one's eyes would hardly be able to sustain the power of vision. The vividness with which each individual building and object stands out in the clear liquid light is one of the first peculiarities which will strike the stranger.

ARCHITECTURE. 131

The dwelling-houses are universally so constructed as to form an open square in the centre, which constitutes the only yard or court that is attached. The house is divided into a living-room, a store-room, chambers, and stable, these all upon one floor, while the family vehicle blocks up in part the only entrance, which is used in common by horses, ladies, slaves, and gentlemen callers. If there is a second story, a broad flight of steps leads to it, and there are the family chambers or sleeping apartments, opening upon a corridor which extends round the court. Peculiar as this manner of building at first seems, it is well adapted to the climate, and one soon becomes satisfied with it.

With such surroundings it is easy to imagine one's self at Granada, in far-off Spain, and it seems almost natural to look about for the Alhambra. An air of rude grandeur reigns over these houses, the architecture being Gothic and Saracenic. In the more ancient portions of the town little picturesque balconies of iron or wood jut out from the second-story windows, where the houses rise to the dignity of two stories. From these balconies hang little naked children, like small performers upon the trapeze, until the passer-by fears for their lives. The travel in the narrow streets is regulated by law, and so divided that only certain ones are used for vehicles going north, and others for those traveling south. Thus, vehicles bound into the city from the Paseo go by the way of Obispo Street, but must return by O'Riley Street, so that no two ever meet in these narrow thoroughfares, — a plan which might be advantageously adopted elsewhere.

The rooms of the houses are lofty and the floors

stuccoed or tiled in marble, while the walls and ceilings are frequently ornamented in fresco, the excellence of the workmanship varying in accordance with the owner's means. The most striking peculiarity of the town-house in Cuba is the precaution taken to render it safe against sudden attack. Every man's house is literally his castle here, each accessible window being secured with stout iron bars, reaching from the top to the bottom, while bullet-proof doors bar the entrance, — the whole seriously suggestive of jails and lunatic asylums. No carpets are used even in the parlors, though a long rug is sometimes placed between the inevitable double row of rocking-chairs. The best floors are laid in white marble and jasper. The great heat of the climate renders even wooden floors quite insupportable. The visitor is apt to find his bed rather unsatisfactory, it being formed by stretching a coarse canvas upon a framework, with an upper and under sheet. Mattresses are not used by the natives, who reject them as being too warm to sleep upon, but the liberality evinced in the shape of mosquito netting is as commendable as it is necessary.

The public vehicle called a victoria is a sort of four-wheeled calash, and it has entirely superseded the volante for city use. There are thousands of them about the town, forming a collection of wretchedly wornout carriages, drawn by horses in a like condition. The drivers occupy an elevated seat, and are composed equally of whites and negroes. The charge for a passage from point to point within the city is forty cents in Cuban paper money, equal to sixteen cents of our currency; three times that sum is charged if engaged for the hour. The streets are in a very bad condition and sadly need repairing. The roads leading out to the suburbs in every direction are full of deep holes, and are badly gullied by the heavy rains. The streets, even about the paseos, are so impregnated with filth, here and there, as to be sickening to the senses of the passer-by. Once in three or four weeks somebody is awakened to the exigency of the situation, and a gang of men is put to work to cleanse the principal thoroughfares, but this serves only a temporary purpose. We were told that the reason for this neglect was that no one was regularly paid for work; even the police had not received any pay for seven months, and many refused to serve longer. The soldiery had not been paid their small stipend for nearly a year, but enlisted men sent out from Spain, forming the army, are more easily kept together and more amenable to discipline than any civil body of officials could be. "With everybody and everything so enormously taxed," we ventured to suggest to our informants, "there should be no lack of pecuniary means wherewith to carry on all departments of the government. Pray what becomes of all this money?" The reply was, "Who can say?" with a significant shrug of the shoulders. With all the exactions of the officials, and with the collection of nearly thirty millions of dollars annually, but a moiety finds its way into the national treasury. Peculation is reduced to a science, and is practiced from the highest to the lowest official sent out by the home government. "Spain has squeezed the orange nearly dry," said a distinguished Cuban to us in Matanzas, "and a collapse is inevitable. We are anxiously waiting to see it come; any change would be for the better. We were long threatened with a war of races, if we did not sustain Spanish rule in the island. That is, if we were not loyal to the Madrid authorities, the slaves should be freed to prey upon us. Blood would flow like water. The incendiary torch would be placed in the hands of the negroes, and they should be incited to burn, steal, and ravish! Cuba should be Spanish or African. There was a time when this threat had great force, and its execution was indeed to be dreaded; but that time is past, and no such fear now exists. The slaves are being gradually freed, and are amalgamating with the rest of the populace. The slow liberation of the blacks has accustomed them to freedom, and any organized outrage from that source has ceased to be feared."

Why all the bells in Havana should be rung furiously and continuously every morning about daylight, one cannot exactly understand. There does not seem to be any concert of action in this awful conspiracy against sleep; but the tumult thus brought about would certainly seem to be sufficient to "wake the isle from its propriety." From every square with its church, and every church with its towers, this brazen-tongued clamor is relentlessly poured forth. In most Christian lands one good bell is all-sufficient for a church steeple, but here they have them in the plural, and all striving to excel each other at the same moment. Of course no one is able to sleep amid such an outburst of noise, or within the radius of a league. Bells and mosquitoes are two of the prevailing nuisances of this thrice-sunny city. Nor must we forget to add to these aggravations the ceaseless, triumphant crowing of the game-cocks, the noisiest and most boastful of birds, large numbers of

HOME-KEEPING LADIES. 135

which are kept by the citizens purely for gambling purposes in the cock-pit. Besides these "professional" birds, every nook and corner is filled with fowls kept for brooding purposes, each bird family with its crower.

We have said that the Cuban ladies rarely stir abroad except in a vehicle, and whatever their domestic habits may be, they are certainly good housekeepers in this respect. While our ladies are busy sweeping the city sidewalks with their trailing dresses, these wisely leave that business to the gangs of criminals detailed from prison to fill that office, with their limbs chained and a heavy ball attached to preserve their equilibrium, — though we should qualify this remark by saying that these condemned men, once so common upon the streets and highways, were not seen during our late visit to Havana. It is, perhaps, owing to the home-keeping habits of the ladies that the feet of the Cuban señoritas are such marvels of smallness and delicacy, seemingly made rather for ornament than for use. You catch a glimpse of them as they step into their victorias, and perceive that they are daintily shod in French slippers, the soles of which are scarcely more substantial than brown paper. Their feet are made for ornament and for dancing. Though they possess a roundness of form that leaves nothing to be desired in symmetry of figure, still they are light as a sylph, — so buoyant, clad in muslin and lace, that it would seem as if a breeze might waft them away like a summer cloud. Passionately fond of dancing, they tax the endurance of the gentlemen in their worship of Terpsichore, stimulated by those Cuban airs which are at once so sweet and so brilliant.

There is a striking and endearing charm about the Cuban ladies, their every motion being replete with a native grace. Every limb is elastic and supple. Their voices are sweet and low, while the subdued tone of their complexions is relieved by the arch vivacity of night-black eyes, that alternately swim in melting lustre, and sparkle in expressive glances. If their comeliness matures, like the fruits of their native clime, early and rapidly, it is sad to know that it also fades prematurely. One looks in vain for that serene loveliness combined with age which so frequently challenges our admiration at the North. Their costume is never ostentatious, though often costly, and sometimes a little too mixed or variegated when seen in public. At home, however, nothing of this sort is observed. There the dress is usually composed of the most delicate muslin, the finest linen, and richest silks. We must admit that one rarely sees elsewhere such contrasts in colors upon the person of the fair sex as are at times encountered upon the Paseo. It would drive a French modiste wild to see the proprieties so outraged. It requires all the proverbial beauty of these señoras and señoritas to carry off respectably such combinations as scarlet and yellow, blue and purple, orange and green; but they do it by sheer force of their beautiful eyes and finely rounded figures. It must be acknowledged that the element of native refinement is too often wanting, and that the whole exhibition of the sex is just a little prononcée. They have no intellectual resort, but lead a life of decided ease and pleasure much too closely bordering upon the sensuous, their forced idleness being in itself an incentive to immorality and intrigue. The indifferent work they perform is light and simple; a little sewing and embroidery, followed by the siesta, divides the hours of the day. Those who can afford to keep their victorias wait until nearly sunset for a drive, and then go to respond by sweet smiles to the salutations of the caballeros on the paseos; afterwards to the Parque de Isabella II., to listen to the military band, and then, perhaps, to join in the mazy dance. That these ladies are capable of deep feeling and practical sympathy on such occasions as would naturally draw these qualities forth, we know by experience. When the patriot forces were poorly armed, with but scant material, and ammunition was short, these fair patriots gave freely of their most valuable jewels as a contribution to the cause of liberty.

A sad instance illustrative of this fact was told us by a resident of Havana. The young ladies and matrons of a certain circle in the city, at the commencement of the year 1872, had put their diamonds and precious stones together to realize money for forwarding supplies to the insurgents under Cespedes, who was then operating in the vicinity of Santiago. The jewels were secretly intrusted to a brother of one of the ladies, a young man who had just reached the age of twenty-two. His part of the business was the most difficult to perform, but he finally succeeded in realizing over four thousand dollars in gold for the gems intrusted to him. Fortunately the money was at once forwarded to the patriot leader through a safe and reliable channel. Hardly had the business been accomplished to the satisfaction of all concerned when the young Cuban was secretly denounced to the Governor-General as a suspected person. The settings and jewels had all been disposed of so as to be beyond recognition, and it is not known to this day how the brother's complicity with his sisters and their friends was divulged, but presumedly it was through the Jew pawnbrokers. The brother was arrested and thrown into Moro Castle, where he was subjected to the closest examination to find out his accomplices. Loyal and affectionate, he could not be made to speak. He was finally offered his freedom and permission to leave the island if he would divulge all. The government reasoned that if they could make a witness of him they would succeed in serving their own interest best, as by sacrificing one prisoner they might gain knowledge of many disaffected people whom they did not even suspect of disloyalty. One of the sisters of the prisoner determined to assume the guilt, and declare that her brother was the unknowing agent of her purpose; but when at last satisfied that this would not free him, she reluctantly gave up the design. The young Cuban maintained his silence. No publicity was given to the matter. He was brought before a military tribunal — so much is known. The sentence never publicly transpired. Like most political prisoners who pass within the walls of Moro Castle, his fate remains a secret.

There are two sides to every picture; even light casts its shadow, and we feel constrained to speak plainly. Social life in the island is certainly at a very low ebb, and unblushing licentiousness prevails. That there are many and noble exceptions only renders the opposite fact the more prominent. This immorality is more particularly among the home Spaniards, whose purpose it is to remain here long enough to gain a certain amount of money, and then to return to the mother country to enjoy it. They look upon all associations contracted here as of a temporary character, and the matter of morality does not affect them in the least. Domestic comforts are few, and, as we have intimated, literature is hardly recognized. The almost entire absence of books or reading matter of any sort is remarkable. A few daily and weekly newspapers, under rigid censorship, supply all the taste for letters. Married women seem to sink far below their husbands in influence. The domestic affections are not cultivated; in short, home to the average Cuban is only a place to sleep, — not of peaceful enjoyment. His meals are rarely taken with his family, but all spare hours are absorbed at the club. Domestic infidelity is prevalent, and female virtue but little esteemed. Priest-craft and king-craft have been the curse of both Spain and Cuba. Here, as in Italy, the outrageous and thinly-disguised immorality of the priesthood poisons many an otherwise unpolluted fount, and thus all classes are liable to infection. Popery and slavery are both largely to be charged with the low condition of morals, though the influence of the former has of late years been much curtailed, both in Spain and in Cuba. The young women are the slaves of local customs, as already intimated, and cannot go abroad even to church without a duenna, — a fact which in itself proves the debased standard of morals. The men appear to have no religion at all, but the women very generally attend early mass and go periodically to confessional. No one seems to think it strange for a white man to have a colony of mulatto children, even though he be also the father of a white family! Many have only the mulatto family, and seem content. These are generally the home Spaniards, already spoken of, and when their fortunes are secured they recklessly sever all local ties and responsibilities and return to Spain. This is no new thing, as there are many families in Cuba of fair position socially, and often of considerable wealth, whose members are by the right of classification quadroons. Miscegenation has greatly complicated social matters, and in half a century, more or less, it may produce a distinctive class, who will be better able to assert and sustain their rights than those who have preceded them.

The class of home Spaniards who have emigrated to Cuba has always been of a questionable character. The description of them by Cervantes in his time will apply in our own day with equal force. He says: "The island is the refuge of the profligates of Spain, a sanctuary for homicides, a skulking-place for gamblers and sharpers, and a receptacle for women of free manners, — a place of delusion to many, of amelioration to few."

One peculiarity which is sure to strike the stranger unpleasantly, and to which allusion has incidentally been made, whether in public or private houses, in the stores or in the streets, is that the colored children of both sexes, under eight and nine years of age, are permitted to go about in a state of nudity. In the country, among the Montero class, this custom also extends to the white children. The colored men who labor in the streets and on the wharves wear only a short pair of linen pantaloons, displaying a muscular development which any white man might envy. The remarkable contrast in the powerful frames of these dusky Africans and the puny Asiatic coolies is extraordinary. On the plantations and small farms the slaves wear but one garment, just sufficient for decency. The great heat when exposed to the sun is the reason, probably, rather than any economical idea.

The populace of Havana is eminently a festive one. Men luxuriate in the café, or spend their evenings in worse places. A brief period of the morning only is given to business, the rest of the day and night to melting lassitude, smoking, and luxurious ease. Evidences of satiety, languor, and dullness, the weakened capacity for enjoyment, are sadly conspicuous, the inevitable sequence of indolence and vice. The arts and sciences seldom disturb the thoughts of such people. Here, as in many European cities, Lazarus and Dives elbow each other, and an Oriental confusion of quarters prevails. The pretentious town-house is side by side with the humble quarters of the artisan, or even the negro hut, about which swarm the naked juveniles of color, a half-clad, slatternly mother appearing now and then. The father of this brood, if there be an acknowledged one, is probably at work upon some plantation not far away, while madame takes in linen to wash, but being possibly herself a slave, pays over one half of her earnings to some city master. High and low life are ever present in strong contrast, and in the best of humor with each other, affording elements of the picturesque, if not of the beautiful. Neatness must be ignored where such human conglomeration exists, and as we all know, at certain seasons of the year, like dear, delightful, dirty Naples, Havana is the hot-bed of pestilence. The dryness of the atmosphere transforms most of the street offal into fine powder, which salutes nose, eyes, ears, and mouth under the influence of the slightest breeze. Though there are ample bathing facilities in and about the city, the people of either sex seem to have a prejudice against their free use. In most hot climates the natives duly appreciate the advantage of an abundance of water, and luxuriate in its use, but it is not so in Cuba. We were told of ladies who content themselves with only wiping neck, face, and hands daily upon a towel saturated with island rum, and, from what was obvious, it is easy to believe this to be true.

Sea-bathing is a luxury which the Northern visitor will be glad to improve, if the natives are not, and for their information let us state that it may be safely enjoyed here. Establishments will be found where baths have been cut in the rock on the shore, west of the Punta fort, along the Calle Ancha del Norte. Here water is introduced fresh from the Gulf Stream, sparkling and invigorating, and characterized by much more salt and iodine than is found in more northern latitudes. It is the purest sea-bathing to be found in any city that we know of, refreshing and healthful, producing a sensation upon the surface of the body similar to that of sparkling soda-water on the palate. The island abounds in mineral springs, both hot and cold, all more or less similar in character, and belonging to the class of sulphur springs. Many of these have considerable local reputation for their curative properties.

In passing through O'Riley, Obispo, Obrapia, or any business streets at about eleven o'clock in the forenoon and glancing into the stores, workshops, business offices, and the like, one is sure to see the master in his shirt-sleeves, surrounded by his family, clerks, and all white employees, sitting in full sight at breakfast, generally in the business room itself. The midday siesta, an hour later, if not a necessity in this climate, is a universal custom. The shopkeeper, even as he sits on duty, drops his head upon his arm and sleeps for an hour, more or less. The negro and his master both succumb to the same influence, catching their forty winks, while the ladies, if not reclining, "lose themselves" with heads resting against the backs of the universal rocking-chairs. One interior seen by the passer-by is as like another as two peas. A Cuban's idea of a well-furnished sitting-room is fully met by a dozen cane-bottom rocking-chairs, and a few poor chromos on the walls. These rocking-chairs are ranged in two even lines, reaching from the window to the rear of the room, with a narrow woollen mat between them on the marble floor, each chair being conspicuously flanked by a cuspidor. This parlor arrangement is so nearly universal as to be absolutely ludicrous.

CHAPTER VIII.

Sabbath Scenes in Havana. — Thimble-Riggers and Mountebanks. — City Squares and their Ornamentation. — The Cathedral. — Tomb of Columbus. — Plaza de Armas. — Out-Door Concerts. — Habitués of Paseo de Isabella. — Superbly Appointed Cafés. — Gambling. — Lottery Tickets. — Fast Life. — Masquerade Balls. — Carnival Days. — The Famous Tacon Theatre. — The Havana Casino. — Public Statues. — Beauties of the Governor's Garden. — The Alameda. — The Old Bell-Ringer. — Military Mass.

ON no other occasion is the difference between the manners of a Protestant and Catholic community so strongly marked as on the Sabbath. In the former, a sober seriousness stamps the deportment of the people, even when they are not engaged in devotional exercises; in the latter, worldly pleasures and religious forms are pursued, as it were, at the same time, or follow each other in incongruous succession. We would not have the day made tedious, and it can only be so to triflers; to the true Christian it will ever be characterized by thoughtfulness and repose. The Parisian flies from the church to the railway station to join some picnic excursion, or to assist at the race-course, or he passes with a careless levity from St. Geneviève to the dance booths of the Champs Elysées. In New Orleans, the Creole who has just bent his knee before the altar repairs to the theatre to pass the evening; and the Cuban goes from the absolution of the priest to the hurly-burly of the bull-ring or the cock-pit.

The influence of fifteen minutes in the church, if

salutary, would seem to be quickly dissipated by the attraction of the gaming-table and the masked ball. Even the Sunday ceremonial of the Church is a pageant: the splendid robes of the officiating priest, changed in the course of the service like the costume of actors in a drama; the music, to Protestant ears operatic and exciting; the clouds of incense scattering their intoxicating perfumes; the chanting in a strange tongue, unknown to the majority of the worshipers, — all tend to give the Roman Catholic services a carnival character. Far be it from us, however, to charge these congregations with an undue levity, or a lack of sincerity. Many a lovely Creole kneels upon the marble floor entirely estranged from the brilliant groups around her, and apparently unconscious for the time of the admiration she excites. There are many, no doubt, who look beyond the glittering symbols to the great truths of the Being whom they are intended to typify. The impression made by the Sabbath ceremonials of the Church strikes us as evanescent, more pleasing to the fancy than informing to the understanding. Still, if the Sabbath in Catholic countries is not wholly devoted to religious observances, neither are the week days wholly absorbed by business and by careless pleasures. The churches are always open, silently but eloquently inviting to devotion, and it is much to be able to step aside at any moment from the temptations, business, and cares of life into an atmosphere of seclusion and religion. The solemn quiet of an old cathedral on a week day is impressive from its very contrast to the tumult outside. Within its venerable walls the light seems chastened, as it falls through stained panes and paints the images of Christian saints and martyrs on the pavement of the aisles. A half unwilling reverence is apt to stimulate us on such an occasion, however skeptical we may be.

The Sabbath in Havana breaks upon the citizens amid the ringing of bells, the firing of cannon from the forts, the noise of trumpets, and the roll of the drum. It is no day of physical rest here, and the mechanical trades are uninterrupted. It is the chosen period for the military reviews, the masked ball, and the bull-fight. The stores are open as usual, the same cries are heard on the streets, and the lottery tickets are vended on every corner. The individuals who devote themselves to this business are in numbers like an army with banners. They rend the air with their cries, promising good luck to all purchasers, while they flourish their scissors with one hand, and thrust the sheet of printed numbers in your face with the other, ready to cut any desired ticket or portion of a ticket. The day proves equally propitious for the omnipresent organ-grinder and his ludicrously-dressed little monkey, à la Napoleon; the Chinese peddler; the orange and banana dealer; and the universal cigarette purveyor. Still, the rough Montero from the country, with his long line of loaded mules or ponies, respectfully raises his broad Panama with one hand while he makes the sign of the cross with the other as he passes the church door. The churches of Havana look very old and shabby compared with those of peninsular Spain, where the splendor of church ornamentation reaches its acme.

In and about the commercial part of the town, the out-door gambler forms a conspicuous feature of the Sabbath, seated upon a cloth spread upon the ground, and armed with cards, dice, cups, and other instruments. With voluble tongue and expressive pantomime urging the passer-by to try his luck, he meets with varying success. Many who are drawn into the net are adroitly permitted to win a little, and afterwards to lose much. Sailors on shore for a day's liberty are profitable game for these thimble-riggers, as they are called with us. Both Spaniards and Creoles patronize them, and occasionally a negro tries his luck with a trifle. In open squares, or at the intersection of several streets, one sometimes sees a carpet spread upon the ground, upon which an athlete accompanied by a couple of expert boys, dressed in high-colored tights ornamented with spangles, diverts the throng by exhibiting gymnastics. At the close of the performance, a young girl in a fancy dress and with long, flowing hair passes among the spectators and gathers a few shillings. Not far away is observed Punch and Judy in the height of a successful quarrel to the music of a harp and a violin. The automatic contestants pound and pommel each other after the conventional fashion.

The city abounds in well-arranged squares, often ornamented by the royal palm, always a figure of majesty and beauty, with here and there a few orange, lime, and banana trees, mingled with the Indian laurel, which forms a grateful shade by its dense foliage. The royal palm is strongly individualized, differing from other trees of the same family. It is usually from sixty to eighty feet in height at what may be called its maturity, and not unfrequently reaches a hundred, the tall trunk slightly swelling near the middle and tapering at either extremity. The upper portion is of a fresh and shining green, contrasting with the lower section, which is of a light slate color. It is crowned by a tuft of branches and leaves at its apex, like a bunch of ostrich feathers drooping in all directions. It seems as though the palm could not be out of place in any spot. It imparts great beauty to the scenery in and about Havana. When it is found dotting a broad stretch of country here and there in isolated groups, or even singly, it is always the first object to catch and delight the eye. It is also a marked and beautiful feature where it forms a long avenue, lining the road on either side leading to a sugar or coffee plantation, but it requires half a century to perfect such an avenue.

The Plaza de Armas, fronting the Governor's palace, is a finely kept square, and until the Parque de Isabella was finished, it was the great centre of fashion, and the place of evening resort. At one corner of this Plaza is an insignificant chapel, built upon the spot where Columbus is said to have assisted at the first mass celebrated on the island; an anachronism easily exposed were it worth the while. The great discoverer never landed at Havana during his lifetime, though his body was brought hither for burial, centuries after his death. There is one fact relating to this site in the Plaza de Armas fully authenticated, and which is not without interest. An enormous old ceiba tree originally stood here, beneath whose branches mass was sometimes performed. This remarkable tree having expired of old age was removed by order of the Governor-General, and the chapel was erected on the spot where its widespread branches had cast their shadow for centuries. We did not see the interior of the chapel, as it is opened but once a year to the public, — on the 16th of November, which is the feast day of San Cristobal, when mass is celebrated in honor of the great discoverer. It is said to contain a marble bust of Columbus, and two or three large historical paintings.

This square is divided into neatly kept paths, and planted with fragrant flowers, conspicuous among which were observed the white and red camellias, while a grateful air of coolness was diffused by the playing of a fountain into a broad basin, ornamented by a marble statue of Ferdinand VII. The Creoles are passionately fond of music, and this park used to be the headquarters of all out-door concerts. Their favorite airs are waltzes and native dances, with not a little of the Offenbach spirit in them. The guitar is the favorite domestic musical instrument here, as in peninsular Spain, and both sexes are as a rule clever performers upon it. Evening music in the open air is always attractive, but nowhere is its influence more keenly felt than under the mellow effulgence of tropical nights. Nowhere can we conceive of a musical performance listened to with more relish and appreciation than in the Plaza de Armas or the Parque de Isabella in Havana. The latter place on the occasion of the concerts is the resort of all classes. Here friends meet, flirtations are carried on, toilets are displayed, and lovers woo. Even the humble classes are seen in large numbers quietly strolling on the outer portions of the Plaza listening to the fine performances of the band, and quietly enjoying the music, "tamed and led by this enchantress still." The balmy nature of the climate permits the ladies to dispense with shawls or wraps of any sort; bonnets they very seldom wear, so that they sit in their vehicles, or alighting appropriate the chairs arranged for the purpose lining the broad central path, and thus appear in full evening dress, bare arms, and necks supplemented by most elaborate coiffures. Even the black lace mantilla, so commonly thrown over the head and shoulders in the cities of Spain, is discarded of an evening on the Plaza de Isabella.

It was very amusing to sit here near the marble statue of the ex-queen (which is, by the way, a wonderful likeness of Queen Victoria), where the band, composed of sixty instrumental performers, discoursed admirable music, and to observe young Cuba abroad, represented by boys and girls of ten and twelve years dressed like young ladies and gentlemen, sauntering arm in arm through the broad paths. These children attend balls given by grown-up people, and are painted and bedizened and decked out like their elders, — a singular fashion in Cuban cities. It is true they not infrequently fall asleep on such occasions in rocking-chairs and in odd corners, overcome by fatigue, as the hours of festivity creep on towards the morning. Childhood is ignored. Youth of a dozen years is introduced to the habits of people thrice that age. We were sadly told, by one who is himself a parent, that most children in the island but twelve years of age know the delicate relations of the sexes as well as they would ever know them. What else could be expected in an atmosphere so wretchedly immoral? Small boys dressed in stovepipe hats and swallow-tail coats, and little misses in long dresses with low necks look like mountebanks.

Opposite the Plaza de Isabella, on the Tacon Theatre side of the square, are situated the most fashionable cafés and restaurants of the capital, where "life" commences at nine o'clock in the evening and rages fast and furious until the small hours of the morning.

In these resorts, which are one blaze of light, every gas-burner reflected by dozens of mirrors, the marble tables are all occupied by vivacious patrons. Some are playing dominoes, some few are engaged at games of chess, others are busy over checkers or cards, and all are gambling. Even the lookers-on at the games freely stake their money on the fortunes of the several players. The whole scene is one of noise and confusion, fifty tongues giving voice at the same time. If a Spaniard or Creole loses a dollar he gesticulates and argues about it as though thousands were involved in the issue. These people represent all classes. Some are in their shirt-sleeves, some roughly clothed, some in full evening dress; Spaniards, Creoles, mulattoes, and occasionally an unmistakable European. They drink often, but not strong liquors, and one is surprised to hear coffee so often called for in place of wine. The games are kept up until two or three o'clock in the morning. Loitering about the doors beggars always form the shadow of the scene; some lame, some blind, mostly negroes and coolies; now and then there is seen among them an intelligent but sad white face, which looks rather than utters its appeal. These are often the recipients of the successful gambler's bounty. Now and again a lottery-ticket vender comes in and makes the circuit of the tables, always disposing of more or less chances, sometimes selling a whole ticket, price one doubloon, or seventeen dollars. As we watch the scene a daintily dressed youth with shining beaver lounges in, accompanied by one of the demi-monde gayly dressed and sparkling with jewelry which betrays her want of modesty. She is of the true Andalusian type, olive complexion, coal-black hair with eyes to match, and long dark lashes; petite in figure and youthful, but aged in experience. Bonnetless, her luxuriant hair is set high upon her head, held by a square tortoise-shell comb, and carelessly thrown off her forehead with a parting on one side. Be sure some sad story underlies her career. She is of just that gypsy cast that painters love to delineate. They sit down at a side table and order ices, cake, and champagne. These are consumed amid jests and laughter, the spurious champagne, at a fabulous cost, is drunk merrily, the hours creep on, and the couple retire to give place to others, after having furnished a picture of the fast, false life of these brilliant, but dissipated haunts.

Some of these cafés are more exclusive than others, where respectable ladies and gentlemen can retire after the band has ceased its performance, and enjoy the cooling influence of an ice. The Louvre, just opposite the Plaza de Isabella and adjoining the Tacon Theatre, is one of such. These establishments couple with their current evening business that of the manufacture of choice preserves for domestic use and also for export, the fruits of the island supplying the basis for nearly a hundred varieties of fruit preserves, which find large sales in our Northern cities and in Europe.

In carnival week these cafés do an immense business; it is the harvest of their year. People who can hardly afford three meals a day pinch themselves and suffer much self-denial that they may have money to spend in carnival week. The public masquerade balls, which then take place, allure all classes. The celebrations of the occasion culminate in a grand public masquerade ball given in the Tacon Theatre. The floor of the parquette is temporarily raised to a level with the boxes and the stage, the entire floor or lower part of the house being converted into a grand ball-room. The boxes and galleries are thrown open free to the public. The music, furnished by two military bands, alternating in their performance, is kept up until broad daylight, while the participants come and go as they please. A little after midnight an organization called the comparzas comes upon the scene. It is composed of men, boys, and women, all masked, who have practiced for the occasion some emblematic dance to perform for their own and the public amusement. The other dancers give way and the new-comers perform, in harlequin fashion, their allotted parts. Towards morning a large paper globe is suspended from the ceiling and lowered to within a certain height from the floor. Blindfolded volunteers of both sexes, furnished with sticks, are permitted to walk towards and try to hit it. Scores fail, others just graze the globe of paper, all amid loud laughter from the spectators. Finally some one hits the globe full and fair, bringing down the contents amid vociferous applause. Then commences a general scramble for the contents, consisting of bonbons, toys, and fancy trinkets.

The celebrated Tacon Theatre faces the Paseo de Isabella, and is built on the corner of San Rafael Street. It is a capacious structure, but extremely plain and unimpressive in its exterior appearance. It has five tiers of boxes and a spacious parquette, the latter furnished with separate arm-chair seats for six hundred persons. The entire seating capacity of the house is a trifle over three thousand, and the auditorium is of the horseshoe shape. The lattice-work finish before the boxes is very light and graceful in effect, ornamented with gilt, and so open as to display the dresses and pretty feet of the fair occupants to the best advantage. The frescos are in good style, and the ornamentation, without being excessive, is in excellent and harmonious taste. A large, magnificent glass chandelier, lighted with gas, and numerous smaller ones extending from the boxes give a brilliant light to this elegant house, which is one of the largest theatres in the world. The scene is a remarkable one when tier upon tier is filled with gayly dressed ladies, powdered and rouged as Cuban women are apt to be, in the most liberal manner. The parquette is reserved for gentlemen, and when the audience is assembled forms a striking contrast to the rest of the house, as they always appear in dark evening dress, and between the acts put on their tall black beaver hats. These audiences have their own special modes of exhibiting appreciation or applause, when captivated by a prima donna's or a danseuse's efforts to please them. At favorable moments during the performance the artist is showered with bouquets; white doves are set free from the boxes, bearing laudatory verses fastened to their wings; gentlemen throw their hats upon the stage, and sometimes even purses weighted with gold. Tiny balloons are started with long streamers of colored ribbon attached; jewelry in the shape of bracelets and rings is conveyed over the footlights; in short, these Spaniards are sometimes extraordinarily demonstrative. A furore has sometimes cost these caballeros large sums of money. But we are describing the past rather than the immediate present, for the scarcity of pecuniary means has put an end to nearly all such extravagances. The Havanese are peculiar in their tastes. While Miss

Adelaide Phillips was more than once the recipient of extravagant favors on the Tacon Theatre stage, Jenny Lind did not pay her professional expenses when she sang there.

The military are always in attendance in large numbers at the theatre, as at all public gatherings in Cuba, their only perceptible use being to stare the ladies out of countenance and to obstruct the passage-ways. In front of the main entrance to the theatre is an open area decorated with tropical plants and trees, where a group of the crimson hibiscus was observed, presenting a gorgeous effect of color. The other places of amusement in Havana, of a dramatic character, are the Payret Theatre, very large, seating twenty-five hundred; the Albisu Theatre, and the Circo, Teatro de Jané, this latter combining a theatre with a circus.

As a place of amusement and instruction combined we should be remiss not to mention the Casino of Havana. It is carried on by an organized society formed on the basis of a club and has, we were told, over one hundred members. The Casino occupies a fine building, fronting Obispo Street, and close to the parks. It supports a free school for teaching the English and French languages and drawing. After some fifteen years of successful existence the society has become one of the institutions of the metropolis. The halls and apartments are large, lofty, and very finely furnished with all domestic conveniences except sleeping accommodations. Here dramatic entertainments are frequently given, mostly by amateurs, and generally for charitable purposes. The main ballroom of the Casino is handsomely decorated and is the scene of occasional masked balls, after the true

Madrid style, where many an intrigue is consummated which does not always end without bloodshed. It is the favorite resort of all the high officials of Havana, who have within their possible reach too few social entertainments not to make the most of those presented at the Casino. During the carnival season the ball-room of the establishment is said to present, in the form of nightly masquerade balls, scenes which for gayety and picturesqueness cannot be surpassed in Europe.

Old Havana is certainly eclipsed by the really fine broad streets and the palatial buildings which have sprung up outside of her ancient limits. In point of picturesqueness the old town has precedence. Near where the Indian Paseo and the Plaza de Isabella II. join each other, a portion of the old wall which once surrounded the city is still to be seen, with its crumbling bastions and ivy-grown débris. Sufficient is left to show that the wall was a remarkably substantial one and an efficient defense against the modes of attack prevalent when it was built. The Indian Paseo commences opposite the Campo de Marte, and is so called from the large marble fountain dedicated to that aboriginal idea. This elaborate structure was executed in Italy at large expense. Its principal figure is an Indian maiden, allegorical of Havana, supporting a shield bearing the arms of the city. These paseos are admirably ornamented on either side by a continuous line of laurel trees whose thick foliage gives admirable shade. On either side of the long central promenade the well-paved streets are broad and handsome, being ornamented with high buildings of a domestic and public character and of good architectural effect. The Matanzas & Havana Railroad depot is situated just opposite one end of the Campo de Marte, its freight yard extending also along the Paseo for an entire block, detracing much from the fine effect of the broad street. The trains and noisy engines being thus brought into the midst of the dwellings and business centre of the city render it very objectionable. The guests of the Telegrafo Hotel can bear testimony as to the nuisance thus created, being awakened at all sorts of unreasonable hours by the engine bell and steam whistle.

The Botanical Garden is situated about a mile from the city proper, adjoining which are the attractive grounds of the Governor General's country-house. Both are open to the public and richly repay a visit. The Governor's grounds are shaded by a great variety of tropical trees and flowers. Here was seen what is called the water rose, pink in color and nearly double the size of our pond lily, recalling the Egyptian lotus, to which family it would seem it must belong. Altogether, the place is a wilderness of blossoms, composed of exotic and native flowers. There is also an interesting aviary to be seen here, and a small artificial lake is covered with curious web-footed birds and brilliant-feathered ducks. The gardens seem to be neglected, but they are very lovely in their native luxuriance. Dead wood and decaying leaves are always a concomitant of such gardens in the low latitudes. If the roses and heliotropes are in full bloom, some other flowering shrub alongside is taking its rest and looks rusty, so that the whole garden is never in a glow of beauty at one time, as is the case with us in June. The noble alley of palms, the great variety of trees, blossoms, and shrubs, the music of the fountains, and the tropical flavor permeating everything were all in the harmony of languid beauty. The coral tree, that lovely freak of vegetation, was in bloom, its small but graceful stem, seven or eight feet in height, being topped above the gracefully pendent leaves with a bit of vegetable coral of deepest red, and in the form of the sea growth from which it takes its name. The star cactus was in full flower, the scarlet buds starting out from the flat surface of the thick leaves after a queer and original fashion. The bread-fruit tree, with its large, melon-like product, hung heavy with the nourishing esculent. The Carolina tree, with gorgeous blossoms like military pompons, blazed here and there, overshadowing the large, pure white, and beautiful campanile, with hanging flowers, like metallic bells, after which the plant is named. Here too was a great variety of the scarlet hibiscus and the garland of night (galan de noche), which grows like a young palm to eight or nine feet, throwing out from the centre of its drooping foliage a cluster of brown blossoms tipped with white, shaped like a mammoth bunch of grapes. It blooms at night and is fragrant only by moon and starlight. Cuba presents an inexhaustible field for the botanist, and in its wilder portions recalls the island of Ceylon in the Indian Ocean. As Ceylon is called the pearl of India so is Cuba the pearl of the Antilles.

To reach the Governor's Garden one turns west from the Campo de Marte and takes the Calzada de la Reina, which followed about a mile in a straight line becomes the Paseo de Tacon, really but a continuation of the former street, commencing at the statue of Carlos III., a colossal monument placed in the middle of the broad driveway. This Paseo forms the favorite evening drive of the citizens, where the ladies in victorias and the gentlemen either as equestrians or on foot pass and repass each other, gayly saluting, the ladies with a coquettish flourish of the fan, and the gentlemen with a peculiar wave of the hand. It is in fact the Champs Elysées of Havana, but the road is sadly out of repair and as dusty as an ash-pit.

The Alameda — every large Spanish city has a spot so designated — skirts the shore of the harbor on the city side, near the south end of Oficios Street, and is a favorite resort for promenaders at the evening hour. Here a refreshing coolness is breathed from off the sea. This Alameda de Paula might be a continuation of the Neapolitan Chiaja. With characteristics quite different, still these shores constantly remind one of the Mediterranean, Sorrento, Amalfi, and Capri, recalling the shadows which daily creep up the heights of San Elmo and disappear with the setting sun behind the orange groves. Sometimes it would seem to be the grand problem of humanity, why the loveliest regions of the earth and the softest climates should be apportioned to the share of slaves and despots.

The cathedral of Havana, on Empedrado Street, is a structure of much interest, its rude pillared front of defaced and moss-grown stone plainly telling of the wear of time. The two lofty towers are hung with many bells, which daily call with their brazen tongues to matins and vespers. Some of these bells are very ancient. The church is not elaborately ornamented, — it rather strikes one with its unusual plainness. It contains a few oil paintings of moderate merit, and also the tomb where the ashes of Columbus so long reposed. All that is visible of this tomb, which is on the right of the altar, is a marble tablet six or eight feet square, upon which, in high relief, is a bust of the great discoverer. As a work of art, the less said of this effigy the better. Beneath the image is an inscription sufficiently bombastic and Spanish in tone, but therein we observed no mention was made of the chains and imprisonment with which an ungrateful country rewarded this man whom history so delights to honor. It will be remembered that Columbus died at Valladolid in 1506. In 1513 his remains were transferred to Seville, preparatory to their being sent, as desired in his will, to St. Domingo, to which city they were removed in 1536. When that island was ceded to France, they were brought with great pomp to Havana in a national ship (January 15, 1796), and deposited in this cathedral in the presence of all the high authorities of the island. These remains have again been removed, and are now interred at Seville, in Spain. The cathedral, aside from this association, is really attractive, and one lingers with quiet thoughtfulness among its marble aisles and confessionals. The lofty dome is supported by pillars of marble and the walls are frescoed. The high altar is a remarkable composition, with pillars of porphyry mingled with a confusion of images, candlesticks, and tinsel. The stalls for the priests are handsomely carved in mahogany. It was annoying to see Gothic grandeur and modern frippery so mingled as was observable in this church. When mass is being performed women attend in goodly numbers, but one rarely sees any of the male population present, unless they be, like the author, strangers come hither from curiosity to see the interior of this Cathedral de la Virgen Maria de la Concepcion.

THE OLD BELL-RINGER. 161

All persons who come to Havana visit the cathedral because it contains the tomb of Columbus, but if they have traveled in Europe they have seen so much finer structures of this class, especially in Spain, that this one challenges but little attention. Let us, gentle reader, go up into the lofty bell tower, where we shall find the most comprehensive view possible of the Cuban capital. The old bell-ringer, seated before a deal table, ekes out a scanty living by making cigars away up here in his circumscribed eyrie. What an original he would have been in the practiced hands of Victor Hugo! This hermit of the tower will call your attention to the ancient bells, which are his sole companions: one bears the date of 1664, with a half-defaced Latin legend; another is dated at London, 1698. He is a queer old enthusiast about these bells, and will tell you on what special occasions of interest he has caused them to speak with metallic tongue to the people: now as a danger signal; then uttering sounds of triumph and announcing a victory; again, tolling the notes of sorrow for the departed, or as merry marriage bells, the heralds of joy. He will tell you how many years, man and boy, he has summoned the devout to matins and to vespers with their resonant voices. If you have a fancy for such things, and some silver to spare, after leaving the bell tower the sacristan will show you the rich vestments, robes, and laces for priestly wear belonging to the church, not forgetting many saintly garments wrought in gold and studded with precious stones. Perhaps you will think, as we did, that such things are but tinsel before Him whom they are supposed to honor. Such dazzling paraphernalia may attract the ignorant or the thoughtless — may make followers, but not converts. Conviction is not the child of fancy, but of judgment.

In an anteroom at the left of the altar there are also to be seen utensils of silver and gold, with many costly ornaments for use before the altar on special church occasions. One of these is a triumph of delicate workmanship and of the silversmith's art. It is in the form of a Gothic tower of very elaborate and artistic design, composed of solid silver, ornamented with gold and precious stones. One regards this thoroughly useless disposal of money with the thought that the articles were better sold and the proceeds bestowed in worthy charity. It would then fulfill a far more Christian purpose than that of adding glitter to church pomp and ceremony.

To witness the observance of Holy Week, commencing with Palm Sunday, in Havana, one would be impressed with a conviction that the people were at heart devout Roman Catholics. The occasion is solemnly observed. On Sunday the old cathedral is crowded by people who come to obtain branches of holy palm from the priests. The old bell-ringer becomes an important agent of the ceremonies, and the solemn spirit of the occasion seems to imbue all classes of the Havanese. On Holy Thursday, just before midday, the bells of all the churches cease to ring, and every vehicle in the city disappears from the streets as if by magic. The garrison marches through the principal thoroughfares in silence, with measured tread and arms reversed. The national flags upon the shipping, and on all the forts from Moro to the Castillo del Principe, are displayed at half mast. The cathedral and the churches are draped in mourning. On Friday, the effigy of our Saviour's body is carried in solemn procession, men and priests marching with heads uncovered, and devout women of the common classes, especially colored ones, kneeling in the street as it passes. On Saturday, at ten o'clock in the morning, the old bell-ringer suddenly starts a merry peal from the cathedral tower — the bells of La Merced, San Agustin, Santa Clara, and Santa Cataline follow; the town awakens to gayety as from a lethargic sleep. Whites and negroes rush through the streets like mad; vehicles of all sorts again make their appearance, the forts and national ships are dressed in holiday flags, and the town is shaken with reiterated salutes from a hundred cannons.

Military mass, as performed within the cathedral, seemed more like a theatrical show than a solemn religious service. On the occasion referred to, the congregation as usual was sparse, and consisted almost exclusively of women, who seem to do penance for both sexes in Cuba. The military band which led the column of infantry marched in, playing a quick operatic air, deploying to one side for the soldiery to pass towards the altar. The time-keeping steps of the soldiery upon the marble floor mingled with drum, fife, and organ. Through all this, one caught now and then the monotonous voice of a shaven-headed priest, reciting his prescribed part at the altar, kneeling and reading at intervals. The busy censer boys in white gowns; the flaring candles casting long shadows athwart the high altar; the files of soldiers kneeling and rising at the tap of the drum; the atmosphere clouded with the fumes of burning incense, — all combined to make up a singularly dramatic picture. The gross mummery witnessed at the temple of Buddha in Ceylon differed only in form, scarcely in degree.

The wealth of the churches of the monks in the island was formerly proverbial, but of late the rich perquisites which the priests were so long permitted to extort from the credulous public have been diverted so as to flow into the coffers of the crown. A military depotism brooks no rival in authority. The priests at one time possessed large tracts of land in Cuba, and their revenue therefrom, especially when they were improved as sugar plantations, was very large. These lands have all been confiscated by the government, and with the loss of their property the power of the monks has declined and their numbers have also diminished. Still the liberty of public worship is denied to all save Roman Catholics. Since the suppression of monastic institutions, some of the convents have been utilized for hospitals, government storehouses, and other public offices in Havana. There are some manifest incongruities that suggest themselves as existing between Church and state upon the island. For instance, the Church recognizes the unity of all races and even permits marriage between all, but here steps in the civil law of Cuba and prohibits marriage between white persons and those having any taint of negro blood. In consequence of this, — nature always asserting herself regardless of conventionalities, — a quasi family arrangement often exists between white men and mulatto or quadroon women, whereby the children are recognized as legitimate. But should either party come under the discipline of the Church, the relationship must terminate. Again, as is perfectly well known, many of the priests, under a thin disguise, lead domestic lives, where a family of children exist under the care of a single mother, who is debarred from the honest name of wife by the laws of celibacy which are stringently held as the inexorable rule of the Church.

If the priesthood keep from cock-fighting and gambling, says a late writer on the subject, notwithstanding many other departures from propriety, they are considered respectable. Can there be any wonder that the masses of men in Cuba recognize no religious obligations, since none save Roman Catholicism is tolerated, and that, through its priesthood, is so disgraced?

CHAPTER IX.

Political Inquisition. — Fashionable Streets of the City. — Tradesmen's Signs. — Bankrupt Condition of Traders. — The Spanish Army. — Exiled Patriots. — Arrival of Recruits. — The Garrote. — A Military Execution. — Cuban Milk Dealers. — Exposure of Domestic Life. — Living in the Open Air. — The Campo Santo of Havana. — A Funeral Cortége. — Punishing Slaves. — Campo de Marte. — Hotel Telegrafo. — Environs of the City. — Bishop's Garden. — Consul-General Williams. — Mineral Springs.

THE Inquisition, as it regards the Church of Rome, is suppressed in Cuba, but the political inquisition, as exercised by the government on the island, is even more diabolical than that of the former Jesuitical organization, because it is more secret in its murderous deeds, not one half of the horrors of which will ever be publicly known. Moro Castle is full of political prisoners, who are thinned out by executions, starvation, and hardships generally, from day to day, only to make room for fresh victims. He who enters those grim portals leaves all hope behind. Political trials there are none, but of political arrests there are endless numbers. The life of every citizen is at the disposal of the Captain-General. If a respectable person is arrested, as one suspected of animosity towards the government, he simply disappears. His friends dare not press his defense, or inquire too closely as to his case, lest they, too, should be incarcerated on suspicion, never again to regain their liberty. A maxim of Spanish law is that every accused person is guilty, until he proves himself innocent! As a large majority of the people, in their hearts, sympathize with the revolutionists, and are revolutionists in secret, they are liable to say or to do some trifling thing unwittingly, upon which the lynx-eyed officials seize as evidence of guilt, and their arrest follows. What fearful stories the dungeons of Moro could reveal had they tongue with which to speak!

Obispo and O'Riley streets are the principal shopping thoroughfares of the metropolis, containing many fine stores for the sale of dry goods, millinery, china, glassware, and jewelry. These shops are generally quite open in front. Standing at the end, and looking along either of these thoroughfares, one gets a curious perspective view. The party-colored awnings often stretch entirely across the narrow streets, reminding one of a similar effect in Canton, where straw matting takes the place of canvas, forming a sort of open marquee. The queer names adopted for the stores never fail to afford a theme of amusement; the drawling cries of the fruit-dealers and peripatetic tradesmen giving an added interest. The merchant in Havana does not designate his establishment by placing his own name upon his sign, but adopts some fancy title, such as Diana, America, The Star, Virtue, The Golden Lion, and so on, which titles are paraded in gilt letters over the door. The Spanish people are always prodigal in names, making the sun, moon and stars, gods and goddesses, all do duty in designating their stores, villas, and plantations. Nearly every town on the island is named after some apostle or saint. The tradesmen are thorough Jews in their style of dealing with the public, and no one thinks of paying them the price which they first demand for an article. It is their practice in naming a price to make allowance for reduction; they expect to be bargained with, or cheapened at least one half. The ladies commonly make their purchases late in the afternoon or evening, stopping in their victorias at the doors of the shops, from whence the articles they desire are brought by the shopmen and deftly displayed on the street. When lighted up at night the stores are really brilliant and attractive, presenting quite a holiday appearance; but customers are sadly wanting in these days of business depression. "I have been compelled to dismiss my salesmen and do their work myself," said a dry-goods merchant to us; "we dare not give credit, and few persons have cash to spare in these times."

One of the principal causes of the present bankrupt condition of the people of Cuba is the critical period of transition through which the island is passing from slave to free labor; besides which there is the exhaustion consequent upon years of civil war and a succession of bad crops. Labor is becoming dearer and sugar cheaper. The Spaniards are slow to adopt labor-saving machinery, or new ideas of any sort, and those not already supplied have neither capital nor credit with which to procure the new machinery for sugar-making. The enormous production of European beet-sugar has cut off all Continental demand for their staple, and has in some degree superseded its use in America. Brigandage is on the increase, as poverty and want of legitimate employment prevail. Money, when it can be borrowed at all, is at a ruinous interest. The army of office-holders still manage to extort considerable sums in the aggregate from the people, under the guise of necessary taxes. Financial ruin stares all in the face.

It is a sad thing to say, but only too true, that among people heretofore considered above suspicion in commercial transactions great dishonesty prevails, pecuniary distress and lack of credit driving men, once in good standing, to defraud their creditors at home and abroad. Estates and plantations are not only heavily mortgaged, but the prospective crops are in the same condition, in many cases. In former prosperous years the planters have been lavish spenders of money, ever ready to use their credit to the full extent, until their interest account has consumed their principal. The expensive habits acquired under the promptings of large profits and a sure market are difficult to overcome, and people who never anticipated the present state of affairs are now forced to exercise economy and self-denial. Cuban planters and their families, in years past, came to our most fashionable watering-places decked with jewels of almost fabulous value, and they lavished gold like water; most of these individuals considered themselves to be rich beyond the chances of fortune. Their profuse style of living was a source of envy; their liberality to landlords and to servants was demoralizing, as it regarded the tariff of hotel prices for more steady-going people. Thousands of human beings were yielding their enforced labor to fill these spendthrifts' purses, and sugar was king. The picture has its reverse. Civil war has supervened, the slaves are being freed, sugar is no longer a bonanza, and the rich man of yesterday is the bankrupt of to-day. Truly riches have wings.

Spain keeps a large and effective force of soldiers upon the island, — an army out of all proportion in numbers to the territory or people she holds in subjection. The present military force must number some forty thousand, rank and file, and the civil department fully equals the army in number; and all are home Spaniards. A large portion of the military are kept in the eastern department of the island, which is and has ever been the locality where revolutionary outbreaks occur. Eighty per cent. of all the soldiers ever sent to Cuba have perished there! It is as Castelar once pronounced the island to be, in the Cortes at Madrid, namely, the Campo Santo of the Spanish army. Exposure, a miserable commissariat, the climate, and insurgent bullets combine to thin the ranks of the army like a raging pestilence. We were informed by a responsible party that twenty-five per cent. of the newly-arrived soldiers died in their first year, during what is called their acclimation. Foreigners who visit Cuba for business or pleasure do so at the most favorable season; they are not subjected to hardships nor exposed in malarial districts. The soldiers, on the contrary, are sent indiscriminately into the fever districts at the worst season, besides being called upon to endure hardships, all the time, which predispose them to fatal diseases.

There are known to be organized juntas of revolutionists at Key West, Florida, in Hayti, and also in New York city, whose designs upon the Cuban government keep the authorities on the island in a state of chronic alarm. A revolutionary spirit is felt to be all the while smouldering in the hearts of this oppressed people, and hence the tyrannous espionage, and the cruelty exercised towards suspected persons. So enormous are the expenses, military and civil, which are required to sustain the government, under these circumstances, that Cuba to-day, notwithstanding the heavy taxes extorted from her populace, is an annual expense to the throne. Formerly the snug sum of seven or eight millions of dollars was the yearly contribution which the island made to the royal treasury, after paying local army, navy, and civil expenses. This handsome sum was over and above the pickings and stealings of the venal officials. As to the Cuban sympathizers at Key West, Florida, a recent visit to that port, just opposite to the island on the hither side of the Gulf Stream, showed us that they formed a large proportion of the population of that thrifty American town. On a day which was the anniversary of some patriotic occasion relating to the island, hundreds of Cuban flags (the single star of free Cuba) were seen displayed upon the dwellings and public places. There are believed to be two thousand Creoles residing here, who have either been expelled from the island for political reasons, or who have escaped from thence as suspected patriots. These people are very generally engaged in the manufacture of the well-known Key West cigars.

The Spanish army is governed with an iron hand. Military law knows no mercy, and it is always more or less a lapse into barbarism where it takes precedence. The ranks are filled by conscription in Spain, and when the men first arrive at Havana they are the rawest recruits imaginable. Soldiers who have been doing garrison duty are sent inland to fill the decimated ranks of various stations, and room is thus made for the recruits, who are at once put to work, enduring a course of severe discipline and drill. They land from the transports, many of them, hatless, barefooted, and in a filthy condition, with scarcely a whole garment among a regiment of them. The writer could hardly believe, on witnessing the scene, that they were not a set of criminals being transported for penal servitude. Fatigue dresses no doubt awaited them at the barracks, and after a while they would be served with a cheap uniform, coarse shoes, and straw hats. They are like sheep being driven to the shambles, and are quite as helpless. Twenty-five per cent. and upwards of these recruits are usually under the sod before the close of a twelve-month!

Sometimes the hardship they have to endure breeds rebellion among them, but woe betide those who commit any overt act, or become leaders of any organized attempt to obtain justice. The service requires frequent victims as examples to enforce the rigid discipline. The punishment by the garrote is a common resort. It is a machine contrived to choke the victim to death without suspending him in the air. At the same time it is fatal in another way, namely, by severing the spinal column just below its connection with the brain. The condemned man is placed upon a chair fixed on a platform, leaning his head and neck back into a sort of iron yoke or frame prepared to receive it. Here an iron collar is clasped about the throat. At the appointed moment a screw is suddenly turned by the executioner, stationed behind the condemned, and instantaneous death follows. This would seem to be more merciful than hanging, whereby death is produced by the lingering process of suffocation, to say nothing of the many mishaps which so often occur upon the gallows. This mode of punishment is looked upon by the army as a disgrace, and they much prefer the legitimate death of a soldier, which is to fall by the bullets of his comrades when condemned to die.

A MILITARY EXECUTION. 173

The writer witnessed one of these military executions, early on a clear April morning, which took place in the rear of the barracks near La Punta. It was a trying experience, and recalled to mind the execution of the mulatto poet and patriot, Valdez, which had occurred a few years before in the Plaza at Matanzas. It was a sight to chill the blood even under a tropical sun. A soldier of the line was to be shot for some act of insubordination against the stringent rules of the army, and that the punishment might prove a forcible example to his comrades the battalion to which he belonged was drawn up on parade to witness the cruel scene. The immediate file of twelve men to which the victim had belonged were supplied with muskets by their officer, and we were told that, according to custom, one musket was left without ball, so that each one might hope that his was not the hand to slay his former comrade. A sense of mercy would still lead them all to aim faithfully, so that lingering pain might be avoided.

The order was given: the bright morning sun shone like living fire along the polished barrels of the guns, as the fatal muzzles all ranged in point at the body of the condemned. "Fire!" said the commanding officer. A quick, rattling report followed, accompanied by a thin cloud of smoke, which was at once dispersed by the sea breeze, showing the still upright form of the victim. Though wounded in many places, no vital spot had been touched, nor did he fall until the sergeant, at a sign from his officer, advanced with a reserved musket, and quickly blew out his brains! His body was removed. The troops were formed into column, the band struck up a lively air, and thus was a human being launched into eternity.

Few current matters strike the stranger as being more peculiar than the Cuban milkman's mode of supplying the required aliment to his town customers. He has no cart bearing shining cans, they in turn filled with milk, or with what purports to be milk; his mode is direct, and admits of no question as to purity. Driving his sober kine from door to door, he deliberately milks then and there just the quantity required by each customer, delivers it, and drives on to the next. The patient animal becomes as familiar with the residences of her master's customers as he is himself, and stops unbidden, at regular intervals, before the proper doors, often followed by a pretty little calf, which amuses itself by gazing enviously at the process, being prevented from interfering by a leather muzzle. Sometimes the flow of milk is checked by an effort of the animal herself, when she seems to realize that the calf is not getting its share of nourishment. The driver then promptly brings the calf to the mother's side, and removes the muzzle long enough to give the little one a brief chance. The cow freely yields her milk while the calf is close to her, and the milkman, muzzling the calf, adroitly milks into his measure. The same mode is adopted in India and the south of Spain. There are at least two good reasons for delivering milk in hot climates after this fashion. First, there can be no adulteration of the article; and second, it is sure to be fresh and sweet. This last is a special desideratum in a climate where ice is an expensive luxury, and the difficulty of keeping milk from becoming acid is very great. The effect upon the cow is by no means salutary, causing the animal to produce much less in quantity than when milked clean at regularly fixed hours, as with us. Goats are often driven about for the same purpose and used in the same manner. It was a surprise not to see more of these animals in Cuba, a country especially adapted to them. Cows thrive best upon grass, of which there is comparatively little in the tropics, — vegetation runs to larger development; but goats eat anything green, and do well nearly anywhere. It is a singular fact that sheep transported to this climate cease gradually to produce wool. After three or four generations they grow only a simple covering, more like hair than wool, and resemble goats rather than sheep.

Glass is scarcely known in Cuban windows; the glazier has yet to make his début in Havana. The most pretentious as well as the humblest of the town-houses have the broad, high, projecting window, reaching from floor to ceiling, secured only by heavy horizontal iron bars, prison-like in effect, through which, as one passes along the narrow streets, it is nearly impossible to avoid glancing in upon domestic scenes that frequently exhibit the female portion of the family en déshabillé. Sometimes a loose lace curtain intervenes, but even this is unusual, the freest circulation of fresh air being quite necessary. The eye penetrates the whole interior of domestic life, as at Yokohama or Tokio. Indeed, the manners of the female occupants seem to court this attention from without, coming freely as they do to the windows to chat with passers-by. Once inside of these dwelling-houses there are no doors, curtains alone shutting off the communication between chambers, sitting-rooms, and corridors. These curtains, when not looped up, are sufficient to keep out persons of the household or strangers, it being the custom always to speak, in place of knocking, before passing a curtain; but the little naked negro children, male and female, creep under these curtains without restraint, while parrots, pigeons, and fowls generally make common use of all nooks and corners of the house. Doors might keep these out of one's room, but curtains do not. The division walls between the apartments in private houses, like those in the hotels, often reach but two thirds of the way up to the walls, thus affording free circulation of air, but rendering privacy impossible. One reason why the Cubans all possess such broad expanded chests is doubtless owing to the fact that their lungs find free action at all times. They live, as it were, in the open air. The effect of this upon strangers is seen and felt, producing a sense of physical exhilaration, fine spirits, and a good appetite. It would be impossible to live in a dwelling-house built in our close, secure style, if it were placed in the city of Havana. The laundress takes possession of the roof of the house during the day, but it is the place of social gathering at night, when the family and their guests enjoy the sea-breeze which sweeps in from the Gulf of Mexico. On a clear, bright moonlight night the effect is very striking as one looks across the house-tops, nearly all being upon a level. Many cheerful circles are gathered here and there, some dancing to the notes of a guitar, some singing, and others engaged in quiet games. Merry peals of laughter come from one direction and another, telling of light and thoughtless hearts among the family groups. Occasionally there is borne along the range of roofs the swelling but distant strains of the military band playing in the Plaza de Isabella, while the moon looks calmly down from a sky whose intensely blue vault is only broken by stars.

A FUNERAL CORTÈGE. 177

The cemetery, or Campo Santo, of Havana is situated about three miles outside of the city. A high wall incloses the grounds, in which oven-like niches are prepared for the reception of the coffins containing the bodies of the wealthy residents, while the poor are thrown into shallow graves, often several bodies together in a long trench, negroes and whites, without a coffin of any sort. Upon them is thrown quicklime to promote rapid decomposition. The cremation which forms the mode of disposing of the bodies of the deceased as practiced in India is far less objectionable.

The funeral cortége is unique in Havana. The hearse, drawn by four black horses, is gilded and decked like a car of Juggernaut, and driven by a flunkey in a cocked hat covered with gold braid, a scarlet coat alive with brass buttons and gilt ornaments, and top boots which, as he sits, reach half-way to his chin. This individual flourishes a whip like a fishing-pole, and is evidently very proud of his position. Beside the hearse walk six hired mourners on either side, dressed in black, with cocked hats and swallow-tail coats. Fifteen or twenty victorias follow, containing only male mourners. The driver in scarlet, the twelve swallow-tails in black, and the occupants of the victorias each and all are smoking cigars as though their lives depended upon the successful operation. And so the cortége files into the Campo Santo.

Not far from La Punta there is a structure, protected from the public gaze by a high wall, where the slaves of either sex belonging to the citizens of Havana are brought for punishment. Within are a series of whipping-posts, to which these poor creatures are bound before applying the lash to their bare bodies. The sight of this fiendish procedure is cut off from the public, but more than one person has told us of having heard the agonizing cries of the victims. And yet there are people who will tell us these poor creatures are far better off than when in their native country. One slave-owner said it was necessary to make an example of some member of all large households of slaves each month, in order to keep them under discipline! Another said, " I never whip my slaves; it may be necessary upon a plantation, but not in domestic circles in town. When they have incurred my displeasure, they are deprived of some small creature comfort, or denied certain liberties, which punishment seems to answer every object." So it will be seen that all slave-holders are not cruel. Some seem as judicious and reasonable as is possible under the miserable system of slavery.

Opposite the Indian Paseo, General Tacon, during his governorship of the island, constructed a broad camp-ground for military parades in what is now becoming the heart of the city, though outside the limits of the old city walls. He called it the Campo de Marte, and surrounded the whole space, ten acres, more or less, with a high ornamental iron fence. It is in form a perfect square, and on each of the four sides was placed a broad, pretentious gateway, flanked by heavy square pillars. That on the west side he named Puerta de Colon; on the north, Puerta de Cortes; on the south, Puerta de Pizarro; and on the east side, facing the city, he gave the gate the name of Puerta de Tacon. His administration has been more praised and more censured than that of any of his predecessors since the days of Velasquez. This

HOTEL TELEGRAFO.

Campo de Marte, which, as stated, was originally intended for military purposes generally, is now converted into a public park, laid out with spacious walks, fountains, handsome trees, and carriage-ways. The gates have been removed, and the whole place thrown open as a thoroughfare and pleasure-ground.

Speaking of this open square brings us to the subject of hotels in Havana, and as we have so often been questioned upon this subject, doubtless a few words upon the matter will interest the general reader. We made our temporary home for nearly a month at the Hotel Telegrafo, but why it is so called we do not know. It is considered to be one of the best in the city, and is centrally situated, being opposite to the Campo de Marte. There was a chief clerk who spoke English, and another who spoke French, and two guides who possessed the same facilities. The price of board was from four to five dollars per day, including meals and service. The rooms were very small, table fair, plenty of fruits and preserves, but the meats were poor. Fish was always fresh and good in Havana. Coffee and tea were poor. If one desires to procure good coffee, as a rule, look for it anywhere rather than in countries where it is grown. Cleanliness was not considered as being an indispensable virtue in the Telegrafo. Drainage received but little attention, and the domestic offices of the house were seriously offensive. The yellow fever does not prevail in Havana except in summer, say from May to October; but according to recognized sanitary rules it should rage there every month in the year. The hotels in peninsular Spain are dirty enough to disgust any one, but those of Havana are a degree worse in this respect. Any of our readers who have chanced in their travels upon the Fonda de Rafaela, for instance, at Burgos, in Spain, will understand us fully. It was of no use to remove elsewhere; after examining the other hotels it was thought best to remain at the Telegrafo, on the principle adopted by the Irishman, who, though not inclined to believe in Purgatory, yet accepted this item of faith lest he should go further and fare worse. There is the San Carlos Hotel, near the wharves, which is more of a family than a travelers' resort; the Hotel Pasaje, in Prado Street, quite central; Hotel Europe, in La Plaza de San Francisco; and Hotels Central and Ingleterra: the last two are opposite the Plaza de Isabella, and are in the midst of noise and gayety. Arrangements can be made at any of these houses for board by the day, or on the European plan; all have restaurants.

There are some very attractive summer resorts in the environs of the city, one of the nearest and prettiest of which is El Cerro (the hill), one league from town. It has a number of remarkably pleasant country-seats, some of which have extensive gardens, rivaling that of the Captain-General in extent. But to reach Cerro one has to drive over a road which is in such want of repair as to be dangerous, gullied by the rains, and exhibiting holes two feet deep, liable to break the horses' legs and the wheels of the vehicles. Here is a road, close to Havana, with stones weighing hundreds of pounds on the surface, in the very wheel-tracks. Handsome hedges of the wild pine, the aloe, and the Spanish bayonet line the road, where an occasional royal palm, the emblem of majesty, stands alone, adding grandeur to all the surroundings. If you drive out to Cerro, put on a linen duster; otherwise you will be likely to come back looking like a miller's apprentice. Not far beyond Cerro there lies some beautiful country, reached by the same miserable road. Puentes Grandes, a small village near the falls of the Almendares River, is but two miles further north than Cerro, and adjoining this place, a couple of miles further, is a small, picturesque village called Ceiba, from the abundance of that species of tree which once flourished there. These two places have some interesting country residences, where the wealthiest citizens of Havana spend their summers. The village of Quemados is also in this immediate neighborhood, about a couple of leagues from town; here is situated the Havana Hippodrome, where horse-races take place in the winter season. We must not forget to mention Vedado, on the seashore, whither the Havanese drive oftenest on Sundays; it is also connected with the city by steam-cars and omnibus. There are some fine villas here, and it is quite a Cuban watering-place, affording excellent bathing facilities. Vedado has wide streets, and, after the city, seems to be remarkably clean and neat.

The Bishop's Garden, so called because some half century since it was the residence of the Bishop of Havana, is about four miles from the city, on the line of the Marianao railroad. It must have been a delightful place when in its prime and properly cared for; even now, in its ruins, it is extremely interesting. There are a score, more or less, of broken, moss-grown statues, stone balustrades, and stone capitals lying among the luxuriant vegetation, indicating what was once here. Its alleys of palms, over two hundred years in age, the thrifty almond-trees, and the gaudy-colored piñons, with their honeysuckle-like bloom, delight the eye. The flamboyant absolutely blazed in its gorgeous flowers, like ruddy flames, all over the grounds. The remarkable fan-palm spread out its branches like a peacock's tail, screening vistas here and there. Through these grounds flows a small swift stream, which has its rise in the mountains some miles inland, its bright and sparkling waters imparting an added beauty to the place. By simple irrigating means this stream is made to fertilize a considerable tract of land used as vegetable gardens, lying between Tulipan and Havana. The Bishop's Garden still contains large stone basins for swimming purposes, cascades, fountains, and miniature lakes, all rendered possible by means of this small, clear, deep river. The neglected place is sadly suggestive of decay, with its moss-covered paths, tangled undergrowth, and untrimmed foliage. Nothing, however, can mar the glory of the grand immemorial palms.

The town of Tulipan, in which is the Bishop's Garden, is formed of neat and pleasant residences of citizens desiring to escape the bustle and closeness of the city. The houses are half European or American in their architecture, modified to suit the climate. Here the American Consul-General has a delightfully chosen home, surrounded by pleasant shade, and characterized by lofty, cool apartments; with bright, snowy marble floors, plenty of space, and perfect ventilation. Mr. Williams is a gentleman unusually well fitted for the responsible position he fills, having been a resident of Cuba for many years, and speaking the language like a native. In his intensely patriotic sentiments he is a typical American. It is not out of place for us to acknowledge here our indebtedness to him for much important information relating to the island.

The most celebrated mineral springs in Cuba are to be found at San Diego, where there are hot sulphur waters, springs bubbling ceaselessly from the earth, and for which great virtues are claimed. The springs are situated west of Havana, between thirty and forty leagues, at the base of the southern slope of the mountains. These waters are freely drank, as well as bathed in, and are highly charged with sulphureted hydrogen, and contain sulphate of lime and carbonate of magnesia. There are some diseases of women for which the San Diego waters are considered to be a specific, and remarkable cures are authenticated. Rheumatism and skin diseases are specially treated by the local physician. There is a very fair hotel at San Diego, located near the baths, and many Americans speak warmly in praise of the place as a health resort.

Next to the springs of San Diego, those of Madruga are notable, situated between Matanzas and Havana, and which can be reached by rail. The character of these springs is very similar to those of San Diego, though of lower temperature. They are used both for bathing and for drinking. Madruga is more easily accessible from the metropolis than is San Diego. There is also a good physician resident in the village.

CHAPTER X.

The Fish-Market of Havana. — The Dying Dolphin. — Tax upon the Trade. — Extraordinary Monopoly. — Harbor Boats. — A Story about Marti, the Ex-Smuggler. — King of the Isle of Pines. — The Offered Reward. — Sentinels in the Plaza de Armas. — The Governor General and the Intruder. — " I am Captain Marti ! " — The Betrayal. — The Ex-Smuggler as Pilot. — The Pardon and the Reward. — Tacon's Stewardship and Official Career. — Monopoly of Theatricals. — A Negro Festival.

THE fish-market of Havana doubtless affords the best variety and quality of this article to be found in any city of the world, not even excepting Madras and Bombay, where the Indian Ocean and the Bay of Bengal enter into rivalry with each other as to their products. The scientist Poey gives a list of six hundred species of fishes indigenous to the shores of Cuba. The supply of the city is not only procured from the neighboring waters, but fishermen come regularly a distance of over a hundred miles to the ports of the island, from Florida and Yucatan, with their small cutters well loaded. It was through the means afforded by these fishing crafts that communication was kept up between the Cuban patriots at Key West and their friends on the island, and no doubt smuggling was also carried on by them, until they came under the strict surveillance of the revenue officers.

The long marble counter of the Marti fish-market, at the end of Mercaderes Street, affords a display of the finny tribe which we have never seen equaled elsewhere. Every hue and combination of iris colors is represented, while the variety and oddity of shapes is ludicrous. Even fishing on the coast and the sale of the article are virtually government monopolies; indeed, everything is taxed and double taxed in Cuba; the air one breathes would be, could it be measured. Fish are brought into this market, as at many other tropical ports, alive, being preserved in wells of salt water which also act as ballast for the fishing vessels. One morning, among others brought to the Marti market a dolphin was observed, but as it is not a fish much used for the table why it came hither was not so clear to us. Being curious as to the accuracy of the poetical simile of changing colors which characterize its dying hours, the just landed dolphin was closely watched. The varying and multiform hues were clearly exhibited by the expiring fish. First its skin presented a golden shade, as if reflecting the sun, this changing gradually into a light purple. Presently the body became silvery white, followed slowly by alternating hues of pearl and yellow, and finally death left it of a dull, lustreless gray.

The market is about two hundred feet long, with one broad marble table extending from end to end. The roof is supported by a series of arches resting upon pillars. One side is entirely open to the street, thus insuring good ventilation. It is not far from the cathedral, and in the vicinity of the shore, but is in some measure superseded by the large central Mercado de Tacon in the Calzada de la Reina, one block from the Campo de Marte. In this latter market we saw shark's flesh sold for food and freely bought by the negroes and Chinese coolies.

The monopoly granted in Tacon's time to the famous smuggler whose name the fish-market on Mercaderes Street still bears has reverted to the government, which requires every fisherman, like every cab driver, to pay a heavy tax for the privilege of following his calling. The boatman who pulls an oar in the harbor for hire is obliged to pay the government for the simple privilege. A writer in a popular magazine lately compared these harbor boats of Havana to Venetian gondolas; but even poetical license will not admit of this. They do, however, almost precisely resemble the thousand and one boats which besprinkle the Pearl River at Canton, being of the same shape, and covered in the stern by a similar arched frame and canvas, the Chinese substituting for this latter the universal matting. The Havana boatmen have so long suffered from the extortion of the Spanish officials that they have learned the trick of it, and practice the same upon travelers who make no bargain with them before entering their tiny vessels.

The fish monopoly referred to was established under the governorship of Tacon, and is of peculiar origin. We cannot do better, perhaps, by way of illustrating his arbitrary rule, than to relate for the reader's benefit the story of its inauguration and enforcement.

One of the most successful rogues whose history is connected with that of modern Cuba was one Marti, who during his life was a prominent individual upon a limited stage of action. He first became known as a notorious and successful smuggler on the coast of the island, a daring and reckless leader of desperate men. At one time he bore the pretentious title of

King of the Isle of Pines, where he maintained a fortified position, more secure in its inaccessibility than for any other reason. From hence Marti dispatched his small fleet of cutters to operate between Key West and the southern coast of Cuba, sometimes extending his trips to Charleston, Savannah, and even to New Orleans. With the duty at ten dollars a barrel on American flour legitimately imported into the island, it was a paying business to smuggle even that prosaic but necessary article from one country to the other, and to transport it inland for consumption. By this business Marti is said to have amassed a large amount of money. He is described as having been a tall, dark man of mixed descent, Spanish, Creole, and mulatto. His great physical strength and brute courage are supposed to have given him precedence among his associates, added to which he possessed a large share of native shrewdness, cunning, and business tact. His masquerading capacity, if we may believe the current stories told of him, was very remarkable, enabling him to assume almost any disguise and to effectually carry it out, so as to go safely among his enemies or the government officials and gain whatever intelligence he desired. Little authentic information can be had of such a man, and one depends upon common report only in making up a sketch of his career; but he is known to have been one of the last of the Caribbean rovers, finally turning his attention to smuggling as being both the safer and more profitable occupation. The southern coast of Cuba is so formed as to be peculiarly adapted to the business of the contrabandists, who even to-day carry on this adventurous game with more or less impunity, being stimulated by the excessive and unreasonable excise duties imposed upon the necessities of life.

When Tacon first arrived in the colony he found the revenue laws in a very lax condition. Smuggling was connived at by the venal authorities, and the laws, which were so stringent in the letter, were practically null and void. It is said that Marti could land a contraband cargo, at that time, on the Regla side of Havana harbor in broad daylight without fear of molestation. The internal affairs of the island were also in a most confused condition; assassinations even in the streets of Havana were frequent, and brigandage was carried on in the near environs of the city. The Governor seemed actuated by a determination to reform these outrages, and set himself seriously about the business. He found that the Spanish vessels of the navy sent hither to sustain the laws lay idly in port, the officers passing their time in search of amusement on shore, or in giving balls and dances on board their ships. Tacon saw that one of the very first moves essential to be made was to suppress the wholesale system of smuggling upon the coast. The heretofore idle navy became infused with life and was promptly detailed upon this service, coasting night and day along the shore from Cape Antonio to the Point of Maysi, but to little or no good effect. A few captures were made, but the result was only to cause a greater degree of caution on the part of the contrabandists. In vain were all the measures taken by the officials. The smuggling was as successful as ever, and the law was completely defied. At last, finding that his expeditions against the outlaws failed, partly from their adroitness and bravery and partly from want of pilots capable of guiding attacking parties among the shoals frequented by the smugglers, a large and tempting reward in gold was offered to any one of them who would desert his comrades and act as pilot to the King's ships. At the same time a double reward was offered for the person of Marti, dead or alive, as he was known to be the leader of the desperate men who so successfully defied the authorities. These offers were fully promulgated, and care was taken that those who were most interested should be made aware of their purport. But the hoped-for result did not ensue. There was either too much honor among the guilty characters to whom the bribe was offered to permit them to betray each other, or they feared the condign punishment which was the portion of all traitors among them. The government had done its best, but had failed to accomplish its object.

It was a dark, cloudy night in Havana, some three or four months subsequent to the offering of the rewards to which we have referred. Two sentinels were pacing back and forth before the main entrance of the Governor's palace which forms one side of the area inclosing the Plaza de Armas. The military band had performed as usual that evening in the Plaza and had retired. The public, after enjoying the music, had partaken of their ices and favorite drinks at La Domenica's and found their way to their homes. The square was now very quiet, the stillness only broken by the music of the fountain mingled with the tread of the two sentinels. The stars looked calmly down from between the rifts of hanging clouds which crowded one another onward as though bound to some important rendezvous, where they were to perform their part in a pending storm. A little before midnight a tall figure, wrapped in a half military cloak, might have been observed watching the two guards from behind the marble statue of Ferdinand. After observing that they paced their apportioned walk, meeting each other face to face, and then separated, leaving a brief moment when the eyes of both were turned away from the entrance they were placed to guard, the stranger seemed to calculate the chances of passing them without being discovered. It was an exceedingly delicate manœuvre, requiring great care and dexterity. Watching for the favorable moment the purpose was, however, accomplished; the tall man in the cloak at a bound passed within the portal and quickly secreted himself in the shadows of the inner court. The sentinels paced on undisturbed.

The individual who had thus stealthily effected an entrance within the gates of the palace now sought the broad marble steps which led to the Governor's business suite of rooms, with a confidence that evinced a perfect knowledge of the place. A second sentinel was to be passed at the head of the stairs, but, assuming an air of authority, the stranger gave a formal military salute and passed quickly forward as though there was not the least question as to his right to do so. The drowsy guard promptly presented arms, doubtless mistaking him for some regular officer of the Governor's staff. The stranger boldly entered the Governor's reception-room and closed the door behind him. In a large chair sat the commander-in-chief before a broad table, engaged in writing, but he was quite alone. An expression of undisguised satisfaction passed across the weather-beaten countenance of the new-comer at this state of affairs, as he coolly cast off his cloak, tossed it carelessly over his arm, and proceeded to wipe the perspiration from his face. The Governor, looking up with surprise and fixing his keen eyes upon the intruder, asked peremptorily : —

" Who enters here unannounced and at this hour ? "

" One who has important information to impart to the government," was the quiet reply.

" But why seek this manner of audience ? "

" For reasons, Excellency, that will soon appear."

" How did you pass the guard unchallenged ? "

" Do not mind that for the present, Excellency."

" But I do mind it very seriously."

" It can be explained by and by."

" Very well," said the Governor, "speak quickly then. What is your business here ? "

" Excellency, you have publicly offered a handsome reward for any information concerning the contrabandists," continued the stranger. " Is it not so ? "

" Ha ! " said the Governor, " is that your errand here ? What have you to say about those outlaws ? Speak, speak quickly."

" Excellency, I must do so with caution," said the stranger, " otherwise I may condemn myself by what I have to communicate."

" Not so," interrupted Tacon, " the offer " —

" I know, Excellency, a free pardon is promised to him who shall turn state's evidence, but there may be circumstances " —

" The offer is unconditional, as it regards pardon."

" True, but "—

" I say you have naught to fear," continued Tacon ; " the offered reward involves unconditional pardon to the informant."

" You offer an additional reward, Excellency, for the discovery of the leader of the contrabandists, Captain Marti."

"Ay."

"It is a full revelation I have come hither to make."

"Speak, then."

"First, Excellency, will you give me your knightly word that you will grant a free pardon to me, a personal pardon, if I reveal all that you require?"

"I pledge you my word of honor," replied the Governor.

"No matter how heinous in the eyes of the law my offenses may have been, still you will pardon me under the King's seal?"

"Why all this reiteration?" asked Tacon impatiently.

"Excellency, it is necessary," was the reply.

"I will do so, if you reveal truly and to any good purpose," answered the Governor, weighing carefully in his mind the purpose of all this precaution.

"Even if I were a leader among these men?"

The Governor hesitated but for a single moment, while he gave the man before him a searching glance, then said: —

"Even then, be you whom you may, if you are able and willing to pilot our ships and reveal the rendezvous of Marti and his followers, you shall be rewarded and pardoned according to the published card."

"Excellency, I think that I know your character well enough to fully trust these words, else I should not have ventured here."

"Speak, then, and without further delay. My time is precious," continued the Governor with manifest impatience, and half rising from his seat.

"It is well. I will speak without further parley

The man for whom you have offered the largest reward — ay, dead or alive — is before you!"

"And you are" —

"Captain Marti!"

Tacon had not expected this, but supposed himself talking to some lieutenant of the famous outlaw, and though no coward he instinctively cast his eyes towards a brace of pistols that lay within reach of his right hand. This was but for a moment; yet the motion was not unobserved by his visitor, who, stepping forward, drew a couple of similar weapons from his own person and laid them quietly on the table, saying: —

"I have no further use for these; it is to be diplomacy for the future, not fighting."

"That is well," responded the Governor; and after a few moments of thought he continued: "I shall keep my promise, be assured of that, provided you faithfully perform your part, notwithstanding the law demands your immediate punishment. For good reasons, as well as to secure your faithfulness, you must remain under guard," he added.

"I have anticipated that, and am prepared," was the reply.

"We understand each other then."

Saying which he rang a small silver bell by his side, and issued a verbal order to the attendant who responded. In a few moments after, the officer of the watch entered, and Marti was placed in confinement, with directions to render him as comfortable as possible under the circumstances. His name was withheld from the officers.

Left alone, the Governor mused for a few moments thoughtfully over the scene which we have described, then, summoning the officer of the guard, demanded that the three sentinels on duty should be relieved and brought at once before him. What transpired between them was not made public, but it was known on the following day that they had been condemned to the chain-gang for a whole month. Military law is rigid.

On the subsequent day, one of the light-draught corvettes which lay under the guns of Moro Castle suddenly became the scene of the utmost activity, and before noon had weighed anchor and was standing out of the harbor. Captain Marti was on board acting as pilot, and faithfully did he guide the government ship in the discharge of her errand among the bays and shoals of the southern coast. For more than a month he was engaged in this piloting to all the secret haunts and storage places of the contrabandists, but it was observed that very few stores were found in them! On this famous expedition one or two small vessels were taken and destroyed in the bays of the Isle of Pines, but not one of the smugglers was captured. Information of the approach of the would-be captors was always mysteriously conveyed to them, and when a rendezvous was reached the occupants, it was found, had fled a few hours previously! The amount of property secured was very small, but still the organization which had so long and so successfully defied the government was broken up, and the smugglers' place of rendezvous became known. Marti returned with the ship to claim his reward. Tacon was well satisfied with the result and with the manner in which the ex-smuggler had fulfilled his agreement. The officials did not look very deeply into the business, and they believed that Marti had really betrayed his former comrades. The Governor-General summoned him to his presence and said to Marti: —

"As you have faithfully performed your part of our agreement, I am prepared to fulfill mine. In this package you will find a free and unconditional pardon for all your past offenses against the law. Mark the word *past* offenses," reiterated the Governor. "Any new disloyalty on your part shall be as promptly and rigorously treated as though these late services had never been rendered. And here is an order upon the treasury for the sum" —

"Excellency, excuse me," said the pardoned smuggler, stepping back, and holding up his hand in significance of declining the reward.

"What does this mean?" asked Tacon.

"Permit me to explain, Excellency."

"What, more conditions?" asked the Governor.

"The pardon, Excellency, I gladly receive," continued Marti. "As to the sum of money you propose to give me, let me make you a proposal."

"Speak out. Let us know what it is."

"The treasury is poor," said the ex-smuggler, "I am rich. Retain the money, and in place of it guarantee me alone the right to fish on the coast of Cuba, and declare the business of supplying the people with fish contraband, except to me and my agents. This will amply compensate me, and I will erect a public market at my own expense, which shall be an ornament to the city, and which at the expiration of twenty-five years shall revert to the government."

"So singular a proposition requires to be considered," said the Governor.

"In the mean time I will await your commands," said Marti, preparing to leave.

"Stay," said the Governor. "I like your proposal, and shall probably accede to it; but I will take a day to give it careful thought."

As Tacon said, he was pleased with the idea from the outset. He saw that he was dealing with a thorough man of business. He remembered that he should always have the man under his control, and so the proposal was finally accepted and confirmed.

The ci-devant smuggler at once assumed all the rights which this extraordinary grant gave to him. Seeking his former comrades, they were all employed by Marti on profitable terms as fishermen, and realized an immunity from danger not to be expected in their old business. Having in his roving life learned where to seek fish in the largest quantities, he furnished the city bountifully with the article, and reaped a large annual profit, until the period expired for which the monopoly was granted, and the market reverted to the government.

Marti, in the mean time, possessing great wealth, looked about him to see in what enterprise he could best invest it. The idea struck him that if he could obtain some such agreement relating to theatricals in Havana as he had enjoyed in connection with the fishery on the coast, he could make a profitable business of it. He was granted the privilege he sought, provided he should build one of the largest and best appointed theatres in the world on the Paseo, and name it the Tacon Theatre. This agreement he fulfilled. The detailed conditions of this monopoly were never made public.

Many romantic stories are told relating to Captain Marti, but these are the only ones bearing upon the subject of our present work which are believed to be authentic.

Of all the Governors-General who have occupied that position in Cuba, none are better known at home or abroad than Tacon, though he filled the post but four years, having been appointed in 1834, and returning to Spain in 1838. His reputation at Havana is of a somewhat doubtful character, for although he followed out with energy the various improvements suggested by Arranjo, yet his modes of procedure were often so violent that he was an object of terror to the people generally rather than one of gratitude. It must be admitted that he vastly improved the appearance of the capital and its vicinity, built a new prison, rebuilt the Governor's palace, constructed several new roads in the environs, including the Paseo bearing his name, and opened a large parade-ground just outside the old city walls, thus laying the foundation of the new city which has sprung up in the formerly desolate neighborhood of the Campo de Marte. Tacon also practically suppressed the public gaming-houses, but this radical effort to check an inherent vice only resulted in transferring the gambling-tables of the private houses devoted to the purpose into the public restaurants, which was not much of an improvement.

In one important matter he was more successful; namely, in instituting a system of police, and rendering the streets of Havana, which were formerly infested with robbers, as secure as those of most of our American cities. But his reforms were all consummated with a rude, arbitrary arm, and in a military fashion. Life or property were counted by him of little value, if either required to be sacrificed for his purpose. Many people fell before his relentless orders. There was undoubtedly much of right mingled with his wrongs, but if he left lasting monuments of energy and skill behind him, he also left many tombs filled by his victims. Notwithstanding all, there seemed to be throughout his notable career a sort of romantic spirit of justice — wild justice — prompting him. Some of the stories still current relating to him go far to show this to have been the case, while others exhibit the possibilities of arbitrary power, as exercised in the contract with Captain Marti.

On January 6th, the day of Epiphany, the negroes of Havana, as well as in the other cities of the island, make a grand public demonstration; indeed, the occasion may be said to be given up to them as a holiday for their race. They march about the principal streets in bands, each with its leader got up like a tambour major, and accompanied by rude African drum notes and songs. They are dressed in the most fantastic and barbarous disguises, some wearing cow's horns, others masks representing the heads of wild beasts, and some are seen prancing on dummy horses. All wear the most gorgeous colors, and go from point to point on the plazas and paseos, asking for donations from every one they meet. It is customary to respond to these demands in a moderate way, and the greatest reasonable latitude is given to the blacks on the occasion; reminding one of a well-manned ship at sea in a dead calm, before the days of steam, when all hands were piped to mischief. But what it all means except improving a special occasion for wholesale noise, grotesque parading, and organized begging, it will puzzle the stranger to make out. Among the colored performers there is but a small proportion of native Africans, that is, negroes actually imported into Cuba; most of them are direct descendants, however, from parents who were brought from the slave coast, but it must be remembered that none have been imported for about thirty years.

The Isle of Pines, which has been more than once alluded to in these notes, is situated less than forty miles south of Cuba, being under the jurisdiction of the Governor-General of Havana. It is forty-four miles long and nearly as wide, having an area of between twelve and thirteen hundred square miles. It is supposed that there are about two thousand inhabitants, though Spanish statistics are not to be relied upon. Like Cuba, it has a mountain range traversing the middle for its whole length, but the highest portion does not reach quite two thousand feet. The island has several rivers and is well watered by springs. The climate is pronounced to be even more salubrious than that of Cuba, while the soil is marvelously fertile. An English physician, who, with a patient, passed a winter at Nueva Gerona, which has a population of only a hundred souls, says the climate is remarkably bland and equable, especially adapted for pulmonary invalids. The coast is deeply indented by bays, some of which afford good anchorage, though the island is surrounded by innumerable rocky islets or keys. The Isle of Pines is very nearly in the same condition in which Columbus found it in 1494, containing a large amount of precious woods, and some valuable mines of silver, iron, sulphur, quicksilver, and quarries of beautifully variegated marble. It is reached by special steamers from Havana, not oftener than once a month.

CHAPTER XI.

The Havana Lottery. — Its Influence. — Hospitality of the Cubans. — About Bonnets. — The Creole Lady's Face. — Love of Flowers. — An Atmospheric Narcotic. — The Treacherous Indian Fig. — How the Cocoanut is propagated. — Cost of Living in Cuba. — Spurious Liquors. — A Pleasant Health Resort. — The Cock-Pit. — Game-Birds. — Their Management. — A Cuban Cock-Fight. — Garden of the World. — About Birds. — Stewed Owl ! — Slaughter of the Innocents. — The Various Fruits.

THERE is a regularly organized lottery in Havana, to which the government lends its name, and which has semi-monthly drawings. These drawings are made in public, and great care is taken to impress the people with the idea of their entire fairness. The authorities realize over a million dollars annually by the tax which is paid into the treasury on these most questionable enterprises. The lottery is patronized by high and low, the best mercantile houses devoting a regular sum monthly to the purchase of tickets on behalf of their firms. One individual of this class told the writer that no drawing had taken place within the last ten years at Havana in which the firm of which he was a member had not been interested to the extent of at least one doubloon, that is, one whole ticket. The mode usually is, however, to purchase several fractional parts of tickets, so as to multiply the chances. On being asked what was the result of the ten years of speculation in this line, the reply was that the books of the firm would show, as it was entered therein like any other line of purchases.

Curious to find an authentic instance as an example, the matter was followed up until the result was found. It seemed that this house had averaged about four hundred dollars per annum expended for lottery tickets, that is, four thousand dollars in the last ten years. On the credit side they had received in prizes about nineteen hundred dollars, making a loss of twenty-one hundred dollars. " But then," remarked our informant, "we may get a big prize one of these days, — who knows?"

The lottery here proves to be as great a curse as it does in Italy, where its demoralizing effects are more apparent. The poorer classes, even including the slaves and free negroes, are regular purchasers, and occasionally a prize is realized among them, which stimulates to increased ventures. A few years since, some slaves upon a plantation near Alquizar purchased a single ticket, clubbing together in order to raise the money. These Africans drew a prize of forty thousand dollars, which sum was honestly paid to them, and they purchased their freedom at once, dividing a very pretty amount for each as a capital to begin business on his own account.

" And pray what became of those liberated men?" we asked of our informant. "Singular to say I can tell you," he answered. " Others felt the same interest you express, and they have been followed in their subsequent career. There were sixteen of the party, who realized equal portions of the prize. They were valuable slaves, and paid an average of fifteen hundred dollars each for their free papers. This left them a thousand dollars each. Two returned to Africa. Four joined the insurgents at Santiago, in 1870, and were probably shot. The remainder drank themselves to death in Havana, or died by fevers induced through intemperate habits." "Did you ever know a man, white or black, who drew a prize of any large amount, who was not the worse for it after a short time?" we asked. "Perhaps not," was his honest reply. A miserable creature came into the vestibule of the Telegrafo Hotel one day begging. After he had departed we were told that a few years ago he was possessed of a fortune. "Why is he in this condition?" we asked. "He was engaged in a good business," said our informant, "drew a large prize in the lottery, sold out his establishment, and gave himself up to pleasure, gambling, and drink. That is all that is left of him now. He has just come out of the hospital, where he was treated for paralysis."

Honestly conducted as these lotteries are generally believed to be, their very stability and the just payment of prizes but makes them the more baleful and dangerous in their influence upon the public. As carried on in Havana, the lottery business is the most wholesale mode of gambling ever witnessed. Though some poor man may become comparatively wealthy through their means, once in twenty years, yet in the mean time thousands are impoverished in their mad zeal to purchase tickets though it cost them the last dollar they possess. The government thus fosters a taste for gambling and supplies the ready means, while any one at all acquainted with the Spanish character must know that the populace need no prompting in a vice to which they seem to take intuitively. No people, unless it be the Chinese, are so addicted to all games of chance upon which money can be staked.

Spaniards, and especially Cuban Spaniards, receive credit for being extremely hospitable, and to a certain extent this is true; but one soon learns to regard the extravagant manifestations which so often characterize their domestic etiquette as rather empty and heartless. Let a stranger enter the house of a Cuban for the first time, especially if he be a foreigner, and the host or hostess of the mansion at once places all things they possess at his service, yet no one thinks for a single moment of interpreting this offer literally. The family vehicle is at your order, or the loan of a saddle horse, and in such small kindnesses they are always generous; but when they beg you to accept a ring, a book, or a valuable toy, because you have been liberal in your praise of the article, you are by no means to do so. Another trait of character which suggests itself in this connection is the universal habit of profuse compliment common among Cuban ladies. Flattery is a base coin at best, but it is current here. The ladies listen to these compliments as a matter of course from their own countrymen or such Frenchmen as have settled among them, but if an American takes occasion to express his honest admiration to a Creole, her delight is at once manifest. Both the French and Spanish are extremely gallant to the gentler sex, but it requires no argument to show that woman under either nationality is far less esteemed and honored than she is with us in America.

The bonnet, which forms so important a part of a lady's costume in Europe and America, is rarely worn by the Creoles, and strangers who appear on the streets of Havana with the latest fashion of this ever varying article are regarded with curiosity, though so many American and English ladies visit the island annually. In place of a bonnet, when any covering is considered desirable for the head, the Cuban ladies generally wear a long black veil, richly wrought, and gathered at the back of the head upon the clustered braid of hair, which is always black and luxuriant. More frequently, however, even this appendage is not seen, and they drive in the Paseo or through the streets with their heads entirely uncovered, save by the sheltering hood of the victoria. When necessity calls them abroad in the early or middle hours of the day, there is generally a canvas screen buttoned to the dasher and extended to the top of the calash, to shut out the too ardent rays of the sun. Full dress, on all state occasions, is black, but white is universally worn by the ladies in domestic life, forming a rich contrast to the olive complexions of the women. Sometimes in the Paseo, when enjoying the evening drive, these fair creatures indulge in strange contrasts of colors in dress. They also freely make use of a cosmetic called cascarilla, made from egg-shells finely powdered and mixed with the white of the egg. This forms an adhesive paste, with which they at times enamel themselves, so that faces and necks that are naturally dark resemble those of persons who are white as pearls.

There is one indispensable article, without which a Cuban lady would feel herself absolutely lost. The fan is a positive necessity to her, and she learns its coquettish and graceful use from childhood. Formed of various rich materials, it glitters in her tiny hand like a gaudy butterfly, now half, now wholly shading her radiant face, which quickly peeps out again from behind its shelter, like the moon from out a passing cloud. This little article, always costly, sometimes very expensive, in her hand seems in its eloquence of motion almost to speak. She has a witching flirt with it that expresses scorn; a graceful wave of complacence; an abrupt closing of it that indicates vexation or anger; a gradual and cautious opening of its folds that signifies reluctant forgiveness; in short, the language of the fan in the hand of a Cuban lady is a wonderfully adroit and expressive pantomime that requires no interpreter, for, like the Chinese written language, it cannot be spoken.

It may be the prodigality of nature in respect to Flora's kingdom which has retarded the development of a love for flowers among the people of the island. Doubtless if Maréchal Niel roses, Jacqueminots, jonquils, and lilies of the valley were as abundant with us in every field as clover, dandelions, and buttercups, we should hardly regard them with so much delight as we do. It is not common to see flowers under cultivation as they are at the North. They spring up too readily in a wild state from the fertile soil. One cannot pass over half a league on an inland road without his senses being regaled and delighted by the natural floral fragrance, heliotrope, honeysuckle, sweet pea, and orange blossoms predominating. The jasmine and Cape rose, though less fragrant, are delightful to the eye, and cluster everywhere among the hedges, groves, and coffee estates. There is a blossoming shrub, the native name of which we do not remember, but which is remarkable for its multitudinous crimson flowers, so seductive to the hummingbirds that they hover about it all day long, burying themselves in its blossoms until petal and wing seem one. At first upright, a little later the gorgeous bells droop downward and fall to the ground unwithered, being poetically called Cupid's tears. Flowers abound here which are only known to us in our hothouses, whose brilliant colors, like those of the cactus, scarlet, yellow, and blue, are quite in harmony with the surroundings, where everything is aglow. There was pointed out to us a specimen of the frangipanni, a tall and nearly leafless plant bearing a milkwhite flower, and resembling the tuberose in fragrance, but in form much like our Cherokee rose. This plant, it will be remembered, was so abundant and so pleasant to the senses as to attract the attention of the early explorers who accompanied Columbus across the sea.

There seems to be at times a strange narcotic influence in the atmosphere of the island, realized more especially inland, where the visitor is partially removed from the winds which commonly blow from the Gulf in the after part of the day. So potent has the writer felt this influence that at first it was supposed to be the effect of some powerful and medicinal plant abounding in the neighborhood; but on inquiry it was found that this delightful sense of ease and indolent luxuriousness was not an unusual experience, particularly among strangers, and was solely attributable to the narcotic of the soft climate. By gently yielding to this influence one seemed to dream while awake, and though the sense of hearing is diminished, that of the olfactories appears to be increased, and pleasant odors float on every passing breeze. One feels at peace with all human nature, and a sense of voluptuous ease overspreads the body. Others have experienced and remarked upon this sensation of idle happiness. The only unpleasant realizing sense during the enjoyment of this condition is the fear that some human voice, or some chance noise, loud and abrupt, may arouse the dreamer from his trance.

Specimens of the Indian fig, as it is called here, will be sure to attract the visitor's eye on his inland excursions. It clasps, entwines, and finally, serpent-like, kills the loftiest forest monarchs, and taking their place, firmly roots itself and becomes a stately tree, fattening upon its ill-gotten possession. Its unfading leaf of vivid green is beautiful to look upon, in spite of its known and treacherous character. In many respects it typifies the Spanish discoverers of this beautiful isle, who gradually possessed themselves of its glorious heritage by the destruction of its legitimate owners.

The manner in which that prolific tree, the cocoanut palm, is propagated was a curious and interesting study for a leisure hour, the germination having been with us heretofore an unsolved riddle. Within the hard shell of the nut, among the mass of rich creamy substance, near the large end, is a small white lump like the stalk of a young mushroom, called the ovule. This little finger-like germ of the future tree gradually forces itself through one of the three eyes always to be found on the cocoanut. What giant power is concealed within that tiny ovule, apparently so soft and insignificant! Having pierced its way through the first shell, it then gradually rends the outer coat of fibrous covering and curves upward towards the light. Into the inner shell which it has vacated, it throws little fibrous threads which slowly absorb the albumen, and thus sustain its new life as it rapidly develops. First a few leaves grow upward, which from the very outset begin to assume the pinnate form of the cocoanut leaf, while, stretching earthward, a myriad of little threads of roots bury themselves in the ground. Though the tree will grow to a height of sixty feet or more, these roots will never individually exceed the size of the fingers on one's hand. In five or six years the tree will produce its first cluster of cocoanuts, and for several years will go on increasing in fruitfulness and yielding a bountiful crop for fifty or sixty years. It was a constant wonder how these cocoanut trees could sustain an upright position with such a weight of ripening fruit clustered beneath the shade of their tufted tops.

As regards the cost of living in the island, it may be said to average higher to the stranger than in the United States. At the city hotels and large boarding houses the charge is modified from four or five dollars per day; if a special bargain is made for a considerable period, it is customary to give a reduction on transient rates of ten or fifteen per cent. Among the small towns in the interior, at the houses of entertainment, which are wretchedly poor as a rule, the charges are exorbitant, and strangers are looked upon as fair game. This, however, is no more so than in continental Europe, where, though the accommodations are better, the general treatment is the same. The luscious and healthful fruits of the country form a large share of the provisions of the table in Cuba, and are always freely provided. A fair quality of claret wine, imported from Spain, is also regularly placed before the guest free of charge, it being the ordinary drink of the people; but beware of calling for other wines, and particularly champagne, unless you are prepared to be swindled by the price charged in your bill. Of course you get only imitation champagne, — that is to be expected; you do the same nearly everywhere. There is not enough pure champagne manufactured in Europe to supply the Paris and London markets alone. The mode of cooking is very similar to the French, plus the universal garlic, which, like tobacco, appears to be a prime necessity to the average Spanish appetite. One does not visit Cuba, however, with the expectation of finding all the niceties of the table which are ordinary comforts at home, and therefore he is quite content to enjoy the delightful fruits of the country, the novel scenery, the curious vegetation, and the captivating climate, which cannot fail to compensate for many small annoyances.

One of the most pleasant and healthful resorts for a temporary home on the island is probably the small but thrifty town of Guines, situated about forty-five miles from Havana, with which it is connected by rail; indeed, this was the first railroad constructed in Cuba, that between Matanzas and Havana being the second. Both were mainly the result of American enterprise and capital. There are now a little over nine hundred miles of railroad in operation, and more is urgently demanded to open internal communication with important sections. The water communication along the southern and northern coasts is mostly depended upon, and a very well organized system is sustained by three or four lines of domestic steamers. The immediate locality of Guines is thought to be one of the most salubrious and best for invalids on the western division of the island, and is largely resorted to by Americans. It has generally more of the comforts considered necessary for persons in delicate health than can readily be obtained in

Havana, and one has here the quiet and retirement which it is impossible to find in the metropolis.

Here will be seen, as in all towns large or small in Cuba, a curious place of amusement of circular form, called a "pit," where the natives indulge their national passion for cock-fighting and gambling combined. It is astonishing how pugnacious and fierce these birds become by careful training; the instinct must be in them or it could not be so developed. When brought together and opposed to each other in battle, one must die, and often both do so, for they will fight as long as they can stand on their feet. The pit is always crowded, and the amount of money which changes hands daily in this cruel mode of gambling is very considerable. Women not infrequently attend these contests, but only those of the pariah class, certain back seats being reserved for them, while here and there may be seen a shovel-hatted priest, as eager in the result as the professionals themselves. The cock-pit is a circular building, thirty or forty feet in diameter, resembling on the outside a huge haystack. The size, however, is regulated according to the population of the immediate neighborhood. The seats are raised in a circle, one above another, about a central ring in which the contest takes place. The ground is covered with sawdust or tan. The birds are of a native game breed, and are subject from chickenhood to a peculiar course of treatment. The English game-cock is prized here only for crossing with the native breed. He cannot equal the Spanish bird in the necessary qualities of pluck and endurance.

The food of the game-cock when in training is regulated with great care, carefully weighed, and a certain number of ounces is given to him three times a day, so that the bird, like a race-horse, is never permitted to grow fat, but is kept in what is called fighting condition. Some days before a contest they are fed with a few ounces of raw meat once during the twenty-four hours, which, being kept always a little hungry, they devour with avidity. Greater care as to diet and exercise could not be taken by pugilists training for a conflict. The feathers of these fighting-cocks are closely cropped in a jaunty style; the neck and head, to the length of three inches, is completely plucked of all feathers, the comb being trimmed close to the crown. The flesh which is thus left bare is daily rubbed with rum until it becomes hardened and calloused. Brief encounters are permitted among them under proper restrictions, when they are young. No fear is felt that they will seriously injure each other, until they are old enough to have the sharp steel gaffs affixed upon the spurs with which nature has supplied them. Then, like men armed with sword and dagger, they attack each other with fatal earnestness, making the blood flow at every stroke. It is singular that the birds are so determined upon the fight that no amount of loud cries, or challenges between the betters, or jeers by the excited audience, disturbs them in the least.

The author witnessed one of these exhibitions at Guines. The fighting-ring of the cock-pit was some twelve feet in diameter, the seating capacity being arranged for about a hundred persons or more, and each bench was fully occupied. The two birds pitted against each other were carefully weighed, and the result was announced to the audience. They were then passed in review, held in the hands of their respective owners, and betting at once commenced as to which would win the victory. In the mean time the two birds seemed quietly awaiting their time, and by the knowing way in which both surveyed the surroundings and the assembled people, they really appeared as if they understood the business in hand. There was no struggling on their part to get out of the hands of those who held them. Presently they were passed into the care of the umpires, two of whom officiated, and who then affixed the steel gaffs to the spurs of the contestants. The two birds were then placed on the ground inside of the ring, opposite each other. No sooner did they feel themselves fairly on their feet than both crowed triumphantly, eying each other with fell intent.

Then commenced a series of bird-tactics, each partially advancing and pretending to retreat as if to draw on his antagonist, pecking the while at imaginary kernels of corn on the ground. In the mean time the audience almost held its breath in anticipation of the cunningly deferred onset. Presently the two birds, as if by one impulse, rushed towards each other, and a simultaneous attack took place. The contest, when the birds are armed with steel gaffs, rarely lasts more than eight or ten minutes before one or both are so injured as to end the fight. The money staked upon the fight is won by those backing the bird which survives, or is longest in dying. When the artificial spurs are not used, and the birds fight in their natural state, the battle sometimes lasts for an hour, but is always fatal in the end to one or the other, or both. Eyes are pecked out, wings and legs broken, necks pierced again and again; still they fight on until death ensues. During the fight the excitement is intense, and a babel of voices reigns within the structure, the betting being loud, rapid, and high. Thus in a small way the cock-fight is as cruel and as demoralizing as that other national game, the terrible bull-fight, indigenous to Spain and her colonies.

Cuba has justly been called the garden of the world, perpetual summer smiling upon its shores, and its natural wealth and possibilities baffling even the imagination. The waters which surround it, as we have seen, abound with a variety of fishes, whose bright colors, emulating the tints of precious stones and the prismatic hues of the rainbow, astonish and delight the eye of the stranger. Stately and peculiar trees enliven the picturesque landscape. Throughout the woods and groves flit a variety of birds, whose dazzling colors defy the palette of the artist. Here the loquacious parrot utters his harsh natural notes; there the red flamingo watches by the shore of the lagoon, the waters dyed by the reflection of his scarlet plumage. It would require a volume to describe the vegetable and animal kingdom of Cuba, but among the most familiar birds are the golden robin, the bluebird, the catbird, the Spanish woodpecker, the gaudy-plumed paroquet, and the pedoreva, with its red throat and breast and its pea-green head and body. There is also a great variety of wild pigeons, blue, gray, and white; the English lady-bird, with a blue head, scarlet breast, and green and white back; the indigo-bird, the golden-winged woodpecker, the ibis, and many smaller species, like the humming-bird. Of this latter family there are said to be sixty different varieties, each sufficiently individualized in size and other peculiarities to be easily identified by ornithologists. Some of these birds are actually no larger in body than butterflies, and with not so large a spread of wing. A humming-bird's nest, composed of cotton interlaced with horse-hair, was shown the author at Buena Esperanza, a plantation near Guines. It was about twice the size of a lady's thimble, and contained two eggs, no larger than common peas. The nest was a marvel of perfection, the cotton being bound cunningly and securely together by the long horse-hairs, of which there were not more than three or four. Human fingers could not have done it so deftly. Probably the bird that built the nest and laid the eggs did not weigh, all fledged, over half an ounce! Parrots settle on the sour orange trees when the fruit is ripe, and fifty may be secured by a net at a time. The Creoles stew and eat them as we do pigeons; the flesh is tough, and as there are plenty of fine water-fowl and marsh birds about the lagoons as easily procured, one is at a loss to account for the taste that leads to eating parrots. The brown pelican is seen in great numbers sailing lazily over the water and dipping for fish.

Strange is the ubiquity of the crows; one sees them in middle India, China, and Japan. They ravage our New England cornfields, and in Ceylon, — equatorial Ceylon, — they absolutely swarm. When one, therefore, finds them saucy, noisy, thieving, even in Cuba, it is not surprising that the fact should be remarked upon, though here the species differs somewhat from those referred to, being known as the Jack-crow or turkey-buzzard. In the far East, like the vulture, the crow is considered a natural scavenger or remover of carrion, and the same excuse is made for him in Cuba and Florida. But is he not more of a freebooter and feathered bandit, — in short, a prowling thief generally? Nature has few birds or animals upon her varied list with which we would find fault, but the crow, — well, having nothing to say in its favor, let us drop the subject. Parrots, paroquets, tiny indigo birds, pedorevas, and robins, — yes, these are all in harmony with mingled fragrance and sunshine, but the coal-black crow, with his bad habits and hoarse bird-profanity, bah! When these West Indian islands were first settled by Spanish emigrants, they were the home of myriads of birds of every tropical variety, but to-day the feathered beauties and merry songsters have been entirely driven away from some of the smaller islands, and decimated on others, by the demand for bird's wings with which to deck ladies' bonnets in Europe and America. Sportsmen have found it profitable to visit the tropics solely for the purpose of shooting these rainbow-colored creatures for ornaments. Aside from the loss to general interest and beauty in nature caused by this wholesale destruction of the feathered tribe, another and quite serious result has been the consequence. A plague of vermin has followed the withdrawal of these little insect-killers. It is so natural to look for them amid such luxuriant vegetation that they become conspicuous by their absence. Now and again, however, the ears are gratefully saluted by the trilling and sustained notes of some hidden songster, whose music is entirely in tune with the surrounding loveliness, but truly delightful song-birds have ever been rare in the low latitudes, where there is more of color than song.

Those agriculturists who possess sufficient means confine themselves solely to the raising of sugar, coffee, and tobacco, the former principally employing capital. Indian corn, which the first settlers found indigenous here, is quite neglected, and when raised at all it is used before ripening, almost universally, as green fodder; very little is ripened and gathered as grain. It is found that horses and cattle can be kept in good condition and strength, while performing the usual labor required of them, by feeding them on a liberal allowance of cornstalks, given in the green state, before the corn has begun to form on the cob. The Cubans will tell you that the nourishing principle which forms the grain is in the stalk and leaves, and if fed in that state before ripening further, the animals obtain all the sustaining properties which they require. The climate is particularly adapted to the raising of oranges, but there is very little attention given to propagating this universally popular fruit, more especially since the increased production which has taken place on the other side of the Gulf Stream in Florida. Three years after the seed of this fruit is deposited in suitable soil in Cuba the tree becomes ten or twelve feet in height, and in the fourth year rarely produces less than a hundred oranges, while at ten years of age it commonly bears three and four thousand, thus proving, with proper care, extremely profitable. It will be remembered that it is the longest lived of succulent fruit trees. There are specimens still extant in Cuba known to be one hundred years old. The oranges produced in Florida are of equally good quality, and bring a better price in the market, but the crop is subject to more contingencies and liability to loss than in Cuba. The frost not infrequently ruins a whole season's yield in the peninsula in one or two severe nights, while frost is never experienced upon the island.

It seems unreasonable that when the generous, fruitful soil of Cuba is capable of producing two or three crops of vegetables annually, the agricultural wealth of the island should be so poorly developed. Thousands upon thousands of acres of fertile soil are still in their virgin condition. It is capable of supporting a population of almost any density, — certainly from eight to ten millions of people might find goodly homes here, and yet the largest estimate at the present time gives only a million and a half of inhabitants. When one treads the fertile soil and beholds the clustering fruits in such abundance, the citron, the star-apple, the perfumed pineapple, the luscious banana, and other fruits for which our language has no name, not forgetting the various noble woods which caused Columbus to exclaim with pleasure, and to mention the palm and the pine growing together, characteristic types of Arctic and equatorial vegetation, we are struck with the thought of how much Providence and how little man has done for this Eden of the Gulf. We long to see it peopled by men who can appreciate the gifts of nature, men who are willing to do their part in recognition of her fruitfulness and who will second her spontaneous bounty.

Nowhere on the face of the globe would well-directed, intelligent labor meet with a richer reward, nowhere would repose from labor be so sweet. The hour of rest here sinks upon the face of nature with a peculiar charm; the night breeze, in never-failing regularity, comes with its gentle wing to fan the weary frame, and no danger lurks in its breath. It has free scope through the unglazed windows, and blowing fresh from the broad surface of the Mexican Gulf, it bears a goodly tonic to the system. Beautifully blue are the heavens and festally bright the stars of a tropical night, where familiar constellations greet us with brighter radiance and new ones charm the eye with their novelty. Preëminent in brilliancy among them is the Southern Cross, a galaxy of stars that never greets us in the North. At midnight its glittering framework stands erect. That solemn hour past the Cross declines. How glorious the nights where such a heavenly sentinel indicates the watches! "How often have we heard our guides exclaim in the savannas of Venezuela," says Humboldt, "or in the deserts extending from Lima to Truxillo, 'Midnight is past, the Cross begins to bend.'" Cuba is indeed a land of enchantment, where nature is beautiful and bountiful, and where mere existence is a luxury, but it requires the infusion of a sterner, a more self-reliant, self-denying and enterprising race to test its capabilities and to astonish the world with its productiveness.

CHAPTER XII.

Traveling by Volante. — Want of Inland Communication. — Americans Profitable Customers. — The Cruel National Game. — The Plaza de Toros. — Description of a Bull-Fight. — The Infection of Cruelty. — The Romans and Spaniards Compared. — Cry of the Spanish Mob: "Bread and Bulls!" — Women at the Fight. — The Nobility of the Island. — The Monteros. — Ignorance of the Common People. — Scenes in the Central Market, Havana. — Odd Ideas of Cuban Beggars. — An Original Style of Dude. — A Mendicant Prince.

THE volante, the national vehicle of Cuba, and until latterly the only one in common use upon the island, has been several times spoken of. It has been superseded, especially in Havana, just as steam launches are crowding out the gondolas on the canals of Venice. Our present notes would be quite incomplete without a description of this unique vehicle. It is difficult without experience to form an idea of its extraordinary ease of motion, or its appropriateness to the peculiarities of the country roads, where only it is now in use. At first sight, with its shafts sixteen feet long, and wheels six yards in circumference, one would think that it must be very disagreeable to ride in; but the reverse is the fact, and when seated the motion is most agreeable, like being rocked in a cloud. It makes nothing of the deep ruts and inequalities upon the execrable roads, but sways gently its low-hung, chaise-like body, and dashes over and through every impediment with the utmost facility. Strange as it may seem, it is very light upon the horse, which the postilion also bestrides. When traveling any distance, a second horse is added on the left, abreast of the first, and attached to the volante by an added whiffletree and traces. When there are two horses the postilion rides the one to the left, thus leaving the shaft-horse free of other weight than the vehicle.

If the roads are very rough, which is their chronic condition, and there is more than usual weight to carry, a third horse is often added, and he is placed abreast with the others, to the right of the shaft horse, being guided by a bridle rein in the hands of the calisero, as he is called. Heretofore the wealthy people took great pride in these volantes, a purely Cuban idea, and they were ornamented for city use at great expense with silver trimmings, and sometimes even in gold. A volante equipped in this style, with the gayly-dressed negro postilion, his scarlet jacket elaborately trimmed with gold or silver braid, his high jack-boots with big silver buckles at the knees, and huge spurs upon his heels, was quite a dashing affair, more especially if a couple of black-eyed Creole ladies constituted the freight.

Were it not for the few railroads and steamboat routes which are maintained, communication between the several parts of the island would be almost impossible. During the rainy season especially, inland travel is impracticable for wheels. China or Central Africa is equally well off in this respect. Nearly all transportation, except it be on the line of the railroads, is accomplished on mule-back, or on the little Cuban horses. The fact is, road making is yet to be introduced into the island. Even the wonderful volante can only make its way in the environs of cities. Most of the so-called roads resemble the bed of a mountain torrent, and would hardly pass for a cow-path in America. Nothing more clearly shows the undeveloped condition of the island than this absence of means for internal communication. In Havana and its immediate environs the omnibus and tramway afford facilities which are liberally patronized, though when the latter was first introduced it was considered such an innovation that it was most bitterly opposed by the citizens. Like the railroads, the tramway was the result of foreign enterprise, and has doubled the value of property in any direction within a couple of leagues of the city proper.

One of the most petty and most annoying experiences to which the traveler is subjected is the arbitrary tax of time and money put upon him by the small officials, of every rank, in the employment of the government. By this system of small taxes upon travelers, a considerable revenue is realized. Where this is known, it keeps visitors away from Cuba, which is just what the Spaniards pretend to desire, though it was found that the Creoles did not indorse any such idea. Americans leave half a million dollars and more annually in Havana alone, an estimate made for us by competent authority. Passports are imperatively necessary upon landing, and if the visitor desires to travel outside of the port at which he arrives a fresh permit is necessary, for which a fee is charged. In vain do you show your passport, indorsed by the Spanish consul at the port from which you embarked in America. The official shrugs his shoulders, and says it is the law. Besides, you are watched and your movements recorded at police headquarters; though in this respect Berlin is quite as uncomfortable for strangers as is the city of Havana. Despots must hedge themselves about in every conceivable way. Be careful about the contents of your letters sent from or received in Cuba. These are sometimes delivered to their address, and sometimes they are not. Your correspondence may be considered of interest to other parties as well as to yourself, in which case an indefinite delay may occur in the receipt thereof.

Of all the games and sports of the Spaniards, that of the bull-fight is the most cruel, and without one redeeming feature to excuse its indulgence. During the winter season, weekly exhibitions are given at Havana on each recurring Sunday afternoon, the same day that is chosen for the brutal sport in Madrid and other Spanish peninsular cities. The arena devoted to this purpose will seat about ten thousand persons. The ground upon which the fight takes place occupies about an acre, and is situated on the Regla side of the harbor, in the Plaza de Toros. The seats are raised one above another, in a complete circle, at a secure height from the dangerous struggle. Sometimes, in his furious onslaughts, the bull throws himself completely over the stout boards which separate him from the spectators, when a wild stampede occurs.

On the occasion of the fight witnessed by the author, after a shrill flourish of trumpets a large bull was let loose from apartments beneath the seats, the door of which opened into the arena. The poor creature came from utter darkness, where he had been kept for many hours, into a blaze of bright sunlight, which confused him for a moment, and he pawed the ground excitedly, while he rolled his big fierce eyeballs as though he suspected some trick had been played upon him. Presently, having become accustomed to the light, he glared from one side to the other as if to take in the situation, and see who it was that dared to oppose him.

In the ring, distributed here and there, were some half a dozen professional fighters on foot, called banderilleros and chulos, besides which there were two on horseback, known as picadors. The former held scarlet flags in their hands, with which to confuse and tease the bull; the latter were armed with a long pole each, at the end of which was a sharp piece of steel capable of wounding the bull, but not deeply or dangerously. These fighters were a hardened set of villains, if the human countenance can be relied upon as showing forth the inner man. They rushed towards the animal and flaunted their flags before his eyes, striving to excite and draw him on to attack them. They seemed reckless, but very expert, agile, and wary. Every effort was made to worry and torment the bull to a state of frenzy. Barbs were thrust into his neck and back by the banderilleros, with small rockets attached. These exploded into his very flesh, which they burned and tore. Thrusts from the horsemen's spears also gave harsh, if not dangerous wounds, so that the animal bled freely at many points.

When the infuriated beast made a rush at one of his tormentors, they adroitly sprang on one side, or, if too closely pressed, these practiced athletes with a handspring leaped over the high board fence. Whichever way he turned the bull met a fresh enemy and another device of torment, until at last the poor creature was frantically mad. The fight then became more earnest, the bull rushing first at one and then another of his enemies, but the practiced fighters were too wary for him; he could not change position so quickly as they could. Finally, the bull turned his attention to the horses and made madly first at the one which was nearest, and though he received a tearing wound along his spine from the horseman's spear, he ripped the horse's bowels open with his horns and threw him upon the ground, with his rider under him. The men on foot rushed to the rescue and drew off the bull by fresh attacks and by flaunting the flags before his eyes. In the mean time, the rider was got out from beneath the horse, which lay dying. The bull, finding that he could revenge himself on the horses, transferred his attention to the other and threw him to the ground with his rider, but received another long wound upon his own back. Leaving the two horses lying nearly dead, the bull again turned upon the banderilleros, rushing with such headlong speed at them that he buried his sharp horns several inches in the timbers of the fence. It was even a struggle for him to extract them. The purpose is not to give the bull any fatal wounds, but to worry and torment him to the last degree of endurance. This struggle was kept up for twenty minutes or more, when the poor creature, bleeding from a hundred wounds, seemed nearly exhausted. Then, at a sign from the director, there was a grand flourish of trumpets, and the matador, a skillful swordsman and the hero of the occasion, entered the ring to close with the bull, singly. The other fighters withdrew and the matador advanced with a scarlet flag in one hand and his naked sword in the other. The bull stood at bay, too much worn by the fight and loss of blood to voluntarily attack this single enemy. The matador advanced and lured him to an attack by flaunting his flag. A few feeble rushes were made by the bleeding animal, until, in a last effort to drive his horns into this new enemy, he staggered heavily forward. This time the matador did not leap to one side, but received the bull upon the point of his Toledo blade, which was aimed at a spot just back of the horns, where the brain meets the spinal column. As the bull comes on with his head bent down to the charge, this spot is exposed, and forms a fair target for a practiced hand. The effect was electrical. The bull staggered, reeled from side to side for an instant, and then fell dead. Four bulls were destroyed in a like manner that afternoon, and, in their gallant fight for their lives, they killed seven horses, trampling their riders in two instances almost fatally, though they are protected by a sort of leather armor on their limbs and body. During the fight with the second bull, which was an extremely fierce and powerful creature, a young girl of eighteen dressed in male attire, who was trained to the brutal business, took an active part in the arena with the banderilleros. One remarkable feat which she performed was that of leaping by means of a pole completely over the bull when he was charging at her. At Madrid, where the author witnessed a similar exhibition, the introduction of a young girl among the fighters was omitted, but otherwise the performance was nearly identical. At the close of each act of the murderous drama, six horses gayly caparisoned with bells and plumes dashed into the arena led by attendants, and chains being attached to the bodies of the dead animals, they were drawn out at great speed through a gate opened for the purpose, amid another flourish of trumpets and the shouts of the excited multitude.

The worst of all this is that the influence of such outrageous cruelty is lasting. It infects the beholders with a like spirit. In fact, it is contagious. We all know how hard the English people became in the time of Henry VIII. and Bloody Mary.

In this struggle of the bull ring there is no gallantry or true bravery displayed on the part of the professional fighters. They run but little personal risk, practiced as they are, sheltered and protected by artificial means and armed with keen weapons, whereas the bull has only his horns to protect himself from his many tormentors. There is no possible escape for him; his fate is sealed from the moment he enters the ring. All the true bravery exhibited is on his part; he is always the attacking party, and were the exhibition to be attempted in an open field, even armed as they are, he would drive every one of his enemies out of sight. The much-lauded matador does not take his position in front of the animal until it is very nearly exhausted by loss of blood and long-continued, furious fighting. In our estimation, he encounters far less risk than does the humblest of the banderilleros or chulos, who torment the bull face to face in the fullness of his physical strength and courage. Still, instances are not wanting wherein these matadors have been seriously wounded and even killed by a frantic and dying bull, who has roused himself for a last final struggle.

Whatever colonial modification the Spanish character may have apparently undergone in Cuba, the Creole is Castilian still in his love for the cruel sports of the arena. Great is the similitude also between the modern Spaniard and the ancient Roman in this respect. As the Spanish language more closely resembles Latin than does the Italian, so do the Spanish people show more of Roman blood than the natives of Italy themselves. *Panem et circenses* (bread and circuses!) was the cry of the old Roman populace, and to gratify their wishes millions of sesterces were lavished, and hecatombs of human victims slain in the splendid amphitheatres erected by the masters of the world in all the cities subject to their sway. And so *pan y toros* (bread and bulls!) is the imperious demand of the Spaniards, to which the government is forced to respond. The parallel may be pursued still further. The proudest ladies of Rome, maids and matrons, gazed with liveliest interest upon the dying gladiators who hewed each other in pieces, or on the Christians who perished in conflict with the wild beasts, half starved to give them battle. So the señoras and señoritas of Madrid, Seville, Malaga, and Havana enjoy, with keen delight, the terrible spectacle of bulls slaughtered by picadors and matadors, and gallant horses ripped up and disemboweled by the horns of their brute adversaries. It is true that the ameliorating spirit of Christianity is evinced in the changes which the arena has undergone. Human lives are no longer designedly sacrificed wholesale in the bloody contests, yet the bull-fight is sufficiently barbarous and atrocious. It is a national institution, indicative of national character.

To look upon the serenity of Cuban ladies, driving in the Paseo or listening to the nightly music in the Plaza de Isabella, one could not possibly imagine them to be lacking in tenderness, or that there was in them sufficient hardihood to witness such exhibitions as we have described, and yet one third of the audience on the occasion spoken of was composed of the gentler sex. They are almost universally handsome, being rather below the average height of the sex with us, but possessing an erect and dignified carriage. Their form, always rounded to a delicate fullness, is quite perfection in point of model. Their dark hair and olive complexions are well matched, — the latter without a particle of natural carmine. The eyes are a match for the hair, being large and beautifully expressive, with a most irresistible dash of languor in them, — but not the languor of illness. It is really difficult to conceive of an ugly woman with such eyes as they all possess in Cuba, — the Moorish, Andalusian eye. The Cuban women have also been justly famed for their graceful carriage, and it is indeed the poetry of motion, singular as it may appear, when it is remembered that for them to walk abroad is such a rarity. It is not the simple progressive motion alone, but also the harmonious play of features, the coquettish undulation of the face, the exquisite disposition of costume, and the modulation of voice, that engage the beholder and lend a happy charm to every attitude and every step.

The gentlemen as a rule are good-looking, though they are much smaller, lighter, and more agile than the average American. The lazy life they so universally lead tends to make them less manly than a more active one would do. It seems to be a rule among them never to do for themselves that which a slave can do for them. This is demonstrated in the style of the volante, where the small horse is made not only to draw the vehicle, but also to carry a large negro on his back as driver. Now, if reins were used, there would be no occasion for the postilion at all, but a Spaniard or Creole would think it demeaning to drive his own vehicle. With abundance of leisure, and the ever present influences of their genial clime, where the heart's blood leaps more swiftly to the promptings of the imagination and where the female form earliest attains its maturity, the West Indians seem peculiarly adapted for romance and for love. The consequent adventures constantly occurring among them often culminate in startling tragedies, and afford plots in which a French feuilletonist would revel.

The nobility of Cuba, so called, is composed of rather homespun material, to say the least, of it. There may be some fifty individuals dubbed with the title of marquis, and as many more with that of count, most of whom have acquired their wealth and position by carrying on extensive sugar plantations. These are sneeringly designated by the humble classes as sugar noblemen, and not inappropriately so, as nearly all of these aristocratic gentlemen have purchased their titles outright for money. Not the least consideration is exercised by the Spanish throne as to the fitness of these ambitious individuals for honorary distinction. It is a mere question of money, and if this be forthcoming the title follows as a natural sequence. Twenty-five thousand dollars will purchase any title. Such things are done in other lands, but not quite so openly. And yet the tone of Cuban society in its higher circles is found to be rather aristocratic and exclusive. The native of Old Spain does not endeavor to conceal his contempt for foreigners of all classes, and as to the Creoles, he simply scorns to meet them on social grounds, shielding his inferiority of intelligence under a cloak of hauteur, assuming the wings of the eagle, but possessing only the eyes of the owl. Thus the Castilians and Creoles are ever at antagonism, both socially and politically. The bitterness of feeling existing between them can hardly be exaggerated. The sugar planter, the coffee planter, the merchant, and the liberal professions stand in the order in which we have named them, as regards their relative degree of social importance, but wealth, in fact, has the same charm here as elsewhere in Christendom, and the millionaire has the entrée to all classes.

The Monteros or yeomanry of the island inhabit the less cultivated and cheaper portions of the soil, entering the cities only to dispose of their surplus produce, and acting as the marketmen of the populous districts. When they stir abroad, in nearly all parts of the island, they are armed with a sword, and in the eastern sections about Santiago, or even Cienfuegos, they also carry pistols in the holsters of their saddles. Formerly this was indispensable for self-protection, but at this time weapons are more rarely worn. Still the arming of the Monteros has always been encouraged by the authorities, as they form a sort of militia at all times available against negro insurrection, a calamity in fear of which such communities must always live. The Montero is rarely a slaveholder, but is frequently engaged on the sugar plantations during the busy season as an overseer, and, to his discredit be it said, he generally proves to be a hard taskmaster, entertaining an intuitive dislike to the negroes.

An evidence of the contagious character of cruelty

was given in a circumstance coming under the author's observation on a certain plantation at Alquizar, where a manifest piece of severity led him to appeal to the proprietor in behalf of a female slave. The request for mercy was promptly granted, and the acting overseer, himself a mulatto, was quietly reprimanded for his cruelty. "You will find," said our host, "that colored men always make the hardest masters when placed over their own race, but they have heretofore been much employed on the island in this capacity, because a sense of pride makes them faithful to the proprietor's interest. That man is himself a slave," he added, pointing to the sub-overseer, who still stood among the negroes, whip in hand.

The Montero sometimes hires a free colored man to help him in the planting season on his little patch of vegetable garden, in such work as a Yankee would do for himself, but these small farmers trust mostly to the exuberant fertility of the soil, and spare themselves all manual labor, save that of gathering the produce and taking it to market. They form, nevertheless, a very important and interesting class of the population. They marry very young, the girls at thirteen and fifteen, the young men from sixteen to eighteen, and almost invariably rear large families. Pineapples and children are a remarkably sure crop in the tropics. The increase among them during the last half century has been very large, much more in proportion than in any other class of the community, and they seem to be approaching a degree of importance, at least numerically, which will render them eventually like the American farmers, the bone and sinew of the land. There is room enough for them and to spare, for hardly more than one tenth of the land is under actual cultivation, a vast portion being still covered by virgin forests and uncleared savannas. The great and glaring misfortune — next to that of living under a government permitting neither civil nor religious liberty, where church and state are alike debased as the tools of despotism, — is their want of educational facilities. Books and schools they have none. Barbarism itself is scarcely less cultured. We were told that the people had of late been somewhat aroused from this condition of lethargy concerning education, and some effort has recently been made among the more intelligent to afford their children opportunities for instruction. But at the present writing, the Egyptian fellah is not more ignorant than the rural population of Cuba, who as a mass possess all the indolence and few of the virtues of the aborigines.

There is one highly creditable characteristic evinced by the Monteros as a class, and that is their temperate habits in regard to indulgence in stimulating drinks. As a beverage they do not use ardent spirits, and seem to have no taste or desire for the article, though they drink the ordinary claret — rarely anything stronger. This applies to the country people, not to the residents of the cities. The latter quickly contract the habit of gin drinking, as already described. There is one prominent vice to which the Monteros are indisputably addicted; namely, that of gambling. It seems to be a natural as well as a national trait, the appliances for which are so constantly at hand in the form of lottery tickets and the cock-pits that they can hardly escape the baleful influences. There are some who possess sufficient strength of character and intelligence to avoid it altogether, but with the majority it is the regular resort for each leisure hour. One of their own statesmen, Castelar, told the Spaniards, not long since, that gambling was the tax laid upon fools.

Perhaps the best place at which to study the appearance and character of the Monteros is at the Central Market, where they come daily by hundreds from the country in the early morning to sell their produce, accompanied by long lines of mules or horses with well-laden panniers. It is a motley crowd that one meets there, where purchasers and salesmen mingle promiscuously. From six to nine o'clock, A. M., it is the busiest place in all Havana. Negroes and mulattoes, Creoles and Spaniards, Chinamen and Monteros, men and women, beggars, purchasers, and slaves, all come to the market on the Calzada de la Reina. Here the display of fruits and vegetables is something marvelous, both in variety and in picturesqueness of arrangement. This locality is the natural resort of the mendicants, who pick up a trifle in the way of provisions from one and another, as people who do not feel disposed to bestow money will often give food to the indigent. This market was the only place in the city where it was possible to purchase flowers, but here one or two humble dealers came at early morn to dispose of such buds and blossoms as they found in demand. A blind Chinese coolie was found sitting on the sidewalk every morning, at the corner of the Calzada de la Reina, just opposite the market, and he elicited a trifle from us now and again. One morning a couple of roses and a sprig of lemon verbena were added to his small gratuity. The effect upon that sightless countenance was electrical, and the poor mendicant, having only pantomime with which to express his delight, seemed half frantic. The money fell to the ground, but the flowers were pressed passionately to his breast.

Did it remind him, we thought, of perfumes which had once delighted his youthful senses in far-off Asia, before he had been decoyed to a foreign land and into semi-slavery, to be deprived of health, liberty, sight, hope, everything?

The Cuban beggars have a dash of originality in their ideas as to the successful prosecution of their calling; we mean those " native and to the manor born." Some of them possess two and even three cadaverous dogs, taught to follow closely at their heels, as they wander about, and having the same shriveled-up, half-starved aspect as their masters. One beggar, who was quite a cripple, had his daily seat in a sort of wheelbarrow, at the corner of Paseo Street, opposite the Plaza de Isabella. This man was always accompanied by a parrot of gaudy plumage, perched familiarly on his shoulder. Now and then the cripple put some favorite bird-food between his own lips, which the parrot extracted and appropriated with such promptness as to indicate a good appetite. Another solicitor of alms, quite old and bent, had an amusing companion in a little gray squirrel, with a collar and string attached, the animal being as mischievous as a monkey, now and then hiding in one of the mendicant's several pockets, sometimes coming forth to crack and eat a nut upon his owner's shoulder. A blind beggar, of Creole nationality, sat all day long in the hot sun, on the Alameda de Paula near the Hotel San Carlos, whose companion was a chimpanzee monkey. The little half-human creature held out its hand with a piteous expression to every passer-by, and deposited whatever he received in his master's pocket. These pets serve to attract attention, if not commiseration, and we observed that the men did not beg in vain.

The acme of originality, however, was certainly reached in the case of a remarkable Creole beggar whose regular post is on the west corner of the Central Market. This man is perhaps thirty-five or forty years of age, and possesses a fine head, a handsome face, and piercing black eyes. He is of small body, and his lower limbs are so withered as to be entirely useless; so he sits with them curled up in a low, broad basket, in which he is daily brought to the spot, locomotion in his case being out of the question. He wears the cleanest of linen, and his faultless cuffs and ruffled shirt-bosom are decked with solid gold studs. He is bareheaded, but his thick black hair is carefully dressed, and parted with mathematical precision in the middle. He wears neither coat nor vest, but his lower garments are neatly adapted to his deformity, and are of broadcloth. This man does not utter a word, but extends his hand pleasantly, with an appealing look from his handsome eyes, which often elicits a silver real from the passer-by. We acknowledge to having been thus influenced more than once, in our morning walks, by a sympathy which it would be difficult to analyze. We had seen a colored dude selling canes at Nassau, but a dude mendicant, and a cripple at that, was a physical anomaly.

CHAPTER XIII.

Introduction of Sugar-Cane. — Sugar Plantations. — Mode of Manufacture. — Slaves on the Plantations. — African Amusements. — The Grinding Season. — The Coffee Plantations. — A Floral Paradise. — Refugees from St. Domingo. — Interesting Experiments with a Mimosa. — Three Staple Productions of Cuba. — Raising Coffee and Tobacco. — Best Soils for the Tobacco. — Agricultural Possibilities. — The Cuban Fire-Fly. — A Much-Dreaded Insect. — The Ceiba Tree. — About Horses and Oxen.

THE first sugar plantation established in Cuba was in 1595, nearly three hundred years since. These plantations are the least attractive in external appearance, but the most profitable pecuniarily, of all agricultural investments in the tropics, though at the present writing there is a depression in prices of sugar which has brought about a serious complication of affairs. The markets of the world have become glutted with the article, owing to the enormous over-production in Europe from the beet. The plantations devoted to the raising of the sugar-cane in Cuba spread out their extensive fields, covered with the corn-like stalks, without any relief to the eye, though here and there the graceful feathery branches of the palm are seen. The fields are divided off into squares of three or four acres each, between which a roadway is left for ox-teams to pass for gathering purposes. On some of the largest estates tramways have been laid, reaching from the several sections of the plantation to the doors of the grinding-mill. A mule, by this means, is enabled to draw as large a load as a pair of oxen on plain ground, and with much more ease and promptness.

About the houses of the owner and the overseer, graceful fruit trees, such as bananas and cocoanuts, with some flowering and fragrant plants, are grouped, forming inviting shade and producing a picturesque effect. Not far away, the low cabins of the blacks are half hidden by plantain and mango trees, surrounded by cultivated patches devoted to yams, sweet potatoes, and the like. Some of the small gardens planted by these dusky Africans showed judgment and taste in their management. Chickens and pigs, which were the private property of the negroes, were cooped up just behind the cabins. Many of these plantations employ from four to five hundred blacks, and in some instances the number will reach seven hundred on extensive estates, though the tendency of the new and improved machinery is to constantly reduce the number of hands required, and to increase the degree of intelligence necessary in those employed. Added to these employees there must also be many head of cattle, — oxen, horses, and mules. The annual running expenditure of one of these large estates will reach two hundred thousand dollars, more or less, for which outlay there is realized, under favorable circumstances, a million five hundred thousand pounds of sugar, worth, in good seasons, five cents per pound at the nearest shipping point.

There are a few of the small estates which still employ ox-power for grinding the cane, but American steam-engines have almost entirely taken the place of animal power; indeed, as we have shown, it will no longer pay to produce sugar by the primitive processes. This creates a constant demand for engineers and machinists, for whom the Cubans depend upon this country. We were told that there were not less than two hundred Bostonians at the present time thus engaged on Cuban estates. A Spaniard or Creole would as soon attempt to fly like a bird as to learn how to run a steam-engine or regulate a line of shafting. It requires more intelligence and mechanical skill, as a rule, than the most faithful slaves possess. A careful calculation shows that in return for the services of this small band of employees taken from our shores, this country takes eighty per cent. of all the sugar produced upon the island! Twelve per cent. is consumed by peninsular Spain, thus leaving but eight per cent. of this product for distribution elsewhere.

During the grinding season, which begins about the first of December and ends in April, a large, well-managed sugar plantation in Cuba is a scene of the utmost activity and most unremitting labor. Time is doubly precious during the harvesting period, for when the cane is ripe there should be no delay in expressing the juice. If left too long in the field it becomes crystallized, deteriorating both in its quality and in the amount of juice which is obtained. The oxen employed often die before the season is at an end, from overwork beneath a torrid sun. The slaves are allowed but four or five hours sleep out of the twenty-four, and being worked by watches during the night, the mill does not lie idle for an hour after it is started until the grinding season is closed. If the slaves are thus driven during this period, throughout the rest of the year their task is comparatively light, and they may sleep ten hours out of the twenty.

four, if they choose. According to the Spanish slave code, — always more or less of a dead letter, — the blacks can be kept at work in Cuba only from sunrise to sunset, with an interval of two hours for repose and food in the middle of the day. But this is not regarded in the sugar harvest season, which period, after all, the slaves do not seem so much to dread, for then they are granted more privileges and are better fed, given more variety of food and many other little luxuries which they are known to prize.

On Sunday afternoons and evenings on most of the plantations the slaves are given their time, and are permitted, even in the harvest season, to amuse themselves after their own chosen fashion. On such occasions the privilege is often improved by the blacks to indulge in native African dances, crude and rude enough, but very amusing to witness. The music for the dancers is supplied by a home-made drum, and by that alone, the negro who plays it being to the lookers-on quite as much of a curiosity as those who perform the grotesque dances. This humble musician writhes, wriggles, twists himself like a corkscrew, and all the while beats time, accompanying his notes with cries and howls, reminding one of the Apache Indian when engaged in a war dance. It is astonishing to witness to what a degree of excitement this negro drummer will work himself up, often fairly frothing at the mouth. A buxom wench and her mate step forward and perform a wild, sensuous combination of movements, a sort of negro can-can, like those dancing girls one sees in India, striving to express sentiments of love, jealousy, and passion by their pantomime, though these negroes are far less refined in their gestures. When these two are exhausted, others take their place, with very similar movements. The same drummer labors all the while, perspiring copiously, and seeming to get his full share of satisfaction out of the queer performance. This is almost their only amusement, though the Chinese coolies who have been distributed upon the plantations have taught the negroes some of their queer games, one, particularly, resembling dominoes. The author saw a set of dominoes made out of native ebony wood by an African slave, which were of finer finish than machinery turns out, delicately inlaid with ivory from alligators' teeth, indicating the points upon each piece. We were told that the only tool the maker had with which to execute his delicate task was a rude jack-knife. We have said that the negroes find in the singular dance referred to their one amusement, but they sometimes engage among themselves in a game of ball, after a fashion all their own, which it would drive a Yankee base-ball player frantic to attempt to analyze.

The sugar-cane yields but one crop in a year. There are several varieties, but the Otaheitan seems to be the most generally cultivated. Between the time when enough of the cane is ripe to warrant the getting-up of steam at the grinding-mill and the time when the heat and the rain spoil its qualities, all the sugar for the season must be made; hence the necessity for great industry on the large estates. In Louisiana the grinding season lasts but about eight weeks. In Cuba it continues four months. In analyzing the sugar produced on the island and comparing it with that of the mainland, — the growth of Louisiana, — chemists could find no difference as to the quality of the true saccharine principle contained in each. The Cuban sugar, compared with beet-sugar, however, is said to yield of saccharine matter one quarter more in any given quantity.

In society the sugar planter holds a higher rank than the coffee planter, as we have already intimated; merely in the scale of wealth, however, for it requires five times the capital to carry on a sugar estate that would serve for a coffee estate. Some of the large sugar plantations have been owned and carried on by Jesuit priests — we were about to write ex-Jesuit priests, but that would not be quite correct, for once a member of this order one is bound to it for all time. The priest or acknowledged member of the organization may be forced for prudential reasons to temporarily change his occupation, but he cannot sever himself from the responsibilities which he has once voluntarily assumed. There was a time when much of the landed and fertile property of the island was controlled by the Church, — in fact owned by it, though often by very questionable titles. The original owners, under cunning pressure, perhaps on a threatened death-bed, were induced to will all to the Church; or as an act of deep penance for some crime divulged at the confessional, they yielded up all. To preserve this property and possibly to cause it to produce an income for the Church, certain priests became active planters. Extreme ecclesiastic rule, as has been said, is greatly modified in Spain and her colonies, the natural reaction of the hateful days of the Inquisition.

As the sugar plantation surpasses the coffee in wealth, so the coffee estate surpasses the sugar in every natural beauty and attractiveness. A coffee plantation, well and properly laid out, is one of the most beautiful gardens that can well be conceived of, in its variety and loveliness baffling description. An estate devoted to this purpose usually covers a hundred acres, more or less, planted in regular squares of one acre or thereabouts, intersected by broad alleys lined with palms, mangoes, bananas, oranges, and other fruits; as the coffee, unlike the sugar cane, requires partial protection from the ardor of the sun. Mingled with the trees are lemons, limes, pomegranates, Cape jasmines, and a species of wild heliotrope, fragrant as the morning. Occasionally in the wide reach of the estate there is seen a solitary, broad-spreading ceiba, in hermit-like isolation from other trees, but shading a fragrant undergrowth. Conceive of this beautiful arrangement, and then of the whole when in flower; the coffee, with its milk-white blossoms, so abundant that it seems as though a pure white cloud of snow had fallen there, and left the rest of the vegetation fresh and green. Interspersed in these fragrant alleys dividing the coffee plants is the red of the Mexican rose, the flowering pomegranate, the yellow jasmine, and the large, gaudy flower of the penon, shrouding its parent stem in a cloak of scarlet. Here too are seen clusters of the graceful yellow flag, and many wild flowers, unknown by name, entwining their tender stems about the base of the fruit trees. In short, a coffee plantation is a perfect floral paradise, full of fragrance and repose.

The writer's experience was mainly gained at and about the estate of the late Dr. Finley, a Scotch physician long resident upon the island. He had named his plantation after the custom with a fancy title, and called it Buena Esperanza. Here was seen the mignonette tree twenty feet high, full of pale yellow and green blossoms, as fragrant as is its little namesake, which we pet in our conservatories. There were also fuchsias, blue, red, yellow, and green, this last hue quite new to us. The night-blooming cereus was in rank abundance, together with the flor de pascua, or Easter flower, so lovely in its cream-colored, wax-like blossom. The Indian poui, with its saffron-colored flowers, was strikingly conspicuous, and there too was that pleasant little favorite, the damask rose. It seemed as if all out-doors was an exotic garden, full of marvelous beauty. What daily miracles nature is performing under our only half-observant eyes! Behold, where the paths intersect each other, a beautiful convolvulus has entwined itself about that dead and decaying tree, clothing the gray old trunk with pale but lovely flowers; just as we deck our human dead for the grave.

It was the revolution in San Domingo which gave the first great stimulus to the culture of the coffee plant in Cuba, an enterprise which has gradually faded out in the last decade, though not absolutely obliterated. The refugees from the opposite shore sought shelter wherever they could find it among the nearest islands of the Archipelago, and large numbers made their new homes in the eastern department of Cuba, near the cities of Trinidad and Santiago. Here they turned lands which had been idle for three and four centuries into smiling gardens, and the production of the favorite berry became very profitable for a series of years, many cargoes being shipped annually to this country from the two ports just named. The production of sugar, however, has always maintained precedence, dividing the honor to-day only with tobacco in the manufactured state. Coffee does not figure to any extent in the statistics of exports. Exorbitant taxation and the cruel ravages of civil war, in the coffee districts especially, are largely the cause of the loss of an important and profitable industry.

Some amusing experiments with a mimosa or sensitive plant served to fill a leisure hour at Buena Esperanza, under our host's intelligent direction. It grew wild and luxuriantly within a few feet of the broad piazza of the country-house. Close by it was a morning-glory, which was in remarkable fullness and freshness of bloom, its gay profuseness of purple, pink, and variegated white making it indeed the glory of the morning. It was a surprise to find the mimosa of such similar habits with its neighbor, the morning-glory, regularly folding its leaves and going to sleep when the shades of evening deepened, but awaking bright and early with the first breath of the morn. So sensitive is this most curious plant, so full of nerves, as our host expressed it, that it would not only shrink instantly, like unveiled modesty, at the touch of one's hand, but even at the near approach of some special organisms, ere they had extended a hand towards it. Five persons tried the experiment before the sixth illustrated the fact that touch was not absolutely necessary to cause the leaves to shrivel up or shrink through seeming fear. Our host even intimated that when the mimosa had become familiar with a congenial person its timidity would vanish, and it could be handled gently by that individual without outraging its sensibility. Of this, however, we saw no positive evidence. If Mr. Darwin had supplemented his chapters on the monkey by a paper relating to the mimosa, he might possibly have enabled us to find a mutual confirmation in them of some fine-spun theory.

THREE STAPLE PRODUCTIONS. 245

The three great staple productions of Cuba are sugar, the sweetener; coffee, the tonic; and tobacco, the narcotic of half the world. The first of these, as we have shown, is the greatest source of wealth, having also the preference as to purity and excellence over any other saccharine production. Its manufacture also yields molasses, which forms an important article of export, besides which a spirituous liquor, called aguardiente, is distilled in considerable quantities from the molasses. The cane, which grows to about the size of a large walking-stick, or well-developed cornstalk, is cut off near the ground and conveyed in the green state, though it is called ripe, to the mill, where it is crushed to a complete pulp between stones or iron rollers. After the juice is thus extracted the material left is spread out in the sun to dry, and is after being thus "cured" used for fuel beneath the steam-boilers, which afford both power to the engine and the means of boiling the juice. Lime-water is employed to neutralize any free acid as well as to separate the vegetable matter. The granulation and crystallization are effected in large flat pans, or now more commonly by centrifugal machines, rotating at great speed. It is then crushed and packed either in hogsheads or in boxes for exportation; canvas bags are also being largely employed, as they are easier to pack on board ship, and also to handle generally. A plantation is renewed when deemed necessary, by laying the green canes horizontally in the ground, when new and vigorous shoots spring up from every joint, showing the great fertility of the soil.

Coffee was introduced by the French into Martinique in 1727, but it did not make its appearance in Cuba until forty years later, or, to be exact, in 1769.

The decadence of this branch of agriculture is due not only to the causes we have already named, but also to the inferior mode of cultivation adopted on the island. It was predicted some years before it commenced, and when the crash came the markets of the world were also found to be greatly overstocked with the article. While some planters introduced improved methods and economy in the conduct of their estates, others abandoned the business altogether, and turned their fields either into sugar-raising, fruits or tobacco. Precisely the same trouble was experienced in the island of Ceylon, which was at one time a great coffee-raising centre, but now its planters are many of them abandoning the business, while others adopt new seed and new methods of culture. In Cuba it was found that the plants had been grown too closely together and subjected to too close pruning, while the product, which was gathered by hand, yielded a mixture of ripe and unripe berries. In the countries where coffee originated, a very different method of harvesting is adopted. The Arabs plant the coffee-shrubs much farther apart, allow them to grow to considerable height, and gather the crop by shaking the tree, a method which secures only the ripe berries. After a few weeks, or even days, the field is gone over a second time, when the green berries have become fit to gather, and readily fall to the ground.

A coffee estate well managed, that is, combined with the rearing of fruits and vegetables intermingled, thus affording the required shade for the main crop, proves fairly profitable in Cuba to-day, and were this industry not hampered and handicapped by excessive taxes, it would attract many new planters. The

COFFEE ESTATES. 247

coffee ripens from August to December, the nuts then becoming about the size of our cherries. The coffee-berry is the seed of the fruit, two of which are contained in each kernel, having their flat surfaces together, surrounded by a soft pulp. The ripe berries are dried by exposure to the sun's rays, then bruised in a mill, by which means the seeds are separated from the berry. They are then screened to cleanse them, after which they are bagged, and the coffee is ready for market. Some planters take great care to sort their crop by hand, in which operation the negro women become very expert. By dividing the berries into first and second qualities as to size and cleanliness, a better aggregated price is realized for the entire harvest. Not only are the coffee estates much more pleasing to the eye than the sugar plantations, but they are also much more in harmony with the feelings of the philanthropist. There is here no such exigency in getting in the harvest, leading to the overwork of the slaves, as on a sugar estate in the grinding season. Indeed, we were assured that it was quite possible to carry on a coffee estate with white labor. When, heretofore, a negro has been brought to the block in Havana, or any other Cuban city, the price realized for him has always been materially affected by the question whether he had been employed on a sugar estate in the grinding season. If he had been thus employed it was considered that his life has been unduly shortened, and he sold accordingly at a lower price. At the present time few negroes are bought or sold, as their market value has become merely nominal. There is no good reason why white labor is not suited to the coffee and tobacco estates. When the field labor upon the sugar estates is almost wholly performed by machinery, that is, the cane cut by a reaper, there will be so much less exposure to the sun that white hands, under proper management, can perform it.

Tobacco, indigenous to both Cuba and the United States, is a great source of revenue upon the island. Its cultivation involves considerable labor and expense, as the soil must be carefully chosen and prepared, and the crop is an exhaustive one to the land; but the cultivation does not require machinery, like sugar-cane, nor quite so much care as does the growing coffee. It is valued in accordance with the locality from which it comes, some sections being especially adapted to its production. That of the greatest market value, and used in the manufacture of the highest-cost cigars, is grown in the most westerly division of the island, known as the Vuelta de Abajo (Lower Valley). The whole western portion of Cuba is not by any means suitable to the production of tobacco. The region of the best tobacco is comprised within a small parallelogram of very limited extent. Beyond this, up to the meridian of Havana, the tobacco is of fine color, but of inferior aroma. From Consolacion to San Christoval the tobacco is very "hot," — to use a local phrase, — harsh, and strong, and from San Christoval to Guanajay the quality is inferior up to Holguin y Cuba, where better tobacco is produced. The fertile valley of Los Guines produces poor smoking-tobacco, but an article excellent for the manufacture of snuff. On the banks of the Rio San Sebastian, are also some estates which produce the very best quality of tobacco. Thus it will be seen that certain properties of soil operate more directly in producing a fine grade of tobacco than any slight variation of climate. Possibly a chemical analysis of the soil of the Vuelta de Abajo would enable the intelligent cultivator to supply to other lands the ingredients wanted to make them produce equally good tobacco. A fairly marketable article, however, is grown in nearly any part of the island. Its cultivation is thought to produce a full ten per cent. upon the capital invested, the annual crop of Cuba being estimated in value at about twenty-three million dollars. The number of tobacco planters is said to be about fifteen thousand, large and small. On many tobacco farms the labor is nearly all performed by white hands. Some coolies and some negroes are also employed even on small estates.

When it is remembered that so small a portion of the land is under cultivation, and yet that Cuba exports annually a hundred million dollars worth of sugar and molasses, besides coffee, tobacco, fruits, and precious woods, it will be realized what might be accomplished, under a liberal system of government, upon this gem of the Caribbean Sea. Cacao, rice, plantains, indigo, and cotton, besides Indian corn and many nutritious vegetables, might be profitably cultivated to a much larger degree than is now done. It is a curious and remarkable fact, suggesting a striking moral, that with the inexhaustible fertility of the soil, with an endless summer that gives the laborer two and even three crops a year, agriculture generally yields in Cuba a lower percentage of profit than in our stern Northern latitudes, where the farmer has to wrench, as it were, the half-reluctant crop from the ground. It must be remembered that in Cuba there are numerous fruits and vegetables not enumerated in these pages, which do not enter into commerce, and which spring spontaneously from the fertile soil. In the possession of a thrifty population the island would be made to blossom like a rose, but as it now is, it forms only a garden growing wild, cultivated here and there in patches. None of the fine natural fruits have ever been improved by careful culture and the intelligent selection of kinds, so that in many respects they will not compare in perfection with our average strawberries, plums, pears, and peaches. Their unfulfilled possibilities remain to be developed by intelligent treatment.

The plantain, which may be said to be the bread of the common people, requires to be planted but once. The stem bears freely, like the banana of the same family, at the end of eight months, and then withering to the ground renews itself again from the roots. Sweet potatoes once planted require care only to prevent their too great luxuriance, and for this purpose a plough is passed through them before the wet season, and as many of the vines as can be freely plucked up are removed from the field. The sugar-cane, on virgin soil, will last and prove productive for twenty years. The coffee shrub or tree will bear luxuriantly for forty or fifty years. The cocoanut palm is peculiar to all tropical climates, and in Cuba, as in the Malacca Straits and India, bears an important share in sustaining the life of the people, supplying milk, shade, and material for a hundred domestic uses. It grows in luxuriant thriftiness all over the island, in high and low land, in forests, and down to the very shore washed by the Gulf Stream. It is always graceful and picturesque, imparting an oriental aspect to everything which surrounds it. It is esti mated that over ten million acres of native forests, covered by valuable wood, still remain untouched by the woodman's axe, especially on and about the mountain range, which extends nearly the entire length of the island, like the vertebræ of an immense whale.

About the coffee plantations, and indeed throughout the rural portions of the country, there is a curious little insect called a cocuyo, answering in its general characteristics and nature to our firefly, though it is quadruple its size, and far the most brilliant insect of its kind known to naturalists. They float in phosphorescent clouds over the vegetation, emitting a lurid halo, like fairy torch-bearers to elfin crews. One at first sight is apt to compare them to a shower of stars. They come in multitudes immediately after the wet season sets in, prevailing more or less, however, all the year round. Their advent is always hailed with delight by the slave children, as well as by children of a larger growth. They are caught by the slaves in any desired numbers and confined in tiny cages of wicker, giving them sufficient light in their cabins at night for ordinary purposes, and forming the only artificial light permitted them. We have seen a string of the little cages containing the glittering insects hung in a slave-cabin in festoons, like colored lamps in fancy-goods stores in America. The effect of the evanescent light thus produced is very peculiar, but the number of insects employed insures a sufficiently steady effect for ordinary purposes. These little creatures are brought into Havana by young Creole children and by women, for sale to the ladies, who sometimes in the evenings wear a small cage hung to the wrist containing a few of the cocuyos, and the light thus produced is nearly equal to a small candle. Some ladies wear a belt of them at night, ingeniously fastened about the waist, others a necklace, and the effect is highly amusing. In the ballroom they are worn in the flounces of ladies' dresses, where they glisten very much like diamonds and other precious stones. Strange to say, there is a natural hook near the head of the firefly, by which it can be attached to the dress without apparent injury to it. The town ladies keep little cages of these insects as pets, feeding them on sugar, of which they appear to be immoderately fond. On the plantations, when a fresh supply is desired, one has only to wait until evening, when hundreds can be secured with a thread net at the end of a pole. By holding a cocuyo up in the out-door air for a few moments, large numbers are at once attracted to the spot. In size they are about an inch long, and a little over an eighth of an inch in breadth.

There is an insidious and much dreaded insect with which the planters have to contend on the sugar and coffee plantations, but which is not met with in the cities; namely, the red ant, a much more formidable foe than any one not acquainted with its ravages would believe. These little creatures possess a power altogether out of proportion to their insignificant size, eating into the heart of the hardest wood, neither cedar, iron-wood, nor even lignum-vitæ being proof against them. They are not seen at the surface, as they never touch the outer shell of the wood whose heart they are consuming. A beam or rafter which has been attacked by them looks as good as when new, to the casual observer, until it is sounded and found to be hollow, a mere shell in fact. Even in passing from one piece of timber to another, the red ant does so by covered ways, and is thus least seen when most busy. The timbers of an entire roof have been found hollowed out and deprived entirely of their supporting strength without the presence of the insect enemy being even suspected until chance betrayed the useless character of the supports. For some unknown reason, upright timbers are rarely attacked by them, but those in a reclining or horizontal position are their choice. These destructive red ants are nearly always to be found in tropical countries, as in India, Batavia, and Sumatra, where they build mounds in the jungle half the size of the natives' cabins. They may be seen marching like an invading army in columns containing myriads across the fields of southern India.

The interior landscape, more particularly of the middle district of the island, is here and there ornamented by fine specimens of the ceiba, or silk-cotton tree, which is often seen a hundred feet in height, with stout and widespread branches, giving the idea of great firmness and stability. It sends up a massive sinewy trunk for some fifty feet, when it divides into branches covered with a dense canopy of leaves, expanded like an umbrella, and forming a perfect shade against the power of the torrid sun. The ceiba is slow of growth, but attains to great age, specimens thriving when Columbus first landed here being, as we were assured, still extant. Next to the royal palm, it is the most remarkable of all the trees which loom up beneath the brilliant purple skies of Cuba. The negroes have a superstition that the ceiba is a magic tree haunted by spirits, a singular notion also shared by the colored people of Nassau, though these two islands are so many hundreds of miles apart and have never had any natural connection. There is certainly something weird in the loneliness and solitary grandeur of the tree. Next to the palm and ceiba in beauty and picturesqueness of effect is the tamarind tree, with its deep green and delicate foliage, presenting a singular and curious aspect when thickly looped on every branch with hanging chocolate-colored pods.

Under the noonday sun, sitting in the deep shade of some lofty ceiba, one may watch with curious eyes the myriads of many-hued, broad-winged butterflies, mingling orange, crimson, and steel-blue in dazzling combinations, as they flit through the ambient atmosphere with a background of shining, evergreen foliage, the hum of insects and the carol of birds forming a soft lullaby inviting sleep. Naturalists tell us that no less than three hundred distinct species of butterflies are found in Cuba, ranging in size from a common house-fly to a humming-bird. The day dies with a suddenness almost startling, so that one passes from sunshine to starlight as if by magic. Then the cocuyo takes up the activity of insect life, flashing its miniature torches over the plantations, and peeping out from among the dense foliage, while the stars sing their evening hymn of silent praise.

The Cubans have a peculiar mode of harnessing their oxen, similar to that seen in the far East and also in some parts of Europe, as at San Sebastian, on the Bay of Biscay. A stout wooden bar is placed at the root of the horns, and so securely bound to them with thongs that the animal draws, or rather pushes, by the head and frontlet, without chafing. The Cuban oxen have a hole pierced in their nostrils, through which a metallic ring is secured, and to this a rope is attached, serving as reins with which to guide the animal. This mode of harnessing certainly seems to enable the oxen to bring more strength to bear upon the purpose for which they are employed than when the yoke is placed, as is the case with us, about the throat and shoulders. The greatest power of horned animals undoubtedly lies in the head and neck, and the question arises whether in placing the yoke on the neck and breast we do not get it out of reach of the exercise of that strength, and cause the animal to draw the load behind him by the mere force of his bodily weight and impetus. The West Indian animal is small, and often of the cream-colored breed, mild-eyed and docile, of which one sees such choice specimens in Italy and especially on the plains of Lombardy.

Not quite satisfied with the conclusion first arrived at, we gave this subject of the harnessing of oxen a second consideration, and in carefully watching the operation of the frontlet-bar we detected at least one very cruel and objectionable feature in this mode of harnessing. The animals are necessarily so bound to the bar that to move their heads one way or the other is a simple impossibility, while our mode of yoking oxen leaves them very much at liberty in the use of their heads, thus enabling them to shake off flies and other biting insects which may tease them, whereas the eyes of a Cuban ox are often seen infested with flies which he cannot get rid of while in harness, however he may be beset by them. This alone, in a climate where biting insects swarm all the year round, is a most serious objection to the frontlet-bar as compared with the yoke.

The Cuban horse deserves more than a mere mention in this connection. He is a remarkably valuable animal, especially adapted to the climate and to the service required of him. Though small and delicate of limb he can carry a great weight, and his gait is not unlike that of our pacing horses, though with much less lateral motion, and is remarkably easy for the rider, certainly forming the easiest gait combined with rapidity of motion possessed by any breed. He has great power of endurance, is a small eater, requiring no grain as a general thing, but is satisfied with the green leaves and stalks of the corn, upon which he keeps in good condition and flesh. He is a docile little creature, easily taught and easily taken care of. The Cuban horse knows no shelter except the heavens above him, for there are no barns in Cuba; but he will no more wander away from his master's door, where he stands at nearly all hours of the day with the saddle on his back, than would a favorite dog. The Montero inherits all the love of his Moorish ancestors for the horse, and never stirs abroad except upon his back. He considers himself established for life when he possesses a good horse, a sharp Toledo blade, and a pair of silver spurs. Being from childhood accustomed to the saddle, it is natural for him to be a good rider, and there are none better even in Arabia. He is apt to tell big stories about his little horse, intimating its descent direct from the Kochlani, or King Solomon's breed, and to endow it with marvelous qualities of speed and endurance. The Montero is never heard to boast of his wife, his children, or any other possession, but he does "blow" for his horse.

 One of this class stood beside his pony one warm afternoon opposite the Hotel Telegrafo, where a few of the guests were seated under the broad veranda. The sleek, well-formed animal elicited some complimentary remarks, which gratified the owner, who spoke English after the style of his people. He indulged in praises of the horse, especially as to the ease and steadiness of his gait, and offered a bet that he could ride round the outside of the Campo de Marte on him and return to the spot where he stood, at ordinary speed, carrying a full glass of water without spilling a tablespoonful of the liquid; such is the ease of motion of these animals trained to what is called the paso gualtrapeo. Four corners were to be turned by the Cuban, as well as half a mile of distance accomplished. The small bet suggested was readily taken, and the full tumbler of water brought out of the house. The Cuban mounted his pony and rode round the park with the speed of a bird, easily winning his bet.

The visitor, as he proceeds inland, will frequently observe on the fronts of the dwellings attempts at representations in colors of birds and various animals, resembling anything rather than what they are apparently designed to depict. The most striking characteristics are the gaudy coloring and the remarkable size. Pigeons present the colossal appearance of ostriches, and dogs are exceedingly elephantine in their proportions. Space would not be adequate to picture horses and cattle. Especially in the suburbs of the cities this fancy may be observed, where attempts at portraying domestic scenes present some original ideas as to grouping. If such ludicrous objects were to be met with anywhere else but in Cuba they would be called caricatures. Here they are regarded with the utmost complacency, and innocently considered to be artistic and ornamental. Noticing something of the same sort in Vevay, Switzerland, not long since, the author found on inquiry that it was the incipient art effort of a Spanish Creole, who had wandered thither from the island.

The policy of the home government has been to suppress, so far as possible, all knowledge of matters in general relating to Cuba; especially to prevent the making public of any statistical information regarding the internal resources, all accounts of its current growth, prosperity, or otherwise. Rigidly-enforced rules accomplished this seclusiveness for many years, until commercial relations with the "outside barbarians" rendered this no longer possible. No official chart of Havana, its harbor, or that of any other Cuban city has ever been made public. Spain has seemed to desire to draw a curtain before this tropical jewel, lest its dazzling brightness should tempt the cupidity of some other nation. Notwithstanding this, our war department at Washington contains complete drawings of every important fortification, and charts of every important harbor in Cuba. Since 1867 we have been connected with Cuba by submarine cable, and through her with Jamaica since 1870. The local government exercises, however, strict surveillance over telegraphic communications.

The political condition of Cuba is what might be expected of a Castilian colony, ruled and governed by such a policy as prevails here. Like the home government, she presents a remarkable instance of the standstill policy, and from one of the most powerful and wealthy kingdoms of Europe, Spain has sunk to the position of the humblest and poorest. Other nations have labored and succeeded in the race of progress, while her adherence to ancient institutions and her dignified contempt for "modern innovations" have become a species of retrogression, which has placed her far below all her sister governments. The true Hidalgo spirit, which wraps itself up in an antique garb and shrugs its shoulders at the advance of other nations, still rules over the realm of Ferdinand and Isabella, while its high-roads swarm with gypsies and banditti, as tokens of decaying power.

CHAPTER XIV.

Consumption of Tobacco. — The Delicious Fruits of the Tropics. — Individual Characteristics of Cuban Fruits. — The Royal Palm. — The Mulberry Tree. — Silk Culture. — The Island once covered by Forests. — No Poisonous Reptiles. — The Cuban Bloodhound. — Hotbed of African Slavery. —Spain's Disregard of Solemn Treaties. — The Coolie System of Slavery. — Ah-Lee draws a Prize. — Native African Races. — Negroes buying their Freedom. — Laws favoring the Slaves. — Example of St. Domingo. — General Emancipation.

THE consumption of tobacco in the form of cigars is almost incredibly large in Cuba, and for the city of Havana alone it has been estimated to amount to an aggregate cost of five million dollars per annum. Every man, woman, and child appears to be addicted to the habit. It strikes a Northerner as rather odd for a lady to sit smoking her cigarette in her parlor, but this is not at all rare. The men of all degrees smoke everywhere, in the dwelling-house, in the street, in the theatre, in the cafés, and in the counting-room ; eating, drinking, and truly it would also seem, sleeping, they smoke, smoke, smoke. At the tables d'hôte of the hotels it is not unusual to see a Cuban take a few whiffs of a cigarette between the several courses, and lights are burning close at hand to enable him to do so. If a party of gentlemen are invited to dine together, the host so orders that a packet of the finest cigarettes is frequently passed to his guests, with a lighted taper, in the course of the meal, and at its close some favorite brand of the more substantial cigar is furnished to all. Thus, tobacco is consumed on every occasion, in the council-chamber, the court, at funerals, in the domestic circles, at feasts, and on the out-door drive. The slave and his master, the maid and her mistress, boy and man, all, all smoke. It seems odd that one does not scent Havana far out at sea before the land is sighted.

We were told that gentlemen who have the means to procure them smoke on an average what is equivalent to a dozen cigars per day, and those of the other sex addicted to the habit consume half that quantity. Of late the larger proportion, however, takes the form of cigarettes, which are far more subtle in effect when used to excess. The consequence of this large home consumption, in addition to the export of the article, is that a very numerous class of the population is engaged in the manufacture, and little stores devoted solely to this business are plentifully sprinkled all about the metropolis. The imperial factory of La Honradez, already described, occupies a whole city square, and is one of its curiosities, producing from three to four million cigarettes per diem. This house enjoys special governmental protection, and makes its annual contribution to the royal household of Madrid of the best of its manufactured goods. A snuff-taker is rarely to be met with, and few, if any, chew the weed, if we except the stevedores and foreign sailors to be seen about the shore and shipping. Havana has no wharves, properly speaking; vessels are loaded and discharged by means of lighters or scows. The negroes become passionately fond of the pipe, inhaling into their lungs the rich, powerful narcotic and driving it out again at their nostrils in slow, heavy clouds, half dozing over the dreamy effect.

The postilion who waits for a fare upon the street passes half his time in this way, dreaming over his pipe of pure Havana, or renewing constantly his cigarette. The price of manufactured tobacco in Cuba is about one half that which we pay for the same article in America, either at wholesale or retail, as shipping expenses, export duty, and import duty must be added to the price charged to the consumer.

In discussing this habit one naturally looks back about four hundred years, recalling the amazement of the Spanish discoverers, when they first landed here, at seeing the Indians smoking a native weed which was called tobacco. The practice was, at that time, entirely unknown in Europe, though now indulged in as a luxury by nearly half the population of the globe.

We have only a partial idea at the North of the true character of tropical fruits, since only a small portion of them are of such a nature as to admit of exportation, and such as are forwarded to us must be gathered in an unripe condition in order to survive a short sea-voyage. The orange which we eat in Boston or New York, therefore, is a very different-flavored fruit from the same when partaken of in Havana or Florida. The former has been picked green and ripened on shipboard, as a general thing; the latter was perhaps on the tree an hour before you ate it, ripened under its native skies and upon its parent stem. So of the banana, one of the most delightful and nutritious of all West Indian fruits, which grows everywhere in Cuba with prodigal profuseness, — though we are told that as regards this fruit it is claimed that, like some varieties of our pear, it ripens as well off the tree as on it; and the same is the case with some other fleshy fruits. After the banana has attained its full growth, the final process of ripening commences, as it were, within itself; that is to say, the fruit ceases to depend upon the tree for sustenance or farther development. The pulp becomes gradually sweetened and softened, chiefly by the change of the starch into more or less of soluble sugar. When the bananas are shipped to our Northern markets they are as green as the leaves of the trees on which they grew. Most of us have seen cartloads of them in this condition landing at our city wharves. Placed in an even temperature and in darkness they will ripen and become as yellow as gold in a very few days.

The banana and plantain differ from each other much as an apple and a potato differ; the latter should always be cooked before eating, but the former may be either eaten raw or cooked, according to the taste. The banana is gathered at three different stages of its growth. At a quarter of its maturity it is rather milky, and contains much starch. Roasted in ashes, or boiled in water, it forms a very nourishing food, and is a good substitute for bread. If eaten at three fourths of its growth it is less nourishing, but contains more sugar. Lastly, when perfectly ripe, it develops an acrid principle, both wholesome and palatable. The fig banana is a favorite species, and forms a universal dessert in the ripe state with the Creoles. A frequent reference is made to it in these notes because of its importance. The enormous productiveness of the plant and its nutritious character assure to the humble classes an abundant subsistence. People may go freely into the wild lands and find edible bananas at any time, without money and without price. In the cities the charge for them is so moderate that a person must be poor indeed who cannot afford a liberal quantity of them daily.

Some of the other fruits are the mango, pomegranate, pineapple, zapota, tamarind, citron, fig, cocoa, lemon, rose-apple, and breadfruit. Japan, India, and Ceylon afford nothing more fascinating or strange in their vegetable kingdoms than this favored isle. The fruits are simply wonderful in variety and perfection. One eats eggs, custard, and butter off the trees. Though all these fruits are universally eaten, the orange seems to be the Creole's favorite, and if he be a person of even ordinary means, he seldom rises in the morning until he has drunk his cup of coffee and eaten a couple of oranges, brought fresh and prepared for him by a servant. The practice is one into which the visitor falls very pleasantly, and finds it no less refreshing than agreeable. It seems to rain oranges in Havana. They are scarcely less cheap than the luscious banana.

The rose-apple grows on one of the most symmetrical trees in Cuba, with strong, oval, glossy leaves. The blossoms are large, white, and of pleasant odor, followed by a round fruit about as large as a well-developed California peach, with a smooth skin, cream-colored within and without. The pulp is as firm as a ripe seckel pear, and the taste is so strong of otto-of-rose that more than one at a time palls upon the palate. It is much used among the Cubans as an agreeable flavoring for soups and puddings. Of the fruit trees the lemon is perhaps the most attractive to the eye; for though small and dwarfish, yet it presents the flowers, small green lemons, and the ripe yellow fruit all together, reminding one of the Eastern alma. The green leaves when young are nearly as fragrant as the lemon verbena.

The mammee is a curious fruit growing on lofty, umbrageous trees, appearing as musk-melons would look if seen hanging in elm-trees. Large and high-flavored, the fruit is solid in texture like the American quince. The flavor of the mammee resembles our peach, though not quite so delicate. Its color when ripe is a light yellow.

The mango is nearly as abundant and prolific as the banana, and yet it came originally from the far East. It grows upon a very handsome tree, the leaves being long, lanceolate, polished, and hanging in dense masses of dark-green foliage. In size it is like a full-grown New England apple tree. The mango is about thrice the size of an egg plum, and when ripe is yellow in color, and grows in long pendant bunches. When this fruit is at its best it is very juicy, and may be sucked away like a grape. The negroes are immoderately fond of it, and when permitted to do so are apt to make themselves ill by their greediness.

The cocoa-nut tree grows to the height of fifty feet and more, differing from the royal palm by its drooping nature. At its summit is a waving tuft of dark green, glossy, pinnate leaves, from ten to fifteen feet in length, like mammoth plumes, immediately under which are suspended the nuts in heavy bunches, often weighing three hundred pounds. When the nut has attained nearly its full size, it is said to be in the milk, and it then furnishes a delightful, cooling, and healthful beverage. In taste it is sweetish, and its effect is that of a slight diuretic.

The sapotilla is a noble fruit tree, with feathery, glossy leaves. The blossoms are white and bell-shaped, with an agreeable perfume like an apple-blossom. The fruit is round, about the size of a peach, the skin being rough and dark like a russet apple or a potato, but when fully ripe it is delicious, and melts away in the mouth like a custard.

The pineapple, that king of fruits, though in itself presenting such a fine appearance, is the plainest of all in its humble manner of growth. It is found wild in Cuba, and there are several varieties cultivated, none quite equal, it seemed to us, to those found in Singapore and other equatorial islands. Its style of growth is the same in either hemisphere. It grows singly upon its low stem, reaching to a height of eighteen or twenty inches above the ground. A single fruit-stem pushes up from the earth, blossoms, and in about eighteen months from the planting it matures a single apple, weighing three or four pounds and upwards; and what a royal fruit it is! A field well covered with the yellow, ripening apples is a very beautiful sight. Though the plant produces but one apple at a time, it will continue to yield an annual crop for three or four years, if cultivated. It is raised from slips, planted much as our farmers set out young cabbages or lettuce.

The custard-apple grows wild, but is also cultivated and thereby much improved. Its color externally is green, and it has a tough skin, is of a subacid flavor, and as full of little flat black seeds as a shad is of bones. It is much used in Cuba for flavoring purposes, and is soft and juicy, each specimen weighing from a pound to a pound and a half. The star-apple is so called because when cut through transversely its centre presents the figure of a star. Even when quite ripe the interior is green in color. Its flavor is exquisite, like strawberries and cream, and it is eaten with a spoon, the outside skin forming as it were a shell or cup.

The guava tree is small and resembles our young cherry trees. The fruit is about the size of the lime, which it much resembles. It is made little use of in its natural condition, but is in universal demand as a preserve; the jelly made from it is famous all over the world. When it is freshly cut, one will scent a whole room for hours with its distinctive flavor.

The pomegranate, a general favorite in the torrid zone, flourishes in Cuba, but is seen in much greater perfection in Africa. It is doubtful if it is indigenous here, though it is now found in such abundance, and as much depended upon for a food supply as apples are with us. Doubtless the reader has seen the bush in bearing in our hothouses, the fruit when cut being full of red seeds glistening like rubies.

The tamarind is a universal and thrifty tree in the island, lofty and umbrageous, a quick grower and yet long-lived. The fruit is contained in a pod, — like a full, ripe pea-pod, — covering mahogany-colored seeds. The pulp when ripe and fresh is as soft as marmalade, and quite palatable; its flavor is sugared acid. Steeped in water it forms a delightful and cooling beverage, much used as a drink in the tropics.

The orange, lime, lemon, and citron are too well known to require detailed description. The wild or bitter orange is much used for hedges: its deep green glossy foliage and its fragrant blossoms and its golden fruit make such hedges strikingly effective. The rind of the bitter orange is used to make a sweetmeat with which we are all familiar.

More than once the Moorish garden of the Alcazar, at Seville, and the garden of Hesperides, at Cannes, were recalled in hours of delightful wanderings among the orange groves of Cuba. Yet these latter are neglected, or at least not generously cultivated, no such care being given to them as is bestowed upon the orange orchards of Florida; but the glowing sun and ardent breath of the tropics ask little aid from the hand of man in perfecting their products. The fruits and flowers of the American Archipelago — " air-woven children of light" — are not only lavishly prolific, but perfect of their kind. No wonder that scientists and botanists become poetical in their descriptions of these regions.

The royal palm, so often alluded to, grows to the height of seventy feet, more or less. It is singular that it should have no substance in the interior of its trunk, though the outside to the thickness of a couple of inches makes the finest of boards, and when seasoned is so hard as to turn a board-nail at a single stroke of the hammer. It is remarkable also that a palm tree which grows so high has such tiny, thread-like roots, which, however, are innumerable. The top of the palm yields a vegetable which is used as food and when boiled is nutritious and palatable, resembling our cauliflower. Though there are many species of palm in Cuba, one seldom sees the fan-palm, which forms such a distinctive feature in equatorial regions as at Penang and Singapore.

Humboldt thought that the entire island was once a forest of palms, mingled with lime and orange trees. The mulberry tree, if not indigenous, was found here at so early a period that it is a matter of doubt as to its having been imported from other lands. It grows to great perfection, and has led to several attempts in the direction of silk-raising, the silkworm also proving more prolific even than in Japan. Some of the fine, hard fancy woods of Cuba were employed in the finish of apartments in the Escurial palace near Madrid. Ebony, rosewood, fustic, lancewood, mahogany, and other choice woods are very abundant, especially the mahogany, which grows to enormous size. The exportation of them has only taken place where these woods were best located for river transportation to harbors on the coast. The interior of the island is so inaccessible that it has hardly been explored. There are fertile valleys there of two hundred miles in length and thirty in width, with an average temperature of 75°, a maximum of 88°, and a minimum of 52°, thus affording a most perfect and healthful climate, favorable to human and to vegetable life, and it should be remembered that malarial diseases or yellow fever are unknown in the districts removed from the coast, and no one ever heard of sunstroke in Cuba.

It is somewhat remarkable that there should be no poisonous animals or reptiles in the island, but so we were creditably informed. Snakes of various species abound, but are considered entirely harmless, though they are sometimes destructive to domestic fowls. During a pleasant trip between San Antonio and Alquizar in a volante with a hospitable planter of that region, this subject happened to be under discussion, when we saw in the roadway a snake six or eight feet long, and as large round as the middle of one's arm. On pointing it out to our friend, he merely told us its species, and declared that a child might sleep with it unharmed. In the mean time it was a relief to see the innocent creature hasten to secrete itself in a lime hedge close at hand. Lizards, tarantulas, and chameleons are frequently seen, but are considered to be harmless. One often awakes in the morning to see lizards upon his chamber wall, searching for flies and insects, upon which they feed.

The Cuban bloodhound, of which we hear so much, is not a native of the island, but belongs to an imported breed, resembling the English mastiff, though with larger head and limbs. He is by nature a fierce, bloodthirsty animal, but the particular qualities which fit him for tracing the runaway slaves are almost entirely acquired by careful training. This is accomplished by experts in the business, who are sometimes Monteros, and sometimes French overseers of plantations who are out of work or regular engagement. Each estate keeps some of these dogs as a precautionary measure, but they are seldom called into use of late, for so certain is the slave that he will be instantly followed as soon as missed, and inevitably traced by the hounds, that he rarely attempts to escape from his master unless under some peculiarly aggravating cause. It may even be doubted whether a slave would be pursued to-day were he to attempt to escape, because slavery is so very near its last gasp. In one respect this is an advantage to the negroes, since the master, feeling this indifference, grants the blacks more freedom of action. So perfect of scent is the Cuban bloodhound that the master has only to obtain a bit of clothing left behind by the runaway and give it to the hound to smell. The dog will then follow the slave through a whole population of his class, and with his nose to the ground lead straight to his hiding-place.

For three centuries Cuba has been the hotbed of African slavery. Few, if any, have been imported during the last thirty years, that is to say since 1855, during which year some cargoes were successfully run. In 1816, the Spanish government, in a solemn treaty, declared its conviction of the injustice of the slave trade. On the 23d of September, 1817, in consideration of four hundred thousand pounds sterling paid as an equivalent by Great Britian, Spain ratified a treaty proclaiming that the slave trade should cease throughout all the dominions of that country on the 30th day of May, 1820, and that it should not afterwards be lawful for any Spanish subject to purchase slaves. It was further declared by the home government that all blacks brought from Africa subsequent to that date should be at once set free, and the vessel on which they were transported should be confiscated, while the captain, crew, and others concerned should be punished with ten years' penal servitude. Yet, as all the world knows, this was nothing more than a dead letter so far as Cuba was concerned, and so late as 1845, statistics show an arrival of imported slaves from Africa of fifteen thousand negroes annually, for the previous twenty years. Tacon, Governor-General from June, 1834, until April, 1838, like his predecessors and successors made no secret of receiving seventeen dollars per head, — that is one doubloon, — on every slave landed. Other officials spent their fees on themselves or hoarded them for a fortune to be enjoyed on returning home to Spain, but Tacon expended his in beautifying Havana and its environs. That the home government secretly fostered the slave trade, notwithstanding the solemn treaty entered into with Great Britain, no one pretends to deny.

The coolie system, which was latterly substituted

for that of the importation of Africans, was commenced in 1847, but it was only slavery under another form, being in point of humanity even more objectionable. Fully seventy per cent. of the Chinese coolies died during the eight years they were bound by their contract to serve their masters! Even after that period was completed, unjust laws and schemes were adopted to retain their services whenever the planters desired it; but the truth is, the planters, after a thorough experience, were generally glad to get rid of the Mongolians. All of them were decoyed from home under false pretenses and large promises, and only arrived in Cuba to find themselves virtually slaves. But there was no help for them. They were thousands of miles from China, in a land of whose language they knew nothing, and so they were obliged to submit. If after their term of service expired they succeeded in reaching Havana, or other Cuban cities, and by becoming fruit peddlers or engaging in any other occupation tried to earn sufficient money to carry them back to their native land, they still were brutally treated by all parties, and were ever at the mercy of the venal police. On the plantations they received perhaps a little more consideration than the blacks, simply because they were less tractable and more dangerous on account of their greater degree of intelligence and keener sense of the wrong done them. The planter, always short of laborers, has heretofore been willing to pay the shipping-agencies four hundred dollars for a newly-arrived coolie, whose services he thus secured for eight years, the coolies at the expiration of the period to receive a mere nominal sum, out of which they have mostly been cheated by some means or other. The whole business of coolie importation is vile beyond measure, and must have included in its aggregate over three hundred thousand Chinese. There are still believed to be some sixty thousand left upon the island, most of whom remain because they have no means of returning to their native land. Half of these subsist by begging. Broken in health and spirits, they await the coming of that final liberator who is the last friend of suffering humanity.

The Chinese are best adapted to the work of the cigar factories, where they excel in the occupation of cigar and cigarette making, and many hundreds are thus employed in Havana. But they are totally unfit for plantation labor, under the hardships of which their feeble frames succumb. They prove themselves very good servants in the cities, being very quick to learn, and ready to adapt themselves to any light occupation. A Chinaman is sly, cunning, and, to a certain degree, enterprising; but he must be trusted cautiously. As a house-servant, footman, cook, or waiter he is admirable. Here, in this to him foreign land, he cannot suppress his instinct for gambling; it seems to be born in him, and he will often lose in an hour the hard accumulation of months, or even years. As to the lottery, he is always the purchaser of portions of tickets at every drawing, and occasionally becomes a winner. A thrifty Chinaman, for there are some such even in Havana, bearing the characteristic name of Ah-Lee, connected with a bricabrac store on the Calzada de la Reina, held a lucky number in the lottery drawn during our brief stay at the Hotel Telegrafo. When the prizes were announced, he found that he was entitled to five hundred dollars. The agents tried to pay Ah-Lee in Cuban currency, but he was too smart for them, and showed them their own announcement promising to cash all prizes, with the usual discount, in gold. So Ah-Lee got his prize finally in gold. We were told by one whose experience was extensive, and whose testimony was worthy of respect, that the coolies would lie and steal with such apparent innocence as to deceive the most wary, and that as regards their moral nature it seemed to be totally undeveloped. For our own part we still sympathize with John. He has been so outrageously cheated and abused from the hour when he stepped on board the transport ship which brought him from China up to the present time that he has learned the trick of it. If he is not strong enough to demand his rights, we certainly hope that he may have sufficient cunning to obtain them by outwitting his adversaries.

In their slave condition the Chinese coolies and the negroes were at times so affected by a spirit of superstition as to cause them to commit suicide, the latter actuated, as it seemed, by a feeling of despair, the former through a vindictive spirit towards their masters. Both were also moved by a superstitious conviction that their spirits would at once be returned to their native land, to inhabit a sort of spirit paradise or intermediate state between earth and heaven. It is very strange that so peculiar and so similar a belief should be indigenous in the minds of such distinctive races. At the period when the free importation from Africa was carried on, the most difficult thing the planters had to contend with was a proneness to suicide on the part of those slaves who were newly imported, and who entertained this same remarkable idea.

Though we abhor the entire system of Cuban labor, yet it cannot be denied that the slaves, so far as material comfort goes, are better lodged, fed, and cared for than four fifths of the population of Ireland and India, and, furthermore, this comparison will hold good as regards a large portion of continental Europe. A well-fed, well-kept negro is twice as valuable, twice as serviceable to his master as a neglected one, and no one knows this better than the master who governs his slaves on purely mercenary grounds, and is yet very careful to supply liberally their physical wants. These slaves are descended from various African tribes, whose characteristics are so marked as to be easily discernible even by strangers. The Congoes are small in stature, but very agile and good workers, and in past years they have been a favorite tribe. The Fantees are a larger race of negroes, hard to manage, and possessing a revengeful nature. Those from the Gold Coast are still more powerful in body, but are good-natured and well-liked by planters. The Ebros are less black than those already named, almost mulatto in complexion, and make favorite house servants. The Ashantees are of another prominent tribe, and are also popular as plantation hands, but not numerous.

The tattooed faces, bodies, and limbs of a large portion of the slaves, especially of the hands upon the plantations, shows their African nativity, while the smooth skin and generally greater degree of intelligence of others show them to have been born in slavery upon the island. These latter are mostly sought for service in the cities. They are remarkably healthy when not overworked, and form the most vigorous part of the population. When an epidemic breaks out among the blacks, it seems to carry them off by wholesale, proving much more fatal than among the whites. Cholera, small-pox, and pneumonia sometimes sweep them off at a fearful rate. It is a curious fact that if a negro is really ill, he requires just twice as much medicine to affect him as a white person.

There are said to be three hundred thousand free negroes on the island, of whom comparatively few are found inland upon the plantations; they are all inclined to congregate in the cities and large towns, where, truth compels us to say, they prove to be an idle and vicious class, and as a body useless both to themselves and to the public. There are believed to be at present in Cuba about one hundred and forty thousand male and about sixty thousand female slaves. To carry on the great industry of the island as systematized by the planters, this number of hands is entirely inadequate. It is sometimes asked how there came to be so many free negroes in the island. It should be clearly understood that the laws which govern Cuba are made by the home government, not by the planters or natives of Cuba, and that indirectly these laws have long favored emancipation of the blacks. For many years any slave has enjoyed the right to go to a magistrate and have himself appraised, and upon paying the price thus set upon himself he can receive his free papers. The valuation is made by three persons, of whom the master appoints one, and the magistrate two. The slave may pay by installments of fifty dollars at a time, but he owes his full service to his master until the last and entire payment is made. If the valuation be twelve hundred dollars, after the slave has paid one hundred he owns one twelfth of himself, and the master eleven twelfths, and so on. Until all is paid, however, the master's dominion over the slave is complete. There has also long been another peculiar law in operation. A slave may on the same valuation compel his master to transfer him to any person who will pay the money in full, and this has often been done where slave and master disagree. This law, as will be seen, must have operated as it was designed to do, as a check upon masters, and as an inducement for them to remove special causes of complaint and dissatisfaction. It has also enabled slaveholders of the better class, in the case of ill-usage of blacks, to relieve them by paying down their appraised value and appropriating their services to themselves. All this relates to the past rather than the present, since, as we have explained, the relationship of slave and master is now so nearly at an end as to render such arrangements inoperative.

There was a law promulgated in 1870, — the outgrowth of the revolution of 1868, which dethroned Isabella II., — declaring every slave in Cuba to be free after reaching the age of sixty, and also freeing the children of all slaves born subsequent to that year. But that law has been ignored altogether, and was not permitted even to be announced officially upon the island. In the first place, few hard worked slaves survive to the age of sixty; and in the second place, the children have no one to look after or to enforce their rights. Spain never yet kept troth with her subjects, or with anybody else, and the passage of the law referred to was simply a piece of political finesse, designed for the eye of the European states, and more particularly to soothe England, which country had lately showed considerable feeling and restlessness touching the disregard of all treaties between herself and Spain.

The slaves who still remain upon the plantations appear in all outward circumstances to be thoughtless and comparatively content; their light and cheerful nature seems to lift them above the influence of brutal treatment when it is encountered. That they have been called upon to suffer much by being overtasked and cruelly punished in the past, there is no doubt whatever, but it may be safely stated that their condition has been greatly improved of late. The owners are obliged by law to instruct the slaves in the Catholic faith, but this has never been heeded to any extent by the planters, though all the children are baptized in infancy. The law relative to the treatment of the negroes also prescribes a certain quantity and quality of food to be regularly furnished to them, but the masters are generally liberal in this respect, and exceed the requirements of the law, as their mercenary interest is obviously in that direction. The masters know by experience that slaves will not work well unless well fed. With no education or culture whatever, their intelligence remains at the lowest ebb. "With plenty of food and sleep," said an owner to us, "they are as easily managed as any other domestic animals."

Until latterly the slaves have been carefully watched at night, but nearly all these precautions against their escaping from servitude seem to have been dropped. They are no longer locked up in corral, their special night quarters. Of course they are kept within certain bounds, but the rigorous surveillance under which they have always lived is no longer in force. The two sexes are nominally separated, but as there is no strict recognition of the marital relation, and free intercommunication between them really exists, the state of morality may be imagined. It has always been customary for mothers to receive certain consideration and partial relief from hard labor during a reasonable period prior to and subsequent to their confinement, with encouraging gifts from the masters, which has caused them generally to covet the condition of maternity. Still the proportion of female slaves on the plantations has always been so small, compared with that of the other sex, that not nearly so many children are born as would be supposed. Female slaves have generally been sent to town service, even when born on the plantations.

It has always been clearly understood that the births on the part of the negroes in Cuba have not nearly kept pace with the number of deaths among them, even under apparently favorable circumstances. One has not far to look for the reason of this. Promiscuous intercourse is undoubtedly the predisposing cause, which is always an outgrowth of a largely unequal division of the sexes. On the plantations the male negroes outnumber the females ten to one. In the cities the males are as five to one. When the slave trade was carried on between Africa and the island, the plan was to bring over males only, but it was hardly practicable to adhere strictly to the rule, so women were not declined when a cargo was being made up and nearly completed. Thus a disparity was inaugurated which has continued to the present day, with only a slight equalizing tendency.

The present plan of freeing the slaves recommends

itself to all persons who fully understand the position, and if it be honestly carried out will soon obliterate the crime of enforced labor upon the island. A sudden freeing of the blacks, that is, all at once, would have been attended with much risk to all parties, although justice and humanity demand their liberation. France tried the experiment in St. Domingo, and the result was a terrible state of anarchy. Not only did she lose possession of the island, but the people settled down by degrees into all the horrors of African savagery, even to cannibalism. England followed, and generously paid the British planters of Jamaica for all their slaves, giving the latter unconditional freedom. Of course this ruined the island commercially, but it was strict justice, nevertheless. Extreme measures are open to objection even in behalf of justice. It was hoped that the freed negroes of Jamaica would become thrifty and industrious, earning fair wages, and that crops would still be remunerative, but it was not so. The negro of the tropics will only work when he is compelled, and in the West Indies he has scarcely more to do, as it regards sustaining life, than to pluck of the wild fruits and to eat. The sugar plantations of Jamaica have simply ceased to exist.

Every reasonable Cuban has long realized that the freedom of the blacks was but a question of time, and that it must soon be brought about, but how this could be accomplished without rendering them liable to the terrible consequences which befell St. Domingo was a serious problem. The commercial wreck of Jamaica had less terror for them as an example, since of late their own condition could in that respect hardly be worse. Therefore, the man-

GENERAL EMANCIPATION.

umitting of one slave in every four annually, so organized that all shall be free on January 1, 1888, is considered with great favor by the people generally, except the most radical of old Spaniards. All are thus prepared for the change, which is so gradually brought about as to cause no great shock. It is not unreasonable to believe that the instantaneous freeing of all the slaves would have led to mutual destruction of whites and blacks all over the island.

CHAPTER XV.

Slave Trade with Africa. — Where the Slavers made their Landing. — An Early Morning Ride. — Slaves marching to Daily Labor. — Fragrance of the Early Day. — Mist upon the Waters. — A Slave Ship. — A Beautiful but Guilty Brigantine. — A French Cruiser. — Cunning Seamanship. — A Wild Goose Chase. — A Cuban Posada. — Visit to a Coffee Estate. — Landing a Slave Cargo. — A Sight to challenge Sympathy and Indignation. — Half-Starved Victims. — Destruction of the Slave Ship.

THE author's first visit to the island of Cuba was during the year 1845, at a period when the slave traffic was vigorously, though surreptitiously carried on between Africa and the island. The trade was continued so late as 1853, and occasional cargoes were brought over even later, slavers having been captured on the south coast two years subsequent to the last named date. The slave vessels generally sought a landing on the south side, both as being nearest and safest for them, but when they were hard pressed they made a port wherever it could be most easily reached. A favorite point at the time of which we speak, was in the Bay of Broa, on the south coast, nearly opposite to the Isle of Pines. It was here in 1845 that the author witnessed a scene which forms the theme of the following chapter. A superior knowledge of all the hidden bays and inlets of the south side gave the contrabandists great advantages over any pursuing vessel, and their lighter draught of water enabled them to navigate their small crafts where it was impossible for a heavy ship to follow.

We were on a brief visit to the coffee estate of Don Herero, near Guines, and having expressed a desire to visit the southern coast, our host proposed that we should do so together on the following day. We were to start on horseback quite early in the morning, so as to accomplish the distance before the heat of the sun should become oppressive.

The early day is almost as beautiful as the evenings of this region, a fact to which we were fully awakened at an early hour, after a refreshing night's sleep. Don Herero was already awaiting us on the broad piazza, which we reached in time to see the slaves, directed by an overseer, file past the house towards the field. "A couple of hours before sunrise," said our host, "is the best time for them to work, and we add these two hours to their noon rest, so that it divides the labor to better advantage and avoids the midday heat." There were perhaps seventy or eighty of this gang of slaves, one fifth only being women. Don Herero went among them and exchanged some pleasant words, mostly with the women, one of whom, evidently in a delicate situation, he singled out and led aside, directing her to return to the huts. It seemed that she had prepared to go to the field, but he did not approve of it, and she acquiesced good naturedly. It was observed also that he gave her a piece of money with a pleasant word, bidding her to purchase some coveted piece of finery, — probably a gaudy "bandana," of whose bright colors the negro women are very fond, binding them turban-fashion about their curly heads. Another passion among the Cuban negresses is a desire for large hoop earrings. Silver, or even brass will answer, if gold cannot be obtained.

As we rode off that delicious morning towards our destination, mounted upon a couple of bright little easy-going Cuban ponies, with their manes and tails roached (that is, trimmed closely, after a South American fashion), the cool, fresh air was as stimulating as wine. At first we passed down the long avenue of palms which formed the entrance of the plantation, and which completely embowered the road, like the grand old oaks one sometimes sees lining the avenues to rural English estates. The delicious fragrance of the morning atmosphere, still moist with dew, the richness of the foliage, and the abundance of fruit and flowers were charming beyond description. We glided along at an easy gait over the roads, which in this thickly populated district were smooth and admirably kept, lined on either side by hedges of the flowering aloe, intermingled with many sweet-scented shrubs, all trimmed with mathematical precision. But the gayest and prettiest hedges were composed of the bitter orange, all aglow with small yellow fruit, hanging in almost artificial regularity and abundance. This immediate district was at that time in possession of wealthy owners, who vied with each other in rendering their surroundings attractive to the eye. Now and again we met little gangs of trusted slaves, who had been sent out on special errands, all of whom recognized Don Herero, and made him a respectful obeisance, which he very carefully returned. There is a strict degree of etiquette sustained in regard to these small matters between the slaves and whites, which goes far in maintaining respect and discipline.

A ride of a couple of leagues or more brought us finally to a gentle rise of ground, which opened to our view the ocean, and a line of coast extending for many miles east and west. It was still quite early, and a morning mist hung over the quiet Caribbean Sea, which stretches away southward towards the Isle of Pines and the more distant isle of Jamaica. A gentle breeze began at that moment to disperse the mist and gradually in conjunction with the sun to lift the veil from the face of the waters. For a considerable time, however, only a circumscribed view was to be had, but Don Herero observed that the mist was quite unusual; indeed, that he had seen such a phenomenon but once or twice before on Cuban shores. He assured us that with the exercise of a little patience we should soon be rewarded by a clear and extensive view. So dismounting and lighting our cigars we leaned upon the saddles of the horses and watched the wreaths of the mist bank gradually dissolving. To the eastward there jutted out a promontory with a considerable elevation, behind which the sun began to show his florid countenance. Presently the indistinct outline of a graceful tracery of spars and cordage greeted the eye through the misty gauze, growing steadily more and more distinct and gradually descending towards the sea level, until at last there lay before us in full view, with a look of treacherous tranquillity, the dark, low hull of a brigantine.

"A slaver!" was the mutual and simultaneous exclamation which burst from our lips as we gazed intently on the small but symmetrical vessel.

Don Herero looked particularly intelligent, but said nothing. There could be no doubt as to the trade which engaged such a clipper craft. No legitimate commerce was suggested by her appearance, no honest trade demanded such manifest sacrifice of carrying capacity. It was very natural that her guilty character should add interest to her appearance and cause us to examine her very minutely. A short distance from where we stood there was gathered a group of a dozen or more persons, who silently regarded the brigantine, but they evinced no surprise at her appearance there so close to the shore. She was of a most graceful model, perfect in every line, with bows almost as sharp as a knife. The rig was also quite unusual and entirely new to us. Her deck was flush fore and aft. Not so much as an inch of rise was allowed for a quarter-deck, a style which gave large stowage capacity below deck, the level of which came up to within a couple of feet of the cappings of the bulwarks. As we have before intimated, it required no interpreter to indicate what business the brigantine was engaged in. A single glance at her, lying in so unfrequented a place, was enough. The rakish craft was of Baltimore build, of about two hundred tons measurement, and, like many another vessel turned out by the Maryland builders, was designed to make successfully the famous middle passage to or from the coast of Cuba, loaded with kidnapped negroes from the shores of Africa. The two requisites of these clippers were great speed and large stowage capacity for a human freight.

At first it appeared as though Don Herero had purposely brought us here to witness the scene, but this he insisted was not the case, declaring that the presence of the slaver was a surprise to him. Be that as it may, it was clear that a cargo of negroes was about to be landed, and certain rapid signals had been exchanged by flags from a neighboring hut ever since the mist lifted. Repulsive as the idea was to a Northerner, still it would do no good to avoid the sight, and so we resolved to witness the disembarkation. Our friend, though a slaveholder, was so more by force of circumstances than through his own choice; he did not defend the institution at all. His solemn convictions were entirely against slavery, and he more than once said he heartily wished that some means might be devised which should gradually and effectually relieve the planters from the entire system and its many troubles. Don Herero now lies in one of the tombs in the Campo Santo, near Havana, but were he living he would doubtless rejoice at the present manner of solving a question which was so involved in perplexity during the last of his days.

While we were exchanging some remarks upon the subject, our attention was suddenly drawn towards another striking object upon the waters of the bay.

Nearly a league beyond the slaver, looming up above the mist, we could now make out three topmasts, clearly defined, the stately set of which, with their firm and substantial rig, betrayed the fact that there floated beneath them the hull of a French or an English man-of-war, such as was commissioned at that time to cruise in these waters for the purpose of intercepting and capturing the vessels engaged in the African slave trade.

"A cruiser has scented the brigantine," said Don Herero.

"It certainly appears so," we affirmed.

"Unless there be sharp eyes on board the little craft, the cruiser will be down upon her before her people even suspect their danger."

"The brigantine can hardly escape, at any rate," we suggested.

"Don't be too sure," said Don Herero.

It was impossible for our friend to suppress the nervous anxiety which so manifestly actuated him as he viewed the new phase of affairs.

"Look! Look!" he exclaimed.

While he spoke, a drapery of snow-white canvas fell like magic from the spars of the slaver, ready to catch the first breath of the breeze which the stranger was bringing down with him, though the larger vessel was still partially wrapped in a thin bank or cloud of fog. A couple of long sweeps were rigged out of either bow of the brigantine, and her prow, which just before was heading shoreward, was swung to seaward, while her canvas was trimmed to catch the first breath of the on-coming breeze.

"This looks like business," said Don Herero with emphasis, at the same time shading his eyes with both hands to get a better view of the situation.

"Can you define the new-comer's nationality?" we asked.

"Not yet."

"See! she is now in full sight."

"French!" exclaimed Don Herero, as the tri-colors were clearly visible hanging from her peak.

"What will the cruiser do with the brigantine?" we asked.

"First catch your hare," said our friend.

Our host then explained that the slaver had evidently intended to land her cargo under cover of the night, but had been prevented by the mist from coming to anchor in time. Fog, being so seldom known on this coast, had not entered into their calculations. She had most likely felt her way towards the shore by soundings, and was waiting for full daylight when we discovered her.

While this explanation was being made, the brigantine had already got steerage way upon her, aided by the steady application of the sweeps, and her sharp bow was headed off shore. Nothing on the sea, unless it were a steamer, could hold speed with these fly-aways, which were built for just such emergencies as the present. The gradually freshening breeze had now dispersed the mist, and the two vessels were clearly in view from the shore and to each other. The remarkable interest of the scene increased with each moment. Don Herero, with all the excitability of his nationality, could hardly contain himself as he walked rapidly back and forth, always keeping his eyes towards the sea.

The cruiser had come down under an easy spread of canvas, wearing a jib, three topsails, fore, main, and mizzen, and her spanker. It did not appear as if she had any previous intimation of the presence of the slaver, but rather that she was on the watch for just such a quarry as chance had placed within reach of her guns. The moment she discovered the brigantine, and at a signal which we could not hear upon the land, a hundred dark objects peopled her shrouds and spars, and sail after sail of heavy duck was rapidly dropped and sheeted home, until the mountain of canvas began to force the large hull through the water with increasing speed.

In the mean time the lesser craft had been by no means idle. In addition to the regular square and fore and aft sails of a brigantine, she had a mizzen-mast stepped well aft not more than four feet from her taffrail, upon which she had hoisted a spanker and gaff-topsail, thus completing a most graceful and effective rig, and spreading a vast amount of canvas for a vessel of her moderate tonnage. It was quite impossible to take one's eyes off the two vessels. It was a race for life with the slaver, whose people worked with good effect at the sweeps and in trimming their sails to make the most out of the light but favorable wind that was filling them. The larger vessel would have made better headway in a stiff breeze or half a gale of wind, but the present moderate breeze favored the guilty little brigantine, which was every moment forging ahead and increasing the distance between herself and her enemy.

"Do you see that commotion on the cruiser's bow?" asked our friend eagerly.

"Some men are gathered on the starboard bow," was our answer.

"Ay, and now she runs out a gun!"

That was plain enough to see. The cruiser trained a bow-chaser to bear on the slaver, and the boom of the gun came sluggishly over the sea a few seconds after the puff of smoke was seen. A quick eye could see the dash of the shot just astern of the brigantine, where it must have cast the spray over her quarter-deck. After a moment's delay, as if to get the true range, a second, third, and fourth shot followed, each ricochetting through and over the slight waves either to starboard or port of the slaver, without any apparent effect. The brigantine, still employing her sweeps, and with canvas well trimmed, took no notice of the shots.

Every time the gun was discharged on board the cruiser, it became necessary to fall off her course just a point or two in order to get a proper aim, and her captain was quick to see the disadvantage of this, as he was only assisting the slaver to widen the distance between them. It would seem to the uninitiated to be the easiest thing possible to cripple the brigantine by a few well directed shots, but when sailing in the wake of an enemy this is by no means so easily done. Besides, the distance between the two vessels, which was considerable, was momentarily increasing. Notwithstanding that the broad spread of canvas on board the slaver made her a conspicuous mark, still, so far as could be seen or judged of by her movements, she remained untouched by half a dozen shots, more or less, which the cruiser sent after her as she slipped away from her big adversary. We could even see that the sweeps were now taken in, showing that the master of the slaver considered the game to be in his own hands.

"The brigantine steers due south," said our friend, rubbing his hands together eagerly. "She will lead the Frenchman a wild goose chase among the Cayman Isles, where he will be most likely to run aground with his heavy draught of water. The sea round about for leagues is underlaid by treacherous coral reefs. We shall see, we shall see," he reiterated.

"But they must certainly have a good pilot on board the cruiser," we ventured to say.

"Undoubtedly," replied Don Herero, "but the brigantine is built with a centre-board, thus having, as it were, a portable keel, and can sail anywhere that a man could swim, while the cruiser, with all her armament, must draw nearly three fathoms. A ship will sometimes follow a chase into dangerous water."

"True," we responded, "the brigantine's safety lies in seeking shoal water."

"You are right, and that will be her game."

In half an hour both vessels were hull down in the

offing, and were soon invisible from our point of view. The early ride and subsequent excitement had developed in us a healthy appetite, and we were strongly reminded of the fact that we had not breakfasted. We were near the little hamlet of Lenore, where there was a small inn, which we had passed on the way, and towards which we now turned our horses' heads. A breakfast of boiled eggs, fried plantains, and coffee was prepared for us and well served, much to our surprise, supplemented by a large dish of various fruits, ripe and delicious. Don Herero had left us for a few moments while the breakfast was preparing, and it must have been owing to his intelligent instructions that we were so nicely served, for, as a rule, country posadas in Cuba are places to be avoided, being neither cleanly nor comfortable. For strangers they are not entirely safe, as they are frequented by a very rough class of people. These idlers do not indulge in spirituous liquors to excess, partaking only of the light Cataline wine in universal use both in Spain and her colonies. Intemperance is little seen outside the large cities, but gambling and quarreling are ever rampant among the class who frequent these posadas. In the present instance there were a dozen and more individuals in the Lenore inn who were more or less connected with the expected arrival of the slave brigantine, and the disappointment caused by the arrival upon the scene of the French cruiser had put them all in a very bad humor. Angry words were being exchanged among them in the large reception apartment, and Don Herero suggested that we should finish our cigars under an inviting shade in the rear of the posada.

At our host's suggestion a neighboring coffee plantation was visited, and its floral and vegetable beauties thoroughly enjoyed. It was in the very height of fragrance and promise, the broad expanse of the plantation, as far as the eye could extend, being in full bloom. Some hours were agreeably passed in examining the estate, the slaves' quarters, and the domestic arrangements, and also in partaking of the hospitalities of the generous owner, after which we rode back to Lenore.

"We must not miss the closing act of our little drama," said Don Herero, significantly.

"The closing act?" we inquired.

"Certainly. You do not suppose we have yet done with the brigantine?"

"Oh, the brigantine. Will she dare to return, now the cruiser has discovered her?"

"Of course she will, after dropping her pursuer. Strange that these French cruisers do not understand these things better; but so it is."

And Don Herero explained that the French cruisers watched the southern coasts of the island, while the English cruised on the northern shore, attempted to blockade it, and also cruised farther seaward, on the line between Africa and Cuba. A couple of American men-of-war, engaged in the same purpose of suppressing the slave trade, patrolled the African coast. It was nearly night before we got through our dinner at the posada. Just as we were preparing to leave the table, the landlord came in and announced to Don Herero that if we desired to witness the close of the morning's business in the bay, we must hurry up to the plateau.

We hastened to our former position, reaching it just in time to see the brigantine again rounding the headland. She now ran in close to the shore, where there seemed to be hardly water sufficient to float her, but the exactness and system which characterized her movements showed that her commander was not a stranger to the little bay in which he had brought his vessel. All was instantly bustle and activity, both on board and on shore. There were not more than twenty people to be seen at the shore, but each one knew his business, and went about it intelligently. There was no more loud talking or disputation. These men, all armed, were accustomed to this sort of thing, and had evidently been awaiting the slaver's arrival for some days. They were a rough-looking set of desperadoes, among whom we recognized several who had been at the posada.

The brigantine was quickly moored as near to the shore as possible, and a broad gangway of wood was laid from her deck to a projecting rock, over which a long line of dark objects was hurried, like a flock of sheep, and nearly as naked as when born into the world. We walked down to the landing-place, in order to get a closer view. The line of human beings who came out from below the deck of the slaver were mostly full-grown men, but occasionally a woman or a boy came out and hastened forward with the rest. As we drew nearer, one or two of the women, it was observed, had infants in their arms, little unconscious creatures, sound asleep, and so very young that they must have been born on the voyage. How the entire scene appealed to our indignation and sympathy! What misery these poor creatures must have endured, cooped up for twenty-one days in that circumscribed space! They were all shockingly emaciated, having sustained life on a few ounces of rice and a few gills of water daily distributed to them. The atmosphere, thoroughly poisoned when so confined, had proved fatal to a large number. As we stood there, one dark body was passed up from below the deck and quietly dropped into the bay. Life was extinct. It was quite impossible to suppress a shudder as we looked upon the disgraceful scene, which being observed Don Herero said, —

"They look bad enough now, but a few days in the open air, with a plenty of fresh vegetables, fruits, and sweet water to drink, will bring them round. They will get a good bath directly at the first river they cross, which is the thing they most require."

While our friend was speaking, four tall, gaunt, fierce-looking negroes passed us, shackled two by two at the wrists. Their eyes rolled curiously about, full of wonder at all they saw, everything was to them so strange. They knew no more than children just born what was in store for them.

"Poor fellows!" we ejaculated. Perhaps they detected sympathy in the tone of voice in which the words were uttered. They could not understand their purport, but all four were observed to turn their eyes quickly towards us, with an intelligent expression.

"These are Ashantees," said Don Herero. "They have thriven but poorly on their small allowance of nourishment, but they will improve rapidly like the rest, now they have landed. They belong to a powerful tribe in Africa, and are rarely captured and sold to the factories on the coast. They are sturdy and serviceable fellows, but they must be humored. The lash will not subdue them. They bring a high price in Havana for harbor workers."

Hastening back to the posada, a large basket of cassava bread and an abundance of ripe bananas and oranges, with half a dozen bottles of wine, were procured. With these, carried by a couple of colored boys, we hastened back to the landing-place in time to distribute the refreshments to all the women and boys. The balance of the provisions were dealt out to the few men who had not already been hurried away from the spot. It is impossible to describe the surprise and grateful expression upon those dusky faces among the half-famished creatures, as they eagerly swallowed a portion of the wine, and ate freely of the delicious fruit and nourishing bread.

We were told afterwards that there were about three hundred and fifty of these poor creatures originally embarked, and over three hundred were landed. Perhaps between thirty and forty had died on the passage, unable to sustain life under such awful circumstances, packed, as they necessarily were, almost like herring in a box. Once a day, in fair weather, thirty or forty at a time were permitted to pass a half hour on deck. That was all the respite from their confinement which they enjoyed during the three weeks' voyage. The horrors of the "middle passage" have not been exaggerated.

"They must have lost many of their number by death, on the voyage," we suggested to Don Herero, as we observed their weak and tremulous condition.

"Doubtless," was the response.

"And what do they do in that case ?"

"They have the ocean always alongside," was his significant reply.

"They throw them over as they did that body just now ?" we asked.

"Exactly. And many a poor sick creature is cast into the sea before life is extinct," he continued.

"That is adding murder to piracy," was our natural and indignant rejoinder.

"Hush!" said Don Herero, "these are sensitive people, and desperate ones, as well. I should find it difficult to protect you if they were to overhear and understand such words."

We realized that his remarks were true enough. We were in a land of slavery, and that meant that everything evil was possible.

The last of the living freight had been landed, and arranged in marching trim they were turned with their faces inland, staggering as they went, their swollen and cramped limbs hardly able to sustain the weight of their bodies. They were all secured with handcuffs, twenty in a lot, between whom, — there being ten on a side, — a pole was placed, and each was fastened by a chain running through the steel handcuffs to the pole. An armed Spaniard directed each lot. The faces of all were quite expressionless. They had just endured such horrors packed beneath the deck of the brigantine that the present change must have been welcome to them, lame as they were.

We had been so completely engaged in watching the colored gangs and in moving up to our lookout station of the early morning that our thoughts had not reverted to anything else, but as the last lot filed by there boomed over the waters of the bay the heavy report of a gun, at once calling our attention seaward. A change had come over the scene. That which has taken some space to relate had transpired with great rapidity. Night had settled over the scene, but the moon and stars were so marvelously bright as to render objects almost as plain as by day. The ocean lay like a sheet of silver, luminous with the reflected light poured upon it by the sparkling skies. Looking towards the southeast, we saw the French cruiser rounding the headland which formed the eastern arm of the little bay, and she had already sent a shot across the water aimed at the brigantine. Don Herero had prognosticated correctly. The slaver had led the cruiser a fruitless chase and lost her among the islands, and then returning to her former anchorage had successfully discharged her cargo. Her tactics could not have been anticipated by the cruiser, yet had an armed party been left behind in boats, the brigantine might have been captured on her return. But then again, if the cruiser had left a portion of her crew at this point, the slaver would have been notified by the friends on shore, and would have sought a landing elsewhere.

The brigantine had cast off her moorings and was now standing seaward, with her sails filled. We could distinctly see a quarter boat leave her side manned by some of her crew, who at once pulled towards the nearest landing. At the same time a bright blaze sprang up on board the slaver just amidships, and in a moment more it crept, like a living serpent, from shroud to shroud and from spar to spar, until the graceful brigantine was one sheet of flame! It was dazzling to look upon, even at the distance where we stood, the body of high-reaching flame being sharply defined against the background of sky and blue water.

While we watched the glowing view the cruiser cautiously changed her course and bore away, for fire was an enemy with which she could not contend. Presently there arose a shower of blazing matter heavenward, while a confused shock and a dull rumbling report filled the atmosphere, as the guilty brigantine was blown to atoms! Hemmed in as she was there could be no hope of escape. Her mission was ended, and her crew followed their usual orders, to destroy the ship rather than permit her to fall a prize to any government cruisers.

CHAPTER XVI.

Antique Appearance of Everything. — The Yeomen of Cuba. — A Montero's Home. — Personal Experience. — The Soil of the Island. — Oppression by the Government. — Spanish Justice in Havana. — Tax upon the Necessities of Life. — The Proposed Treaty with Spain. — A One-Sided Proposition. — A Much Taxed People. — Some of the Items of Taxation. — Fraud and Bankruptcy. — The Boasted Strength of Moro Castle. — Destiny of Cuba. — A Heavy Annual Cost to Spain. — Political Condition. — Pictures of Memory.

EVERYTHING in Cuba has an aspect of antiquity quite Egyptian. The style of the buildings is not unlike that of the Orient, while the trees and vegetable products increase the resemblance. The tall, majestic palms, the graceful cocoanut trees, the dwellings of the lower classes and many other peculiarities give to the scenery an Eastern aspect quite impressive. It is impossible to describe the vividness with which each object, artificial or natural, house or tree, stands out in the clear liquid light where there is no haze to interrupt the view. Indeed, it is impossible to express how essentially everything differs in this sunny island from our own country. The language, the people, the climate, the manners and customs, the architecture, the foliage, the flowers, all offer broad contrasts to what the American has so lately left behind him. It is but a long cannon shot, as it were, off our southern coast, yet once upon its soil the stranger seems to have been transported to another quarter of the globe. It would require but little effort of the imagination to believe one's self in distant Syria, or some remoter part of Asia.

One never tires of watching the African population, either in town or country. During the hours which the slaves are allowed to themselves, they are oftenest seen working on their own allotted piece of ground, where they raise favorite fruits and vegetables, besides corn for fattening the pig penned up near by, and for which the drover who regularly visits the plantations will pay them in good hard money. Thus it has been the case, in years past, that thrifty slaves have earned the means of purchasing their freedom, after which they have sought the cities, and have swelled the large numbers of free negroes who naturally tend towards these populous centres. Some become caleseros, some labor upon the water-front of the town as stevedores, porters, and the like, but the majority are confirmed idlers. In the cities even the slaves have always had a less arduous task to perform than those on the plantations. They are less exposed to the sun, and are as a rule allowed more freedom and privileges. The women never fail to exhibit the true negro taste for cheap jewelry. A few gaudy ribbons and a string of high-colored glass beads about the neck are greatly prized by them. Sometimes the mistress of a good looking negress takes great pleasure in decking her immediate attendant in grand style, with big gold finger rings, large hoop earrings, wide gold necklace, and the like. A bright calico gown and a flaring bandana kerchief bound about the head generally complete the costume of these petted slaves. There was one sight observed in the church of Santa Clara of significance in this connection. Before the altar all distinction ceased, and the negress knelt on the same bit of carpet beside the mistress.

The native soil of Cuba is so rich that a touch of the hoe prepares it for the plant. It is said to be unsurpassed in the world in this respect, and only equaled by Australia. The Monteros have little more to do than to gather produce, which they carry daily to the nearest market, and which also forms their own healthful and palatable food. Nowhere are the necessities of life so easily supplied, or are men so delicately nurtured. And yet to our Northern eye these Monteros seemed rather a forlorn sort of people, forming a class by themselves, and regarded with disdain by the Spaniards and most Creoles, as our Southern slaveholders used to regard the poor whites of the South. If one may judge by appearances they are nearly as poor in purse as they can be. Their home, rude and lowly, consists generally of a cabin with a bamboo frame, covered by a palm-leaf roof, and with an earthen floor. There are a few broken hedges, and numbers of ragged or naked children. Pigs, hens, goats, all stroll ad libitum in and out of the cabin. The Montero's tools — few and poorly adapted — are Egyptian-like in primitiveness, while the few vegetables are scarcely cultivated at all. The chaparral about his cabin is low, tangled, and thorny, but it is remarkable what a redeeming effect a few graceful palms impart to the crudeness of the picture.

The Montero raises, perhaps, some sweet potatoes, which, by the bye, reach a very large size in Cuban soil. He has also a little patch of corn, but *such* corn. When ripe it is only three or four feet in height, or less than half the average of our New

England growth, the ears mere nubbins. This corn grows, however, all the year round, and is fed green to horses and cattle. All this is done upon a very small scale. No one lays in a stock of anything perishable. The farmer's or the citizen's present daily necessities alone are provided for. Idleness and tobacco occupy most of the Montero's time, varied by the semi-weekly attractions of the cock-pit. The amount of sustaining food which can be realized from one of these little patches of ground, so utterly neglected, is something beyond credence to those who have not looked bountiful nature in the face in Cuba.

While traveling in the vicinity of Guines, the author stopped at one of these lonely Montero homes to obtain water and refreshment for his horse. These were promptly furnished in the form of a pail of water and a bundle of green cornstalks. In the mean time the rude hospitality of the cabin was proffered to us, and we gladly sat down to partake of cocoanut milk and bananas. One of the family pets of the cabin consisted of a tall white bird of the crane species, which, regardless of goat, kid, hens, chickens, and children, came boldly to our side as though accustomed to be petted, and greedily devoured the banana which was peeled for him and cut into tempting bits. One wing had evidently been cut so that the bird could not fly away, but his long, vigorous legs would have defied pursuit, had he desired to escape. Four children, two of each sex, two of whom were white and two mulatto, quite naked, and less than ten years of age, kept close to the Montero's Creole wife, watching us with big, wondering eyes, and fingers thrust into their mouths.

What relationship they bore to the household was not clearly apparent. On rising to depart and attempting to pay for the entertainment, the master of the cabin, with true Cuban hospitality, declined all remuneration; but a handful of small silver divided among the children satisfied all, and we parted with a hearty pressure of the hand.

The richest soil of the island is black, which is best adapted to produce the sugar-cane, and is mostly devoted, if eligibly located, to that purpose. To a Northerner, accustomed to see so much enrichment expended upon the soil to force from it an annual return, this profuseness of unstimulated yield is a surprise. The red soil of Cuba, which is impregnated with the oxide of iron, is less rich, and is better adapted to the coffee plantation. The mulatto-colored earth is considered to be inferior to either of the others named, but is by no means unproductive, being preferred by the tobacco growers, who, however, often mingle a percentage of other soils with it, as we mingle barnyard refuse with our natural soil. Some tobacco planters have resorted by way of experiment to the use of guano, hoping to stimulate the native properties of the soil, but its effect was found to be not only exhausting to the land, but also bad for the leaf, rendering it rank and unfit for delicate use.

Coal is found near Havana, though it is of rather an inferior quality, and, so far as we could learn, is but little used, the planters depending mostly upon the refuse of the cane with which to run their boilers and engines. Trees have been only too freely used for fuel while accessible, but great care is now taken to utilize the cane after the juice is expressed. Trees, which are so much needed in this climate for shade purposes, have mostly disappeared near Havana. When Columbus first landed here he wrote home to Spain that the island was so thickly wooded as to be impassable.

The lovely climate and beautiful land are rendered gloomy by the state of oppression under which they suffer. The exuberant soil groans with the burdens which are heaped upon it. The people are not safe from prying inquiry at bed or board. Their every action is watched, their slightest words noted and perhaps distorted. They can sing no song of liberty, and even to hum an air wedded to republican verse is to provoke suspicion. The press is muzzled by the iron hand of power. Two hours before a daily paper is distributed on the streets of Havana, a copy must be sent to the government censor. When it is returned with his indorsement it may be issued to the public. The censorship of the telegraph is also as rigorously enforced. Nor do private letters through the mails escape espionage. No passenger agent in Havana dares to sell a ticket for the departure of a stranger or citizen without first seeing that the individual's passport is indorsed by the police. Foreign soldiers fatten upon the people, or at least they eat out their substance, and every town near the coast is a garrison, every interior village a military depot.

Upon landing, if well advised, one is liberal to the petty officials. Chalk is cheap. A five-dollar gold-piece smooths the way wonderfully, and causes the inspector to cross one's baggage with his chalk and no questions asked. No gold, no chalk! Every article must be scrupulously examined. It is cheapest to pay, humiliating as it is, and thus purchase immunity.

As a specimen of the manner in which justice is dispensed in Havana to-day, a case is presented which occurred during our stay at the Telegrafo Hotel. A native citizen was waylaid by three men and robbed of his pocket-book and watch, about fifty rods from the hotel, at eight o'clock in the evening. The rascal who secured the booty, threatening his victim all the while with a knife at his throat, instantly ran away, but the citizen succeeded in holding on to the other two men until his outcries brought the police to the spot. The two accomplices were at once imprisoned. Three days later they were brought before an authorized court, and tried for the robbery. Being taken red-handed, as it were, one would suppose their case was clear enough, and that they would be held until they gave up their accomplice. Not so, however. The victim of the robbery, who had lost a hundred and sixty dollars in money and a valuable gold watch, was coolly rebuked for carrying so much property about his person, and the case was dismissed! Had the sufferer been a home Spaniard possibly the result would have been different. The inference is plain and doubtless correct, that the official received half the stolen property, provided he would liberate the culprits. Sometimes, as we were assured, the victim outbids the rogues, and exemplary punishment follows!

Flour of a good commercial quality sells at present in Boston for six dollars per barrel. Why should it cost fourteen dollars in Havana and other ports of Cuba? Because Spain demands a tax of one hundred per cent. to be paid into the royal treasury upon this prime necessity of life. This one example is sufficient to illustrate her policy, which is to extort from the Cubans every possible cent that can be obtained. The extraordinary taxation imposed upon their subjects by the German and Austrian governments is carried to the very limit, it would seem, of endurance, but taxation in Cuba goes far beyond anything of the sort in Europe. Spain now asks us to execute with her a "favorable" reciprocity treaty. Such a treaty as she proposes would be of very great benefit to Spain, no doubt, but of none, or comparatively none, to us. Whatever we seemingly do for Cuba in the matter of such a treaty we should do indirectly for Spain. She it is who will reap all the benefit. She has still upon her hands some fifty to sixty thousand civil and military individuals, who are supported by a miserable system of exaction as high and petty officials in this misgoverned island.

It is for the interest of this army of locusts in possession to keep up the present state of affairs, — it is bread and butter to them, though it be death to the Cubans. Relieved of the enormous taxation and oppression generally which her people labor under in every department of life, Cuba would gradually assume a condition of thrift and plenty. But while she is so trodden upon, so robbed in order to support in luxury a host of rapacious Spaniards, and forbidden any voice in the control of her own affairs, all the treaty concessions which we could make to Spain would only serve to keep up and perpetuate the great farce. Such a treaty as is proposed would be in reality granting to Spain a subsidy of about thirty million dollars per annum! This conclusion was arrived at after consultation with three of the principal

United States consuls on the island. Cuba purchases very little from us; she has not a consuming population of over three hundred thousand. The common people, negroes, and Chinese do not each expend five dollars a year for clothing. Rice, codfish, and dried beef, with the abundant fruits, form their support. Little or none of these come from the United States. The few consumers wear goods which we cannot, or at least do not produce. A reciprocity treaty with such a people means, therefore, giving them a splendid annual subsidy.

Taxed by the government to the very last extreme, the landlords, shopkeepers, and all others who work for hire have also learned the trick of it, and practice a similar game on every possible victim. Seeing a small desirable text book in a shop on the Calle de Obrapia, we asked the price.

" Two dollars, gold, señor," was the answer.

" Why do you charge just double the price one would pay for it in Madrid, Paris, or New York ? " we asked.

" Because we are so heavily taxed," was the reply, and the shopman went on to illustrate.

Each small retail store is taxed three hundred dollars for the right to do business. As the store increases in size and importance the tax is increased. A new tax of six per cent. on the amount of all other taxation has just been added, to cover the cost of collecting the whole! A war tax of twenty-five per cent. upon incomes was laid in 1868, and though the war has been ended ten years it is still collected. Every citizen or resident in Havana is obliged to supply himself with a document which is called a cedula, or paper of identification, at an annual cost of five

SOME ITEMS OF TAXATION. 809

dollars in gold. Every merchant who places a sign outside of his door is taxed so much per letter annually. Clerks in private establishments have to pay two and one half per cent. of their quarterly salaries to government. Railroads pay a tax of ten per cent. upon all passage money received, and the same on all freight money. Petty officials invent and impose fines upon the citizens for the most trifling things, and strangers are mulcted in various sums of money whenever a chance occurs, generally liquidating the demand rather than to be at the cost of time and money to contest their rights. The very beggars in the streets, blind, lame, or diseased, if found in possession of money, are forced to share it with officials on some outrageous pretext. All these things taken into consideration show us why the shopkeeper of Havana must charge double price for his merchandise. We have only named a few items of taxation which happen to occur to us, and which only form a commencement of the long list.

It is nearly impossible at present to collect a note or an account on the island. Several of the guests at the Telegrafo had come from the United States solely upon these fruitless errands, each having the same experience to relate. Dishonest debtors take advantage of the general state of bankruptcy which exists, and plead utter inability to meet their obligations, while others, who would gladly pay their honest debts if it were possible, have not the means to do so.

There is considerable counterfeit paper money in circulation, and we were told that the banks of the city of Havana actually paid it out knowingly over their own counters, mixed in with genuine bills, — a presumed perquisite of the bank officers! This unprecedented fraud was not put a stop to until the merchants and private bankers threatened to have the doors of the banks closed by popular force if the outrage was longer continued. Could such a public fraud be carried on under any other than a Spanish government? It is not pleasant to record the fact, but it is nevertheless true that the Spaniards in Cuba are artful, untruthful, unreliable even in small things, with no apparent sense of honor, and seeking just now mainly how they can best avoid their honest obligations. As evil communications are contagious, the Cubans have become more or less impregnated with this spirit of commercial dishonesty. It must be admitted that of true, conscientious principles neither party has any to spare.

The writer has often been asked about Moro Castle. Much has been said about its "impregnable" character, but modern military science will not recognize any such theory. A thousand chances are liable to happen, any one of which might give the place into the hands of an invading force. Has it not already been twice taken? Though it may be said that auxiliary forts have been added since those experiences, nevertheless modern artillery would make but short work of the boasted defenses of Havana, and would knock the metropolis itself all to pieces in a few hours, while lying out of range from Moro Castle. No invading force need attack from the seaward side, unless it should be found particularly desirable to do so. The place could be easily taken, as the French took Algiers, by landing a sufficient force in the rear. With the exception of the fortresses in and about Havana, the island, with its two thousand miles of coast line and nearly one hundred accessible harbors, is certainly very poorly prepared to resist an invading enemy. Cuba's boasted military or defensive strength is chimerical.

That the island naturally belongs to this country is a fact so plain as to have been conceded by all authorities. In this connection one is forcibly reminded of the words of Jefferson in a letter to President Monroe, so long ago as 1823, wherein he says: "I candidly confess that I have ever looked on Cuba as the most interesting addition which could be made to our system of States. The control which, with Florida Point, this island would give us over the Gulf of Mexico and the countries and the isthmus bordering it, would fill up the measure of our political well-being." Is it generally known that Cuba was once freely offered to this government? During the presidency of Jefferson, while Spain was bowed beneath the yoke of France, the people of the island, feeling themselves incompetent to maintain their independence, sent a deputation to Washington city proposing its annexation to the federal system of North America. The President, however, declined to even consider the proffered acquisition. Again, in 1848, President Polk authorized our minister at Madrid to offer a hundred million dollars for a fee simple of the island, but it was rejected by Spain.

Completely divided against itself, the mystery is how Cuba has been so long sustained in its present system. Spain has crowded regiment after regiment of her army into the island. It was like pouring water into a sieve, the troops being absorbed by death almost as fast as they could be landed. The combined slaughter brought about by patriot bullets, hardships, exposure, fever, and every possible adverse circumstance has been enormous beyond belief. In spite of all this sacrifice of human life, besides millions of gold expended annually, what does Spain gain by holding tenaciously to her title of the island? Nothing, absolutely nothing. The time has long passed when the system of extortion enforced upon the Cubans served to recuperate the royal treasury. The tide has entirely changed in this respect, and though the taxation has been increased, still the home government is mulcted in the sum of six or eight millions of dollars annually to keep up the present worse than useless system. The deficit of the Cuban budget for the present year, as we were credibly informed, could not be less than eight millions of dollars. How is Spain to meet this continuous drain upon her resources? She is already financially bankrupt. It is in this political strait that she seeks a one-sided treaty with the United States, by means of which she hopes to eke out her possession of the island a few years longer, through our liberality, — a treaty by which she would gain some thirty millions of dollars annually, and we should be just so much the poorer.

As regards the final destiny of Cuba, that question will be settled by certain economic laws which are as sure in their operation as are those of gravitation. No matter what our wishes may be in the matter, such individual desires are as nothing when arraigned against natural laws. The commerce of the island is a stronger factor in the problem than mere politics; it is the active agent of civilization all over the world. It is not cannon, but ships; not gunpowder, but peaceful freights, which settle the great questions of mercantile communities. Krupp's hundred-ton guns will not control the fate of Cuba, but sugar will. We have only to ask ourselves, Whither does the great commercial interest of the island point? It is in the direction in which the largest portion of her products find their market. If this were England, towards that land her industry and her people would look hopefully, but as it is the United States who take over ninety per cent. of her entire exports, towards the country of the Stars and Stripes she stretches out her hands, and asks for favorable treaties.

At the present moment she has reached a crisis, where her condition is absolutely desperate. The hour is big with fate to the people of Cuba. As long as European soil will produce beets, the product of the cane will find no market on that side of the Atlantic. Cuba must in the future depend as much upon the United States as does Vermont, Mississippi, New York, Ohio, or any other State. The effort to bring about a reciprocal treaty of commerce with us is but the expression of a natural tendency to closer bonds with this country. Thus it will be seen that as regards her commercial existence, Cuba is already within the economic orbit of our Union, though she seems to be so far away politically. The world's centre of commercial gravity is changing very fast by reason of the great and rapid development of the United States, and all lands surrounding the union must conform to the prevailing lines of motion.

It is with infinite reluctance that the temporary sojourner in Cuba leaves her delicious shores. A brief residence in the island passes like a midsummer night's dream, while the memories one brings away seem almost like delusive spots of the imagination. Smiling skies and smiling waters; groves of palms and oranges; the bloom of the heliotrope, the jasmine and the rose; flights of strange and gaudy birds; tropic nights at once luxurious and calm; clouds of fireflies floating like unsphered stars on the night breeze; graceful figures of dark-eyed señoritas in diaphanous drapery; picturesque groups of Monteros, relieved by the dusky faces and stalwart forms of the sons of Africa; undulating volantes, military pageants, ecclesiastical processions, frowning fortresses, grim batteries, white sails, fountains raining silver; all these images mingle in brilliant kaleidoscopic combinations, changing and varying as the mind's eye seeks to fix their features. Long after his departure from the enchanting island, the traveler beholds these visions in the still watches of the night, and again listens to the dash of the sea-green waves at the foot of the Moro and the Punta, the roll of the drum and the crash of arms upon the ramparts, or hears in fancy the thrilling strains of music from the military band in the Paseo de Isabella.

If it were possible to contemplate only the beautiful that nature has so prodigally lavished on this Eden of the Gulf, shutting out all that man has done and is doing to mar the blessings of heaven, while closing our eyes to the myriad forms of human misery that assail them on every hand, then a visit to or a residence in Cuba would present a succession of unalloyed pleasures, delightful as a poet's dream. But the dark side of the picture will force itself upon us. The American traveler, keenly alive to the social and political aspects of life, appreciates in full force the evils that challenge his observation at every step. If he contrasts the natural scenery with the familiar pictures of home, he cannot help also contrasting the political condition of the people with that of his own country. The existence, almost under the shadow of the flag of the freest institutions the earth ever knew, of a government as purely despotic as that of the autocrat of Russia is a monstrous fact that must startle the most indifferent observer.

To go hence to Cuba is not merely to pass over a few degrees of latitude, — it is to take a step from the nineteenth century back into the dark ages. In the clime of sunshine and endless summer, we are in the land of starless political darkness. Lying under the lee of a land where every man is a sovereign is a realm where the lives, liberties, and fortunes of all are held at the will of a single individual, who acknowledges fealty only to a nominal ruler more than three thousand miles across the sea.

In close proximity to a country where the taxes are self-imposed and so light as to be almost unfelt is one where each free family pays over five hundred dollars per annum, directly and indirectly, for the support of a system of bigoted tyranny, scarcely equaled elsewhere, — forming an aggregate sum of over twenty-six millions of dollars. For all this extortion no equivalent is received. No representation, no utterance, for tongue or pen are alike proscribed; no share of public honors, no office, no emolument. The industry of the people is crippled, their intercourse with other nations is hampered in every conceivable manner, and every liberal aspiration of the human soul stifled in its birth. Can good morals and Christian lives be expected of a people who are so down-trodden?

Salubrious in climate, varied in production, and most fortunately situated for commerce, there must yet be a grand future in store for Cuba. Washed by the Gulf Stream on half her border, while the Mississippi pours out its riches on one side and the Amazon on the other, her home is naturally within our own constellation of stars, and some of those who read these pages may live to see such a consummation.

www.ingramcontent.com/pod-product-compliance
Lightning Source LLC
Chambersburg PA
CBHW030735230426

43667CB00007B/720